About the Author

James G. Blase is a 35-year experienced estate planning attorney with offices in St. Louis County and St. Charles County, Missouri. Jim spent the first half of his legal career with the St. Louis law firms Thompson Coburn (then Thompson Mitchell) and Armstrong Teasdale, the latter where he also served as chair of the firm's Trusts & Estates department.

Jim is a 1981 graduate of Notre Dame Law School, where he served as Managing Editor of the *Notre Dame Law Review*, and is a 1982 graduate of the New York University Law School Graduate Program in Taxation, where he served as Graduate Editor of the *Tax Law Review*. Jim is also an adjunct professor of estate planning at the St. Louis University School of Law, and owns a Certified Public Accountant certificate from the State of Missouri.

The author of over 40 articles for various tax and estate planing professional publications, Jim incorporates the analysis of all of these articles here, and adds forms which the attorney may consider in responding to his or her clients' estate planning goals and needs.

© James G. Blase 2017

Table of Contents

Chapter 1

The Goal of Optimum Estate Planning

The word "optimum" means "most likely to lead to a favorable outcome." And in the estate planning context, that favorable outcome is for our clients to be able to have their cake, and eat it too. Clients want to minimize taxes for themselves and for their families, but they also want to protect their assets from lawsuits and to retain as much control as possible - both in themselves and in their family members. The objective of optimum estate planning is to create conditions for our clients which will most likely achieve all of their estate planning goals, not just some or most of them.

Too often today we are forced to "settle" as estate planners. For example, ever since 1986 Congress has imposed unfair and outrageous income taxes on trusts, so for this reason we tend either to use trusts less often or, when we do utilize them, direct in the trust document that all trust income be distributed to the trust beneficiary. This is often contrary to the clients' wishes that the unused income of the trust be controlled and protected from estate taxes, lawsuits, rights of a divorced spouse or of a spouse the beneficiary may remarry, minor, young or otherwise spendthrift children, special needs children, etc., as well as from all issues associated with second marriage situations.

We also avoid establishing protective trusts for a surviving spouse or a child because Congress tells us that the underlying assets of these trusts will not receive a "stepped-up income tax basis" at the spouse or child's death. Is this even true? The surviving spouse in a community property state receives a full income tax basis step-up when the first spouse dies, but surviving spouses in non-community property states do not. Can something be done about this unfairness?

The growth in a non-qualified portfolio of investments escapes income tax in the hands of the heirs after the owner's death, but the recipients of IRAs and other forms of qualified plan benefits and non-qualified annuities not only pay income tax on the same after the owner's death, but they do so at ordinary (normally higher) income tax rates. Again, is there any way to avoid this unfairness?

Through the release of several private letter rulings the Internal Revenue Service steers planners towards leaving all IRA and qualified plan benefits either outright to individuals, or to so-called "conduit trusts" (which basically amount to the same thing as outright, in the long run), even though the owner's preference may be that these amounts be protected for his or her spouse and/or children, via a trust. Is there any way to achieve the owner's objectives that these benefits be eligible for income tax deferral and also be protected from estate taxes, potential creditors, rights of a divorced spouse, etc.?

An individual receives a charitable income tax deduction when he or she donates to charity during his or her lifetime, but generally there is no income tax deduction when he or she donates under his or her will? Is there a way to obtain such a deduction?

When an individual makes lifetime gifts to his or her children of an interest in a closely-held business or real estate, the children take the donor's income tax basis in the same, yet when the same individual waits to give the stock or real estate to his or children at death, the children receive a "stepped-up" income tax basis. Is it possible to receive an income tax basis step-up for business and real estate interests which are gifted to children during the donor's lifetime?

And is it possible to transfer control over the clients' business to the clients' children, but retain in the clients the ability for them to change their minds later?

These are just some of the examples of the myriad of unfair tax laws and traps in the estate planning area which this book is intended to address, and then solve. Although as mere advisors we hesitate to cast invectives at Congress and the Internal Revenue Service when they seem to be continually "out for" our estate planning clients and their families, our reticence should not prevent us from taking positive action to estate plan around this inherent unfairness.

We don't need to act as legal revolutionaries, but we do need to avoid a state of indifference in our planning and drafting. As mentioned at the outset of this chapter, we want our clients to "have their cake, and eat it to." We want them to enjoy all of the estate planning benefits of trusts which are

6

available under the law, while minimizing all of the potential negatives.

Optimum estate planning also means that our estate plans today need to be flexible. The one thing we all learned over 15 years ago, with the passage of President's Bush "estate tax repeal bill" in May of 2001, was that the future of the estate tax laws were no longer certain, and that, through the use of independent trustees or trust protectors, our trust documents now needed to incorporate flexibility to deal with future tax law and other changes. The results of the 2016 Presidential, Senate and House elections serve only to heighten the need for flexibility in our estate planning, given the now very real possibility of federal estate tax repeal in the not too distant future.

Finally, optimum estate planning is also about retaining control for our clients, both during their lifetimes and after their deaths, as well as for the clients' children at an appropriate time after the clients' deaths.

This is an intermediate level book intended for the experienced estate planner who has become frustrated in not being able to accomplish all of his or her clients' estate planning objectives within a single estate plan. Asset protection and preservation concerns must be sacrificed in order to lower income taxes, while income tax savings must be sacrificed in order to protect and preserve assets. It's all become a vicious circle, due primarily to the punitive manner in which Congress has chosen to tax trusts.

In short, optimum estate planning concerns itself with achieving *all four* of these desirable results, but with no risk, and with a minimum level of complexity:

- **Asset protection** - both during the client's lifetime and for the client's heirs after his or her death.

- **Income tax protection** - both during the client's lifetime and for the client's heirs after his or her death.

- **Estate tax protection** - both at the client's death and at the death of the client's heirs.

- **Maximum control** - both for the client and for the client's heirs.

A simple example involving the spousal portability election (also discussed later in Chapter 3) will serve to illustrate. Because of the election, it is often said that traditional bypass or credit shelters trusts are no longer necessary, nor advisable. The trusts are not necessary because the surviving spouse already receives the deceased spouse's unused estate tax exemption, and they are not desirable because the trust is taxed at high income tax rates and further the assets of the trust will not receive an income tax basis step-up at the surviving spouse's death.

The problem with this approach to estate planning for married couples is that it is risky, and inaccurate. One significant concern with relying on the spousal portability election - at least in potential taxable estate situations - is that the surviving spouse loses the portability amount if he or she remarries and his or her new spouse again predeceases.

Relying on the portability election also exposes the "ported" assets to the surviving spouse's creditors, including the potential claims of a new spouse. Even more concerning is the fact that assuming all of this increased risk is usually unnecessary. As we will discuss in Chapter 3, it is actually possible to structure a bypass or credit shelter trust so that its income is not taxed at a high rate, and also so that income tax basis step-up at the surviving spouse's death is achieved.

The surviving spouse would thus have control over and an economic interest in the bypass or credit shelter trust's principal and income, as trustee and beneficiary, but the trust corpus and income will now be protected from potential creditor claims against the survivor, as well as from potential claims by a new spouse. The trust assets are *guaranteed* to be removed from the survivor's taxable estate, and with little or no potential adverse income tax consequences when compared to proceeding under the portability election route. The decedent spouse also retains a level of control regarding the ultimate disposition of the trust assets. All is accomplished with zero risk, and only a minimal level of added complexity.

This book will not inundate the experienced estate planner with basic concepts he or she already utilizes on a daily basis. Rather, for the most part at least, this text is intended to provide the reader with some "fresh perspectives" on how he or she might go about applying all of the above-outlined principles to develop an optimum estate plan for his or her client, in all of the most common estate planning situations, e.g., planning for married couples, planning for children and other non-spouse beneficiaries, planning for retirement benefits, planning for business owners and professionals, and lifetime gift planning.

Chapter 2

Important Tax Principles

Before beginning the seemingly herculean task of "defeating" the great titans - Congress and the Internal Revenue Service - we need to study and master several provisions of the Internal Revenue Code ("the Code") and regulations ("the regulations") which we do not often encounter in our daily practice. These are the dreaded "portion regulations" under Section 671 of the Code, and the only slightly more appealing estate and gift tax portion regulations under Chapters 11 and 12. Let's start with a discussion of the less employed rules.

Income Tax Portion Regulations

Most planners make the mistake of referring to a trust as either a "grantor trust" or a "non-grantor trust." In reality, the Internal Revenue Code and regulations never employ either term, and for a very good reason. The key Code section is Section 671, with emphasis supplied:

Where it is specified in this subpart that the grantor or another person shall be treated as the owner of *any portion* of a trust, there shall then be included in computing the taxable income and credits of the grantor or the other person those items of income, deductions, and credits against tax of the trust which are attributable to *that portion* of the trust to the extent that such items would be taken into account under this chapter in computing taxable income or credits against the tax of an individual. *Any remaining portion* of the trust shall be subject to subparts A through D. No items of a trust shall be included in computing the taxable income and credits of the grantor or of any other person solely on the grounds of his dominion and control over the trust under section 61 (relating to definition of gross income) or any other provision of this title, except as specified in this subpart.

A simple application of this "portion" concept is found in Section 676(a), again with emphasis supplied:

The grantor shall be treated as the owner of *any portion* of a trust, whether or not he is treated as such owner under any other provision of this part, where at any time the power to revest in the grantor title *to such portion* is exercisable by the grantor or a non-adverse party, or both.

Thus, under this simplest of examples, if a grantor can only revoke half of a trust, then only half of the trust's income and capital gains will be taxable to the grantor, under Section 671, and the balance of the trust's income and capital gains will be taxable under Subparts A through D of Subchapter J.

Oh, but only if the Internal Revenue Service was always this generous, because the reading and application of the portion regulations quickly gets a lot more difficult. The leading "guru" in this complex and murky tax area is Professor Leo L. Schmolka of the New York University School of Law Graduate Program in Taxation. Unfortunately, however Professor Schmolka does not appear to have published on this subject since an article he authored for the 1975 Heckerling Institute on Estate Planning.

Professor Schmolka's remarkable scholarly work of the time, "Selected Aspects of the Grantor Trust Rules," is now 42 years old, which means that most estate planning attorneys who were fortunate enough to have attended the 1975 Heckerling Institute are now either retired or nearing retirement age. Largely a theoretical piece when it was first published more than four decades ago, as a direct consequence of the unfair trust income tax rules which were passed by Congress in 1986, Professor Schmolka's masterful work has now become an essential tool for every estate planning attorney to have at his or her ready disposal.

The starting point for the study of the portion regulations is Section 1.671-3, with emphasis added:

(a) When a grantor or another person is treated under subpart E (section 671 and following) as the owner of *any portion* of a trust, there are included in computing his tax liability those items of income, deduction, and credit against tax attributable to or included in *that portion. For example*[1]:

> (1) *If a grantor or another person is treated as the owner of an entire trust (corpus as well as ordinary income)*, he takes into account in computing his income tax liability all items of income, deduction, and credit (including capital gains and losses) to which he would have been entitled had the trust not been in existence during the period he is treated as owner.

> (2) *If the portion treated as owned consists of specific trust property and its income*, all items directly related to that property are attributable to the portion. Items directly related to trust property not included in the portion treated as owned by the grantor or other person are governed by the provisions of subparts A through D (section 641 and following), part I, subchapter J, chapter 1 of the Code. Items that relate both to the portion treated as owned by the grantor and to the balance of the trust must be apportioned in a manner that is reasonable in the light of all the circumstances of each case, including the terms of the governing instrument, local law, and the practice of the trustee if it is reasonable and consistent.

> (3) *If the portion of a trust treated as owned by a grantor or another person consists of an undivided fractional interest in the trust, or of an*

---

1. The words "for example" are very instructive. It is not intended that, set forth below, are the only possibilities.

interest represented by a dollar amount, a pro rata share of each item of income, deduction, and credit is normally allocated to the portion. Thus, where the portion owned consists of an interest in or a right to an amount of corpus only, a fraction of each item (including items allocated to corpus, such as capital gains) is attributed to the portion. The numerator of this fraction is the amount which is subject to the control of the grantor or other person and the denominator is normally the fair market value of the trust corpus at the beginning of the taxable year in question. The share not treated as owned by the grantor or other person is governed by the provisions of subparts A through D. See the last three sentences of paragraph (c) of this section for the principles applicable if the portion treated as owned consists of an interest in part of the ordinary income in contrast to an interest in corpus alone.

(b) *If a grantor or another person is treated as the owner of a portion of a trust, that portion may or may not include both ordinary income and other income allocable to corpus. For example[2]:*

(1) *Only ordinary income is included by reason of an interest in or a power over ordinary income alone.* Thus, if a grantor is treated under section 673 as an owner by reason of a reversionary interest in ordinary income only, items of income

---

2. Again, the words "for example" are instructive. It is not intended that these are the only possible applications of the basic principle.

allocable to corpus will not be included in the portion he is treated as owning. Similarly, if a grantor or another person is treated under sections 674-678 as an owner of a portion by reason of a power over ordinary income only, items of income allocable to corpus are not included in that portion. (See paragraph (c) of this section to determine the treatment of deductions and credits when only ordinary income is included in the portion.)

(2) *Only income allocable to corpus is included by reason of an interest in or a power over corpus alone, if satisfaction of the interest or an exercise of the power will not result in an interest in or the exercise of a power over ordinary income which would itself cause that income to be included.* For example, if a grantor has a reversionary interest in a trust which is not such as to require that he be treated as an owner undersection 673, he may nevertheless be treated as an owner under section 677(a)(2) since any income allocable to corpus is accumulated for future distribution to him, but items of income included in determining ordinary income are not included in the portion he is treated as owning. Similarly, he may have a power over corpus which is such that he is treated as an owner under section 674 or 676 (a), but ordinary income will not be included in the portion he owns, if his power can only affect income received after a period of time such that he would not be treated as an owner of the income if the power were a reversionary interest. (See

paragraph (c) of this section to determine the treatment of deductions and credits when only income allocated to corpus is included in the portion.)

(3) *Both ordinary income and other income allocable to corpus are included by reason of an interest in or a power over both ordinary income and corpus, or an interest in or a power over corpus alone which does not come within the provisions of subparagraph (2) of this paragraph.* For example, if a grantor is treated under section 673 as the owner of a portion of a trust by reason of a reversionary interest in corpus, both ordinary income and other income allocable to corpus are included in the portion. Further, a grantor includes both ordinary income and other income allocable to corpus in the portion he is treated as owning if he is treated under section 674 or 676 as an owner because of a power over corpus which can affect income received within a period such that he would be treated as an owner under section 673 if the power were a reversionary interest. Similarly, a grantor or another person includes both ordinary income and other income allocable to corpus in the portion he is treated as owning if he is treated as an owner under section 675 or 678 because of a power over corpus.

(c) *If only income allocable to corpus is included in computing a grantor's tax liability*, he will take into account in that computation only those items of income, deductions, and credit which would not be included under subparts A through D in the computation of the tax liability of the current income beneficiaries if all distributable net income had actually been distributed to those beneficiaries. On the other hand, if the grantor or another person is treated as an owner solely because of his interest in or power over ordinary income alone, he will take into account in computing his tax liability those items which would be included in computing the tax liability of a current income beneficiary, including expenses allocable to corpus which enter into the computation of distributable net income. If the grantor or other person is treated as an owner because of his power over or right to a dollar amount of ordinary income, he will first take into account a portion of those items of income and expense entering into the computation of ordinary income under the trust instrument or local law sufficient to produce income of the dollar amount required. There will then be attributable to him a pro rata portion of other items entering into the computation of distributable net income under subparts A through D, such as expenses allocable to corpus, and a pro rata portion of credits of the trust. For examples of computations under this paragraph, see paragraph (g) of § 1.677(a)-1.

As we will discuss in the remaining chapters of this book, all of the above portion rules developed by Congress and the IRS will become relevant when we examine how we can minimize the effects of the punitive federal income tax rates imposed on trusts. Further, and as discussed in Chapter 5, it is also possible to divide a trust into two separate portions for income tax purposes, in order to ensure that payments of IRA and other qualified plan benefits to the trust may be deferred over the income beneficiary's lifetime, without forcing the payments out to the beneficiary, which would remove them from the protection of the trust.

Estate Tax Portion Regulations

Section 2033 of the Code provides simply: "The value of the gross estate shall include the value of all property to *the extent of the interest therein of the decedent* at the time of his death." (Emphasis supplied.) The various transfer with retained interest sections of the Code are similar, such as Section 2036(a): " The value of the gross estate shall include the value of all property *to the extent of any interest therein . . .."* (Emphasis supplied.)

The regulations expand on the "portion aspects" of Chapter 11 with examples such as this one from section 20.2036-1(c)(1)(i) (emphasis supplied):

> If the decedent retained or reserved an interest or right with respect to all of the property transferred by him, the amount to be included in his gross estate under section 2036 is the value of the entire property, less only the value of any outstanding income interest which is not subject to the decedent's interest or right and which is actually being enjoyed by another person at the time of the decedent's death. *If the decedent retained or reserved an interest or right with respect to a part only of the property transferred by him*, the amount to be included in his gross estate under section 2036 is only a *corresponding proportion* of the amount described in the preceding sentence.

The regulations under section 20.2041-1(b)(3) provide similar rules for taxable powers of appointment (emphasis supplied):

> *If a power of appointment exists as to part of an entire group of assets or only over a limited interest in property, section 2041 applies only to such part or interest.* For example[3], if a trust created by S provides for the payment of income to A for life, then to W for life, with power in A to appoint the remainder by will and in default of appointment for payment of the remainder to B or his estate, and if A dies before W, section 2041 applies only to the value of the remainder interest excluding W's life estate. If A dies after W, section 2041 would apply to the value of the entire property. If the power were only over one-half the remainder interest, section 2041 would apply only to one-half the value of the amounts described above.

As will be discussed in the remaining chapters of this book, the above regulations become relevant when examining how to intentionally cause federal income tax basis step-up in situations where it would not otherwise exist.

Gift Tax Portion Rules

At least one gift tax "portion rule" will become relevant in our planning to reduce the unfair income taxes on trusts. IRC Section 2514(e) provides that "[t]he lapse of a power of appointment created after October 21, 1942, during the life of

---

3. Note again the instructive aspects of one example, among different possibilities.

the individual possessing the power shall be considered a release of such power [i.e., a potential taxable gift]. *The rule of the preceding sentence shall apply with respect to the lapse of powers during any calendar year only to the extent that the property which could have been appointed by exercise of such lapsed powers exceeds in value the greater of the following amounts: (1) $5,000, or (2) 5 percent of the aggregate value of the assets out of which, or the proceeds of which, the exercise of the lapsed power could be satisfied.*" (Emphasis supplied.)

A careful and precise reading of the last clause of Section 2514(e) - *5 percent of the aggregate value of the assets out of which, or the proceeds of which, the exercise of the lapsed power could be satisfied* - will become important in our planning to minimize the punitive income taxes on trusts without creating unnecessary estate, gift and generation-skipping transfer tax risks.

Chapter 3

Optimum Planning for Married Couples

Perhaps no aspect of estate planning has been transformed more over the past 15+ years, than has estate planning for married couples, including same sex marriages. Prior to the passage of President Bush's "estate tax repeal" legislation in May of 2001, the dominant plan in married couple estate planning was the "two-share" plan, i.e., the husband's share and the wife's share, which we advisors pushed with much brio. The primary reason for this style of estate planning, of course, was the federal estate tax exemption level, which in May of 2001 stood at only $675,000.

If a married couple wished to exempt up to $1,350,000 in assets from the federal estate tax, it was essential that they separate their assets into two shares, and then fund a "bypass," or "credit shelter" trust at the death of the first spouse, with assets equal in value to no more than the federal estate tax exemption amount in effect at the time of first spouse's death. The balance of the first spouse to die's assets passed either outright to the surviving spouse or to some form of marital deduction trust. For couples with estates (including life insurance and retirement benefits) in excess of $675,000, deviating from this standard marital estate plan (sometimes referred to as an "A/B plan") was not an option if the couple wanted all or most of their assets to be available to the surviving spouse. There was no room for alteration.

One Share or Two?

In the world of $5 million plus federal estate tax exemptions and spousal portability elections, the obvious starting point in optimum estate planning for married couples is therefore to decide whether the couple needs to divide their assets in order to achieve two estate tax deductions, and not just one. Further, even if the couple should not divide their assets for federal estate tax reasons, are there other reasons they should consider doing so anyway? The resolution to each of these "one share or two" issues depends on a number of factors.

It depends on the size of the couples' estate. It depends on whether the clients' state of residence has an estate or inheritance tax exemption which is smaller than the federal estate tax exemption. It depends on whether the state recognizes tenancy by the entirety property (and, if so, whether that recognition extends to personalty as well as real property). It depends on whether state law has enacted a statute similar to those of Delaware[4] and Missouri[5] which allow tenancy by the entirety assets to be divided and transferred in trust (sometimes

---

4. 12 Del. C. § 3334. *See also* Md. Est. & Tr. Code Sec. 14-113; T.C.A. Sec. 35-15-510; W.S. 4-10-402(c)-(e).

5. RSMo § 456.950.

referred to as a "qualified spousal trust," or "QST") yet still be entitled to tenancy by the entirety type creditor protection. It may also depend on whether the couple owns significant IRA and/or other qualified plan benefits which can benefit from maximum tax deferral and rollover treatment, and therefore from the federal (and, if available, state) spousal portability election. Finally, it may depend on how long the couple has been married and whether this is a second marriage for either or both of the spouses - and, if so, whether either or both of the spouses has or have a child or children from the previous marriage(s).

"Smaller" Estates

If the couple's estate is "small" (e.g., under $1 million, excluding typical life insurance amounts), normally there is no need to complicate matters by dividing the couple's assets into two shares; one joint share is sufficient. If the couple opts for an estate plan which incorporates a revocable living trust in order to avoid probate at the second spouse's death, the primary issue instead will be whether to fund the revocable trust while both spouses are living.

If the couple does not reside in a tenancy by the entirety state, the only possible disadvantage to funding the trust is that it could create some complexities down the road, e.g., if the couple transfers their home to the trust and they later decide to refinance or sell the home. If the couple resides in a tenancy by the entirety state (as to personalty and/or real property), on the other hand, transferring title to the tenancy by the entirety property to a revocable trust will normally destroy the creditor protection aspects of the transferred property.

An exception to the "credit protection destruction rule" may exist if the couple happens to reside in one of the growing numbers of states which have enacted a qualified spousal trust ("QST") statute, described later in this chapter. If the couple resides in a tenancy by the entirety state which has not passed a QST statute, the couple should keep the property in joint names, and add a transfer on death ("TOD") or payable on death ("POD") designation for the property, to the trust. Of course, if the couple's state of residence or the location of any real property does not permit a TOD or POD designation for the particular type of property at issue, transferring the same to the trust may be the couple's only option if they wish to avoid probate at the second death, and the couple's personal liability insurance will become more relevant.

If the couple happens to reside in a tenancy by the entirety state, their automobiles should each be titled in the name of the principal driver, coupled with a transfer on death designation to the other spouse or to their joint trust, if permitted under state law. This will minimize the chances of a successful joint lawsuit against the couple, e.g., in a situation where defective tires or brakes contributed to an automobile accident.

"Hybrid" Joints Trusts

Even if it is not necessary (for estate tax reduction purposes) to divide the couple's assets into two shares during their lifetime, in a significant percentages of cases it may still be advisable to create a second share when the first spouse dies. This would be the situation where, for example, either or both spouses owns a substantial amount of insurance (e.g., $500,000 or more) on his or her own life, or owns other assets which cannot be titled in joint names.

The insured could simply leave the insurance proceeds or other separately owned assets outright to his or her spouse, but then the same would not be protected from potential future creditor claims against the surviving spouse. A trust (similar to a standard bypass or credit shelter trust) including a spendthrift clause for the benefit of the surviving spouse and/or children, on the other hand, would provide such protections, in most states, even if the surviving spouse serves as trustee of the trust - at least as long as standards for the distribution of income and principal to or for the spouse's benefit are included in the trust document. It would also provide an extra layer of protection against potential encroachments by and elective share rights of a new spouse, should the surviving spouse remarry, and allow the decedent spouse some control over the ultimate disposition of the life insurance proceeds or other separately owned assets.

Leaving the life insurance proceeds or other separately owned assets in trust will also insulate the same from estate taxes, should this become an issue for the surviving spouse later on (e.g., due to future changes in federal or state estate tax laws, the acquisition of additional wealth, etc.). Because the surviving spouse may serve as trustee of this "bypass" trust, it also allows for control.

The "hybrid" joint revocable trust protects the insurance proceeds from estate taxes at the survivor's death, but without having to rely on the spousal portability election. A significant disadvantage stemming from relying on the portability election can arise if the surviving spouse remarries and his or her new spouse also predeceases, since in this situation the spousal portability election amount is no longer available. Another major disadvantage of the spousal portability election is that it has the effect of exposing all of the surviving spouse's assets to lawsuits, potential encroachments by a new spouse, and potential elective share rights of a new spouse. The decedent spouse also lacks any control over the ultimate disposition of the "ported" assets.

Note that leaving life insurance to a trust for the surviving spouse and other family in this fashion will not create an estate tax issue at the surviving spouse's death. This is because the full amount of the life insurance will be includible in the insured spouse's gross estate under Code Section 2042, and therefore any contributions which the surviving spouse may have made toward the payment of premiums during the insured's lifetime will not constitute an estate tax includible transfer under Section 2036 or 2038.

Flexible Drafting Required in Light of the 2016 Election Results

As will be discussed further in the Epilogue to this text, although this should have always been the case, especially as a result of the 2016 Presidential, Senate and House elections, all favoring Republicans who have as part of their platform the repeal of the federal estate tax, whenever a two-share estate plan is adopted the plan should also build in the potential for this repeal during either or both spouses' lifetimes. Flexible planning for the potential repeal of the estate tax is also needed, *now*, at the first spouse to die's death.

At least three reasons exist for this conclusion. First, it is always possible that a spouse could have a stroke or other disabling life event, and after this event (but during the spouse's lifetime) the federal estate tax is repealed. Second, it is just a matter of plain fairness to our clients to draft for the possibility of estate tax repeal, since we now know that this could actually happen, thus potentially eliminating the need to charge the clients additional legal fees for future revisions which can be anticipated today. Finally, a more practical point is that, should the federal estate tax in fact be repealed in the future, attorneys are going to need an abundance of time to amend a potentially very significant number of estate plans.

Sample Form

Here is the sample language we put into place in our office after the federal estate tax was reinstated in early 2011, the goal being to "lock in" estate tax repeal should there be no federal estate tax at the first spouse's death, but a future administration brings back the tax. This form language does not necessarily mean future changes will not still be needed, depending on how future laws are drafted, but at least constitutes our best efforts using what we know at this time, based on the situation which existed for one year, in 2010:

1.2 <u>If There is Not a Federal Estate or Generation-Skipping Transfer Tax</u>. In the event the grantor's wife/husband survives the grantor and there is neither a federal estate tax nor a federal generation-skipping transfer tax in effect and which applies to the grantor's estate at the time of the grantor's death, the trustee shall hold or distribute the Remaining Trust Property as follows:

a.   <u>Section 691 Income in Respect of a Decedent</u>. First, any asset classified as income in respect of a decedent under Section 691 of the Internal Revenue Code, or any successor section thereto, shall be set aside and held in trust with income and principal administered and distributed pursuant to the provisions of ARTICLE __ hereof.

b.   <u>Section 1022 Portion</u>.   Next, in the event that Section 1022 of the Internal Revenue Code (as it existed in the year 2010), or any similar provision, is in effect and applicable to the grantor's estate at the time of the grantor's death, the trustee shall hold or distribute the following trust assets, as follows:

i.   <u>Section 1022(b) Portion</u>. The trustee shall set aside and allocate to the trust under ARTICLE__ hereof **[A TRADITIONAL BYPASS TRUST]**, those remaining trust assets, if any, beginning with the asset or assets having the least amount of built-in appreciation (calculated by subtracting the grantor's income tax basis from the fair market value on the date of death of the grantor), as a percentage of the fair market value of the assets on the date of death of the grantor, necessary to achieve the maximum basis step-up provided for in Section 1022(b) of the Internal Revenue Code (as it existed in the year 2010), or any similar provision, or any successor section thereto, at the time of the grantor's death, which is not allocated to assets passing outside of this trust, or until all of such remaining trust assets have been allocated to the trust under ARTICLE __ hereof, if earlier.

    ii.   Section 1022(c) Portion. Next, the trustee shall [set aside and allocate to the trust under ARTICLE __ hereof - **A TRADITIONAL QTIP TRUST**] [distribute to the grantor's wife, outright and free from trust], those remaining trust assets, if any, beginning with the asset or assets having the least amount of built-in appreciation (calculated by subtracting the grantor's income tax basis from the fair market value on the date of death of the grantor), as a percentage of the fair market value of such asset or assets on the date of death of the grantor, necessary to achieve the maximum basis step-up provided for in Section 1022(c) of the Internal Revenue Code (as it existed in the year 2010), or any similar provision, or any successor section thereto, at the time of the grantor's death, which is not allocated to assets passing outside of this trust, or until all of such remaining trust assets have been [allocated to the trust under ARTICLE __ hereof] [distributed to the grantor's wife/husband, outright and free from trust], if earlier. If the grantor's wife/husband or the grantor's wife's/husband's personal representative shall disclaim or renounce the grantor's wife's/husband's interest under this subparagraph 1.2.b.ii, in whole or in part, then the portion of this gift to which the disclaimed interest attaches shall be held by the trustee pursuant to the provisions of ARTICLE __ hereof.

c.   Residual Portion.   Finally, the balance of the Remaining Trust Property not set aside pursuant to the provisions of paragraphs 1.2.a and1.2.b, above, if any, shall be held in trust with income and principal administered and distributed pursuant to the provisions of ARTICLE __ hereof **[A TRADITIONAL BYPASS TRUST]**. [Finally, the balance of the Remaining Trust Property not disposed of pursuant to the provisions of paragraphs 1.2.a and 1.2.b, above, if any, shall be distributed to the grantor's wife/husband, outright and free from trust (or, at the direction of the grantor's wife/husband or the grantor's wife's/husband's legal representatives, to the trustee or trustees of any revocable trust established by the grantor's wife/husband); PROVIDED, HOWEVER, if the grantor's wife/husband or the grantor's wife's/husband's personal representative shall disclaim or renounce the grantor's wife's/husband's interest under this paragraph 1.2.c, in whole or in part, then the portion of this gift to which the disclaimed interest attaches shall be held by the trustee pursuant to the provisions of ARTICLE __ hereof **[A TRADITIONAL BYPASS TRUST**.]

d.   Reduction of State Transfer Taxes. Notwithstanding the preceding provisions of this subsection 1.2, to the extent any state estate tax, state inheritance tax or other state transfer tax payable as a result of the grantor's death could be reduced by causing any portion of the assets passing under paragraphs 1.2.a through 1.2.c, above, to be either held in trust pursuant to the provisions of ARTICLE __ hereof [**A TRADITIONAL QTIP TRUST**] (with all necessary elections to minimize said taxes assumed to have been made) or distributed to the grantor's wife, outright and free from trust, the trustee shall hold that portion necessary to minimize such state transfer taxes in trust with income and principal administered and distributed pursuant to the provisions of ARTICLE __ hereof [**A TRADITIONAL QTIP TRUST**]; PROVIDED, HOWEVER, if transferring any asset(s) to the grantor's wife/husband, outright and free from trust, would reduce such state transfer taxes more than if such asset(s) were held in trust with income and principal administered and distributed pursuant to the provisions of ARTICLE __ hereof [**A TRADITIONAL QTIP TRUST**] (with all necessary elections to minimize said taxes assumed to have been made), the trustee shall transfer such asset(s) to the grantor's wife/husband, outright and free from trust. If the grantor's wife/husband or the grantor's wife's/husband's personal representative shall disclaim or renounce the grantor's wife's/husband's interest under this paragraph 1.2.d, in whole or in part, then the portion of this gift to which the disclaimed interest attaches shall continue to be held by the trustee pursuant to the provisions of ARTICLE __hereof [**A TRADITIONAL BYPASS TRUST**]. The portion to be set aside pursuant to this paragraph

1.2.d shall, to the extent possible, consist first of assets otherwise passing under paragraph 1.2.a, above, next with assets otherwise passing under paragraph 1.2.c, above, and finally with assets otherwise passing under subparagraph 1.2.b.i, above. **[WARNING - Outright gift may not be desired and/or Federal Estate Tax might be reinstated]**

USE THIS ALTERNATIVE WHEN MARITAL GIFT IS OUTRIGHT.

[d. <u>Reduction of State Transfer Taxes</u>. Notwithstanding the preceding provisions of this subsection 1.2, to the extent any state estate tax, state inheritance tax or other state transfer tax payable as a result of the grantor's death could be reduced by causing any portion of the assets passing under paragraphs 1.2.a through 1.2.c, above, to be distributed to the grantor's wife/husband, outright and free from trust, the trustee shall transfer to the grantor's wife/husband, outright and free from trust, that portion of trust assets necessary to minimize such state transfer taxes. If the grantor's wife/husband or the grantor's wife's/husband's personal representative shall disclaim or renounce the grantor's wife's/husband's interest under this paragraph 1.2.d, in whole or in part, then the portion of this gift to which the disclaimed interest attaches shall continue to be held by the trustee pursuant to the provisions of ARTICLE __hereof **[A TRADITIONAL BYPASS**

TRUST]. The portion to be set aside pursuant to this paragraph 1.2.d shall, to the extent possible, consist first of assets otherwise passing under paragraph 1.2.a, above, next with assets otherwise passing under paragraph 1.2.c, above, and finally with assets otherwise passing under subparagraph 1.2.b.i, above.]

1.3   Additional Funding Provisions

a.   In setting aside the property to be allocated to the shares provided for in this Section 1, and except as otherwise provided, the trustee shall not be required to fractionalize each asset and may, in the trustee's discretion, allot to such shares any asset or any undivided interest therein.

b.   In the sole and absolute discretion of the trustee, the gifts under subparagraphs 1.2.b.i and 1.2.b.ii, above, need not be funded in full, but only to the extent necessary to avoid the creation of fractional interests in assets.

Minimizing Federal Income Taxes on Bypass Trusts

The suggestion that the advisor consider use of these "hybrid joint trusts," as well as bypass and credit shelter trusts (discussed below) generally, immediately reminds us of the significant federal income tax disadvantages associated with holding assets inside a non-grantor trust. These unfair trust income tax laws include:

- A maximum federal income tax rate of 39.6 percent on trusts applicable to levels of trust taxable income in excess of only $12,400 (in 2016), whereas single individuals don't reach the 39.6 percent bracket until their taxable incomes exceed $413,050 (in 2016);

- A 5 percent surtax on capital gains and qualified dividends of trusts applicable when trust taxable income is in excess of only $12,400 (in 2016), whereas single individuals don't pay the same surtax until their taxable incomes exceed $413,500 (in 2016);

- A 3.8 percent surtax on items of net investment income of trusts when adjusted gross income (AGI) exceeds only $12,400 (in 2016), whereas single individuals don't pay the same surtax until their AGIs exceed $200,000 (in 2016); and

- A loss of a new income tax basis on non-IRD assets when these types of trusts terminate as a result of the death of the life beneficiary, whereas non-IRD assets owned outright by an individual generally receive a new income tax basis at the individual's death.

Minimizing the effects of the current high income tax rates on trusts, without neutralizing all of the above-outlined advantages of holding assets in trust (e.g., estate tax protection, divorce or remarriage protection, lawsuit protection, and the obvious protections for a minor or otherwise younger child[6]) by making unnecessary outright distributions of trust income and capital gains, involves utilizing Internal Revenue Code Section 678 and the trust income tax portion rules outlined in Chapter 2. The aim is to cause the trust beneficiary, rather than the trust, to be taxed on the portion of the trust's taxable income, including capital gains, taxed at the high or penalty rates. A potential additional transfer tax benefit of the arrangement is that the Section 678 beneficiary's annual payment of the tax on the income of the trust will not constitute a taxable gift.[7] The beneficiary's gross estate is thus reduced by the compounded effect of the cumulative amount of the income taxes paid over his or her lifetime.

IRC Section 678 provides that "[a] person other than the grantor shall be treated as the owner of any portion of a trust with respect to which: (1) such person has a power exercisable solely by himself to vest the corpus or the income therefrom in himself, or (2) such person has previously partially released or otherwise modified such a power and after the release or modification retains such control as would, within the principles of sections 671 to 677, inclusive, subject the grantor

---

6. Note that in a particular situation a successful plaintiff or divorced spouse may still attempt to attach the trust assets to the extent that a beneficiary's withdrawal power over income has lapsed in previous years. Depending upon state law, at a very minimum the trust device has made this process much more involved and difficult for the claimant, and in any event is obviously preferential to parking all of the previous year's compound trust income in the beneficiary's personal bank or brokerage account.

7. Rev. Rul 2004-64, 2004 C.B. 7.

of a trust to treatment as the owner thereof."[8]

If desired, an estate planner can limit the beneficiary's withdrawal power to the types of trust income that are taxed at the highest federal income tax rates only, for example, by excluding qualified dividends and capital gains taxed at still favorable income tax rates, as well as items of federally tax-exempt income. The withdrawal power holder would naturally possess the ability to withdraw any income necessary to pay his additional income taxes resulting from the Section 678 power, or an independent trustee could reimburse the power holder for this amount.

The trust income tax "portion rules" outlined in Chapter 2 are what allow for this "tax tracing" treatment.[9] Although there is no specific example in the regulations squarely on point, this conclusion is reached by analyzing the principles

---

8. *See also* James G. Blase, "Recent Tax Acts Require Focus on Income Tax Aspects of Estate Planning," 30 ETPL 617(December2003); James G. Blase, "Drafting Tips That Minimize the Income Tax on Trusts—Part 1,"40ETPL28(July2013); James G. Blase, "The Minimum Income Tax Trust," *Trusts & Estates* (May 2014), at p. 32.

9. Despite the clear language of Section 678 relating to a "sole power to vest" trust income, and the trust income tax portion regulations described in Chapter 2, some commentators apparently feel the only Section 678 power which will cause the income of the bypass trust to be taxed to the surviving spouse is a "right to withdraw the trust principal," which obviously could cause the entire trust to be included in the gross estate of the surviving spouse. By effectively combining the trust income tax portion rules and the gift tax portion rules described in Chapter 2 and here, however, estate tax inclusion is limited to a maximum of five percent of the trust's assets. *Cf.* Gans, Blattmachr and Zeydel, "Supercharged Credit Shelter Trust," *Probate & Property* (July/August 2007) 52 at 54.

which the regulations do address. For example, again from Chapter 2:

(1) *Only ordinary income is included by reason of an interest in or a power over ordinary income alone.* Thus, if a grantor is treated under section 673 as an owner by reason of a reversionary interest in ordinary income only, items of income allocable to corpus will not be included in the portion he is treated as owning. Similarly, if a grantor or another person is treated under sections 674-678 as an owner of a portion by reason of a power over ordinary income only, items of income allocable to corpus are not included in that portion. (See paragraph (c) of this section to determine the treatment of deductions and credits when only ordinary income is included in the portion.)

(2) *If the portion treated as owned consists of specific trust property and its income*, all items directly related to that property are attributable to the portion. Items directly related to trust property not included in the portion treated as owned by the grantor or other person are governed by the provisions of subparts A through D (section 641 and following), part I, subchapter J, chapter 1 of the Code. Items that relate both to the portion treated, as owned by the grantor and to the balance of the trust must be apportioned in a manner that is reasonable in the light of all the circumstances of each case, including the terms of the governing instrument, local law, and the practice of the trustee if it is reasonable and consistent.

(3) *If the portion of a trust treated as owned by a*

grantor or another person consists of an undivided fractional interest in the trust, or of an interest represented by a dollar amount, a pro rata share of each item of income, deduction, and credit is normally allocated to the portion. Thus, where the portion owned consists of an interest in or a right to an amount of corpus only, a fraction of each item (including items allocated to corpus, such as capital gains) is attributed to the portion. The numerator of this fraction is the amount which is subject to the control of the grantor or other person and the denominator is normally the fair market value of the trust corpus at the beginning of the taxable year in question. The share not treated as owned by the grantor or other person is governed by the provisions of subparts A through D. See the last three sentences of paragraph (c) of this section for the principles applicable if the portion treated as owned consists of an interest in part of the ordinary income in contrast to an interest in corpus alone.

In the instant case, the Section 678 "portion" is a combination of the rules described in paragraph (1) through (3), above. It is only over trust income (as sometimes defined below, to include capital gains and 100 percent of IRA and qualified plan receipts) which exceeds a certain amount (e.g., the point where the income would otherwise be in the maximum tax bracket), and if desired only certain types of income which is generally not taxed at less than the maximum federal rate, e.g., not qualified dividends.

Remember that the examples included in the regulations are just that, only examples. Section 671 of the Code contains this overriding *general* principle (emphasis supplied):

Where it is specified in this subpart that the grantor or another person shall be treated as the owner of *any portion* of a trust, there shall then be included in computing the taxable income and credits of the grantor or the other person those items of income, deductions, and credits against tax of the trust which are attributable to *that portion* of the trust to the extent that such items would be taken into account under this chapter in computing taxable income or credits against the tax of an individual.

And remember also that Section 678(a) contains this overriding *specific* principle already quoted above (emphasis supplied):

A person other than the grantor shall be treated as the owner of *any portion* of a trust with respect to which: (1) such person has a power exercisable solely by himself to vest the corpus or the income therefrom in himself, or (2) such person has previously partially released or otherwise modified such a power and after the release or modification retains such control as would, within the principles of sections 671 to 677, inclusive, subject the grantor of a trust to treatment as the owner thereof.

The trust document is intentionally drafted to limit the Section 671/678 Chapter 2 "portion"to the income taxed at the punitive trust income tax rates, which definitely includes all trust income taxed at the maximum income tax rate on ordinary income, but, if desired by the trust drafter, also income (including capital gains defined as trust income, in the manner described below) subject to the 5 percent and 3.8 percent surtaxes which became effective in 2013.

Estate planners should ensure that no provision of the trust document will infringe on the power holder's Section 678 "sole power to vest" the trust income for the current tax year (including, if desired, capital gains). For example, in the case of a surviving spouse, a disinterested trustee may possess the power to suspend the spouse's withdrawal power if he or she is the subject of a lawsuit, but only if the exercise of the trustee's suspension power is not effective until the first date of the trust's next tax year. Similarly, in the case of a child beneficiary, a disinterested trustee may be given the power to suspend's the child's Section 678 power in the event of unwise or immature use of trust funds by the child, or in the event of a lawsuit or divorce involving the child, but only effective at the beginning of the next tax year of the trust.

Avoiding Annual Taxable Gifts

The relevant gift tax portion rule discussed in Chapter 2, IRC Section 2514(e), provides that "[t]he lapse of a power of appointment created after October 21, 1942, during the life of the individual possessing the power shall be considered a release of such power [i.e., a potential taxable gift]. The rule of the preceding sentence shall apply with respect to the lapse of powers during any calendar year only to the extent that the property which could have been appointed by exercise of such lapsed powers exceeds in value the greater of the following amounts: (1) $5,000, or (2) 5 percent of the aggregate value of the assets out of which, or the proceeds of which, the exercise of the lapsed power could be satisfied."

Therefore, to avoid an annual taxable transfer by the beneficiary, the beneficiary's withdrawal power over trust income should be limited to a portion of the trust assets equal to 5 percent of the value of the trust, per year. The extent of the 5 percent limitation (i.e., "the assets out of which, or the proceeds of which, the exercise of the lapsed power could be satisfied") should also normally be broadened to its fullest extent possible, by making it clear in the trust document that the trustee may satisfy the beneficiary's withdrawal right by liquidating any asset of the trust, including those payable to the trust over time, such as benefits payable under individual retirement accounts, qualified plans and nonqualified annuities. This important step will create the largest possible portion of the trust income which can be taxed at the beneficiary's income tax rates, rather than at the trust's rates, without potential adverse estate and gift tax consequences.

Note also that, if a portion of the trust is invested in federally income tax-exempt securities, it will be unlikely that the ordinary income of the trust will ever exceed the 5 percent limitation, at least in anything close to today's interest rate environment. However, if the goal is to also tax the trust beneficiary on capital gains, without requiring outright distributions of the same to the beneficiary, the larger 5 percent limitation amount will be important.

In fact, the primary reason for not enlarging the withdrawal power beyond 5 percent in "small" estate situations is the fact that, as above demonstrated, this will normally not be necessary. The other concern is that, just because it may appear at first blush that we are dealing with a small estate situation, one never knows what kind of wealth the survivor may marry into, the future of the federal estate tax exemption, etc., thus creating a potential federal gift tax issue where one did not otherwise exist. Finally, and as discussed further below, the trustee will always retain the ability to make distributions which carry out trust income (including, where desired, capital gains) and which exceed the 5 percent limitation.

Application of Section 678(a)(2)

Section 678(a)(2) of the Code provides that a person other than the grantor shall be treated as the owner of any portion of a trust with respect to which "such person has previously partially released or otherwise modified [a Section 678(a) power] and after the release or modification retains such control as would, within the principles of sections 671 to 677, inclusive, subject the grantor of a trust to treatment as the owner thereof." There is an argument, based solely on private letter rulings, that this means the Section 678 power holder may then be taxed on more than just the trust income subject to the power holder's withdrawal power during the current tax year of the trust.

The first question which this argument elicits seems to be: Is it a bad thing or a good thing for the beneficiary to be taxed on trust income which exceeds the current year 5 percent limitation? Remembering the high income tax rates on *all* trust income today, including even qualified dividends and capital gains, it would be hard to argue that this is a bad thing in most cases, especially since paying the tax on a larger percentage of the trust income is nothing more than a disguised transfer to the trust, allowing for greater asset protection, estate tax protection, etc.

More importantly, and under normal statutory construction rules, there would appear to be less than a convincing argument for taxing the trust beneficiary on this additional income. The argument in favor of the additional inclusion is that when the power of withdrawal lapses each year, this is the same as though the beneficiary "has previously partially released or otherwise modified" the Section 678 power of withdrawal. Aside from the obvious need for positive action on the part of the trust beneficiary, which the (a)(2) language mandates, it is even more significant that, on the gift tax side, Congress chose to include specific Code language which deemed certain lapses to be releases, in Section 2514(e), while on the income tax side Congress did not choose to do the same.

Sample Forms

Set forth below is the first portion of a sample "bypass" trust established under a hybrid joint trust at the first spouse to die's passing, the purpose being to illustrate the basic Section 678 trust drafting technique. The other portions of the form will be discussed later in this chapter.

Note that the form contains built-in warnings to the drafter for potential situations where the couple may not want to include an income tax withdrawal power, irrespective of the potential income tax savings involved (for example, second marriage situations or in the case of a spendthrift child), or because under the particular facts no income or transfer tax savings are anticipated to ensue from the insertion of the withdrawal power into the trust document (for example, in the case of a non-exempt generation-skipping trust where the beneficiary is already in a high income tax bracket).

Note also that this form intentionally breaks out separately (as a separate subsection 1.2) the various new (in 2013) 5 percent excise taxes on "excess" dividends and capital gains, as well as items subject to the 3.8 net investment income tax. The reason for this is to ensure that the first income items captured by the 5 percent maximum withdrawal power are the items which are normally taxed at the highest rate of income tax, e.g., taxable interest and rents, and distributions from IRAs, qualified plans and nonqualified annuities.

The form deems all qualified plan, IRA and nonqualified annuity distributions as part of "trust accounting income" for purpose of defining the scope of the beneficiary's withdrawal power over income, because otherwise the beneficiary's withdrawal over these types of benefits would be subject to state law definitions of trust accounting income. The special structure of the trust to allow the receipt of qualified plan and IRA benefits to qualify for "stretch" income tax deferral treatment is addressed in Chapter 5.

The form also includes some of the optional disinterested trustee "suspension" powers addressed above.

Due to the requisite complexity in these trust forms, it is obviously imperative that clients' draft documents be accompanied with well-written attorney summary explanation letters. It is just as important for the drafting attorney to not refrain from using the best trust language possible, out of fear that this will require the addition of a well-drafted summary explanation letter, somewhat longer trust documents, and sometimes longer client meetings. And remember too that the author is not suggesting that the drafter utilize *any* of these sample forms; but rather only that thought be given to estate planning solutions which address the unfair taxation of trusts, without adversely affecting the client's other legitimate estate planning goals, such as estate and asset protection.

Section 1.   Distribution and Use of Income and Principal During Surviving Grantor's Lifetime

1.1   During the surviving grantor's lifetime the surviving grantor (including any legal representative acting on behalf of the surviving grantor) shall have the annual noncumulative power to withdraw all or any portion of the trust accounting income on or before December 31 of the calendar year; PROVIDED, HOWEVER, that (i) the foregoing power of withdrawal shall not extend to the portion of the trust accounting income which, for the calendar year, would be either exempt from federal income tax or subject to federal income tax to the trust, after all deductions and exemptions (but determined as though the trustee made no other income or principal distributions or encroachments during the year other than for trust expenses and taxes), at less than the general maximum federal income tax rate applicable to trusts (and for this purpose said excluded portion (I) shall begin with any dividends, capital gains or other items of trust accounting income which are subject to a maximum federal income tax rate which is lower than the general maximum federal income tax rate applicable to trusts, (II) shall next include any items of trust accounting income filling out the lower income tax brackets of the trust which do not constitute "net investment income" as defined in Section 1411(c) of the Internal Revenue Code, or any successor section thereto, (III) shall next include any additional items of trust accounting income filling out the lower income tax brackets of the trust which constitute "net investment income" as defined in Section 1411(c) of the Internal Revenue Code, or any successor section thereto, and (IV) shall assume that all items of federal gross income of the trust which do not constitute trust accounting income and which are not subject to a maximum federal income tax rate which is lower than the general maximum federal income tax rate applicable to trusts, are using up the lower income tax brackets of the trust first, before the aforesaid items of trust accounting income) and (ii) if Section 2514(e) of the Internal Revenue Code, or any successor section thereto, is in effect during the calendar year, the amount of trust accounting income subject to the foregoing power of withdrawal during the calendar year shall not exceed five percent (5%) (or such other percentage as shall be provided for in Section 2514(e)(2) of the Internal Revenue Code, or any successor section thereto) of the combined value of the principal and income of the trust on December 31 of the calendar year (or on the date of the surviving grantor's death, if earlier). If more than one item of trust accounting income is withdrawable by the surviving grantor pursuant to the foregoing provisions of this subsection 1.1 (for example, taxable interest from corporate bonds and distributions from retirement assets (as defined in ARTICLE __, below)), but the above-described limitation of Section 2514(e) of the Internal Revenue Code, or any successor section thereto, shall apply, the surviving grantor's power of withdrawal shall extend to a pro rata portion of each of such items based upon the ratio in which the total amount of each of such items bears to the total amount of all of such items (assuming the above-described limitation of Section 2514(e) of the Internal Revenue Code, or any successor section thereto, does not apply). Any such withdrawable trust accounting income which is not withdrawn by the surviving grantor or by the surviving grantor's legal representative by the end of any calendar year (or by the time of the surviving grantor's death, if earlier) shall be added to the principal of the trust estate, and the surviving grantor's power of withdrawal for such calendar year shall lapse. For purposes of this subsection 1.1, the term "trust accounting income" shall include all retirement assets (as defined in ARTICLE __, below, but ignoring the last proviso of the definition) paid to the trust during the year regardless of whether all of said retirement assets paid to the trust during the year are otherwise considered to be trust accounting income, and the principal of the trust shall include the underlying value of all retirement assets (as defined in ARTICLE __, below, but ignoring the last proviso of the definition) and other assets which are payable to the trust over time and not yet paid to the trust. The trustee other than a trustee having any beneficial interest in the trust (other than solely as a contingent taker under ARTICLE __, below) may, in the sole and absolute discretion of said trustee, suspend the surviving grantor's withdrawal power under this subsection 1.1, in whole or part, by instrument in writing executed by said trustee before January 1 of the calendar year in which such withdrawal power would otherwise exist. Reasons for such suspension may include, but shall not be limited to, overall tax savings for the trust and its beneficiaries (including remainder beneficiaries) and creditor protection for the surviving grantor. In the event the surviving grantor shall have the surviving grantor's power of withdrawal suspended, in whole or in part, the trustee other than a trustee having any beneficial interest in the trust (other than solely as a contingent taker under ARTICLE __, below) may also, in the sole and absolute discretion of said trustee, restore the surviving grantor's withdrawal power under this subsection 1.1, in whole or part, at any time, by instrument in writing executed by said trustee. **[MAY NOT WANT TO USE 5% WITHDRAWAL WHEN 1) SECOND SPOUSE, 2) SPENDTHRIFT CHILD, OR 3) HIGH NET WORTH CLIENT AND NO TAX BENEFIT FOR SUCH POWER OVER NON-GST TAX-EXEMPT TRUST]**

      1.2   During the surviving grantor's lifetime the surviving grantor (including any legal representative acting on behalf of the surviving grantor) shall also have the annual noncumulative power to withdraw all or any portion of the "net investment income" of the trust (as defined in Section 1411(c) of the Internal Revenue Code, or any successor section thereto) which is not already withdrawable pursuant to the provisions of subsection 1.1, above, and which is not described in clause (III) of subsection 1.1, above (hereinafter "the excess net investment income"), on or before December 31 of the calendar year; PROVIDED, HOWEVER, that (i) the foregoing power of withdrawal shall not extend to the portion of the excess net investment income of the trust which, for the calendar year, is less than the dollar amount at which the highest tax bracket in section 1(e) of the Internal Revenue Code, or any successor section thereto, begins for such calendar year (but with said dollar amount being reduced, but not below zero, by (A) any net investment income, as defined in Section 1411(c) of the Internal Revenue Code, or any successor section thereto, which is not withdrawable by the surviving grantor pursuant to the provisions of clause (III) of paragraph 1.1, above, and (B) an amount equal to the total of any costs which are deductible for purposes of determining the taxable income of the trust but not for purposes of determining the adjusted gross income of the trust, after the application of Section 67(e) of the Internal Revenue Code, or any successor section thereto), and (ii) if Section 2514(e) of the Internal Revenue Code, or any successor section thereto, is in effect during the calendar year, the amount of the excess net investment income subject to the foregoing power of withdrawal during the calendar year shall not exceed (A) five percent (5%) (or such other percentage as shall be provided for in Section 2514(e)(2) of the Internal Revenue Code, or any successor section thereto) of the combined value of the principal and income of the trust on December 31 of the calendar year (or on the date of the surviving grantor's death, if earlier), less (B) any amount which is withdrawable by the surviving grantor during the calendar year pursuant to the provisions of subsection 1.1, above. If more than one item of excess net investment income is withdrawable by the surviving grantor pursuant to the foregoing provisions of this subsection 1.2 (for example, capital gains from the sale of various corporate stocks and dividend distributions on various corporate stocks), but the above-described limitation of Section 2514(e) of the Internal Revenue Code, or any successor section thereto, shall apply, the surviving grantor's power of withdrawal shall extend to a pro rata portion of each of such items based upon the ratio in which the total amount of each of such items bears to the total amount of all of such items (assuming the above-described limitation of Section 2514(e) of the Internal Revenue Code, or any successor section thereto, does not apply). Any such withdrawable excess net investment income which is not withdrawn by the surviving grantor or by the surviving grantor's legal representative by the end of any calendar year (or by the time of the surviving grantor's death, if earlier) shall not be withdrawable by the surviving grantor in any subsequent calendar year. For purposes of this subsection 1.2, the principal of the trust shall include the underlying value of all retirement assets (as defined in ARTICLE __, below, but ignoring the last proviso of the definition) and other assets which are payable to the trust over time and not yet paid to the trust. The trustee other than a trustee having any beneficial interest in the trust (other than solely as a contingent taker under ARTICLE __, below) may, in the sole and absolute discretion of said trustee, suspend the surviving grantor's withdrawal power under this subsection 1.2, in whole or part, by instrument in writing executed by said trustee before January 1 of the calendar year in which such withdrawal power would otherwise exist. Reasons for such suspension may include, but shall not be limited to, overall tax savings for the trust and its beneficiaries (including remainder beneficiaries) and creditor protection for the surviving grantor. In the event the surviving grantor shall have the surviving grantor's power of withdrawal suspended, in whole or in part, the trustee other than a trustee having any beneficial interest in the trust (other than solely as a contingent taker under ARTICLE __, below) may also, in the sole and absolute discretion of said trustee, restore the surviving grantor's withdrawal power under this subsection 1.2, in whole or

50

part, at any time, by instrument in writing executed by said trustee. **[MAY NOT USE WHEN: 1) SECOND SPOUSE, 2) SPENDTHRIFT CHILD, OR 3) HIGH NET WORTH AND NO TAX BENEFIT FROM POWER OVER NON-GST TAX-EXEMPT TRUST]**

Trustee Powers Article

In the administration of each trust hereunder the trustee shall have the power to make distributions of income and principal in cash or in kind, or partly in cash and partly in kind, without any requirement to make pro rata distributions of specific assets and without any requirement to allocate equitably the basis of property for income tax purposes; PROVIDED, HOWEVER, that satisfactions of any right of withdrawal in any beneficiary hereunder must be made in cash, although the trustee may liquidate any asset of the trust (including but not limited to by withdrawing retirement assets (as defined in ARTICLE __ hereof, but ignoring the last proviso of the definition) and other assets which are payable to the trust over time and not yet paid to the trust) in order to generate said cash. In order to make any division of trust assets to be distributed to two or more persons the trustee may determine the fair market value of those assets to be distributed in kind on the approximate date of distribution and may allot the same as between the various distributees, and the values placed on such assets and the particular assets selected by the trustees for distribution to any particular distributee shall be binding upon all persons having an interest in this trust estate.

Definitions Article

The term "retirement assets" shall mean any asset classified as part of a qualified plan pursuant to Section 401 of the Internal Revenue Code, or any successor section thereto, as part of a nonqualified annuity, as part of an annuity payable under Section 403(a) or 403(b) of the Internal Revenue Code, or any successor sections thereto, as part of an individual retirement account (including a simplified employee pension) pursuant to Section 408 of the Internal Revenue Code, or any successor section thereto, as part of a ROTH IRA pursuant to Section 408A of the Internal Revenue Code, or any successor section thereto, as part of an inherited IRA established by the trustee pursuant to Section 402(c)(11) of the Internal Revenue Code, or any successor section thereto, as part of a retirement plan pursuant to Section 457 of the Internal Revenue Code, or any successor section thereto, or as part of any similar qualified retirement arrangement under the Internal Revenue Code; [PROVIDED, HOWEVER, that any of the aforementioned assets shall not be deemed to be a "retirement asset" for purposes of this agreement if it is not permissible (other than as a result of this proviso), under the governing instrument or otherwise, to make payments to the trust in a form other than in a lump sum or over a maximum term certain (other than a maximum term certain based on the life expectancy of any of the grantors' descendants, of any heir-at-law of either of the grantors, or of any actual or hypothetical spouse of any of the grantors' descendants).] **[BRACKETED PROVISO NOT NECESSARY IF NO SHARE A/B -**

AS DISCUSSED IN CHAPTER 5, BELOW.]

Trustee Powers Article

No one can possibly predict what Congress, the Internal Revenue Service or any other federal or state agency has in store for our clients next. As a result, the above form language may need to be revised after the client's death to ensure a better set of tax results. It may also need to be revised for other non-tax reasons, e.g., to better qualify a child/beneficiary for college financial aid. The client may therefore wish to grant an independent trustee or trust protector the power to make necessary changes to the trust document. Set forth below is just one example of some sample form language which may be used to accomplish this objective:

> Except as provided below, the trustee of any trust hereunder (including any trustee appointed pursuant to the provisions of paragraph __ of ARTICLE __ hereof) other than (i) the primary current beneficiary of the trust, (ii) any descendant of either of the grantors, and (iii) any other person or entity who is "related or subordinate," within the meaning of current Section 672(c) of the Internal Revenue Code, to the primary current beneficiary of the trust (substituting "the primary current beneficiary of the trust" for "the grantor" in said Section) may exercise, in a fiduciary capacity, any of the following powers:
>
> a.   To amend any administrative provisions of the trust;

b.   To amend the trust to comply with and to take advantage of any changes in the law;

c.   To change the situs and governing law of the trust;

d.   To amend the trust to maintain or increase federal and/or state tax advantages for the trust and/or its beneficiaries (including potential remainder beneficiaries), provided that no such amendment may affect a beneficiary's power to withdraw income during the current calendar year or a beneficiary's right to receive income currently;

e.   Except for any trust hereunder wherein the income is required to be distributed currently to the primary current beneficiary of the trust, to place greater restrictions on the trustee's power to make distributions of income and/or principal, for the purposes of: (i) assisting the primary current beneficiary in becoming eligible to receive a greater amount of federal or state governmental assistance benefits, including, but not limited to, Social Security Administration benefits, Veterans Administration benefits, Medicaid benefits and Supplemental Security Income benefits,

(ii) qualifying the trust as a "qualified disability trust" under Section 642(b)(2)(C) of the Internal Revenue Code, or any successor section thereto, and (iii) assisting the primary current beneficiary in becoming eligible to receive the benefit of any college-related (including graduate school) financial aid from the federal government, state government or any educational institution; and

f. Except for any trust hereunder wherein the income is required to be distributed currently to the primary current beneficiary of the trust, to give one or more descendants of the grantors a power of withdrawal over any portion of the income and/or principal of the trust during the calendar year, in conjunction with giving the trustee the discretionary power to reimburse such individual for any income tax liability accruing to such individual as a result of possessing such power of withdrawal. In exercising the trustee's power under this paragraph, the trustee shall be primarily concerned with minimizing overall income taxes to the trust and its beneficiaries (including potential remainder beneficiaries).

Notwithstanding the foregoing provisions of this Section __, a trustee shall not possess any of the foregoing powers (i) if the trustee was appointed pursuant to the provisions of paragraph 2 of ARTICLE __ hereof and the trustee making such appointment shall be deemed to possess the powers of the appointed trustee for federal or state estate tax, gift tax, generation-skipping transfer tax, inheritance tax or other transfer tax purposes, (ii) to the extent that the exercise or non-exercise of such powers would cause any individual to make a taxable gift for federal or state gift tax purposes or disqualify any gift hereunder for the federal or state estate tax marital deduction or any other transfer tax marital deduction, or (iii) if possession of such powers would render the trust not "irrevocable" after the death of either of the grantors for purposes of Sections 1.401(a)(9)-4, A-5(b)(2) and 1.408-8, A-1(b) of the Treasury Regulations, including any successor sections thereto. The trustee shall be entitled to rely on the advice of legal counsel with respect to any matter under this Section; PROVIDED, HOWEVER, that if said legal counsel's opinion is subsequently determined to be invalid as applied to this Section, either as a result of a subsequently passed Internal Revenue Code provision or a subsequently promulgated Department of Treasury regulation or published ruling, or as a result of judicial decision, the trustee's limitations under this Section, if any, shall be determined based on such subsequent development and not in accordance with said legal counsel's opinion. All trustees of any trust hereunder shall be exonerated from any liability relating to any action taken by a trustee pursuant to the provision of this Section.

Distributions Over 5 Percent

If distributions in excess of 5 percent of the trust value are determined to be desirable in any given year (for example, because the trust has a significant amount of capital gains or IRA/qualified plan receipts during the year), a disinterested trustee may be given the authority to make such excess distributions to the beneficiary. Capital gains, however, must first be properly allocated to the distributable net income (DNI) of the trust; otherwise, they won't "carry out" to the beneficiary.

The IRS regulations establish alternatives for recognizing capital gains as part of DNI by providing that an allocation to income of all or a part of the gains from the sale or exchange of trust assets will, generally, be respected if it's made pursuant to either: (1) the terms of the governing instrument and applicable local law, or (2) a reasonable and impartial exercise of a discretionary power granted to the fiduciary by applicable local law or by the governing instrument, if not prohibited by applicable local law.[10]

---

10. Treas. Regs. Section 1.643(a)-3(b), 1.643(b)-1. See also James G. Blase, "Drafting Tips That Minimize the Income Tax on Trusts—Part 2," 40 ETPL 22 (August 2013) (Drafting Tips—Part 2). The regulations also include two additional situations in which capital gains allocated to the principal of the trust may be included in the trust's distributable net income, if permissible under local law, or the trust instrument, if not prohibited by local law, but these alternatives tend to be difficult to work with and somewhat inflexible: "(2) Allocated to corpus but treated consistently by the fiduciary on the trust's books, records, and tax returns as part of a distribution to a beneficiary; or (3) Allocated to corpus but actually distributed to the beneficiary or utilized by the fiduciary in

57

Allocations   pursuant   to   terms   of governing instrument and local law

The Uniform Principal and Income Act (UPAIA) unequivocally recognizes the allocation of capital gains to income if the allocation is required under the terms of the trust instrument.[11] As long as the trust instrument doesn't require that all income be distributed currently to the beneficiaries (which could potentially overfund trust distributions), this technique for characterizing capital gains as trust accounting income will, generally, be a successful strategy, at least for trusts governed by state income and principal rules similar to the UPAIA. Because the disinterested trustee won't be required to distribute the capital gains to the beneficiaries, the disinterested trustee will be able to monitor the situation to make the most prudent decisions possible, including, for example, situations in which a beneficiary: (1) is likely to be subject to federal estate tax, (2) turns out to be a spendthrift or otherwise unfit to receive the additional distributions, or (3) has special needs.

Allocations pursuant to impartial exercise of discretionary power

If the trust instrument requires that all income be distributed currently to the beneficiaries, it may not be a wise drafting strategy to have all capital gains automatically

_____

determining the amount that is distributed or required to be distributed to a beneficiary." Treas.Regs.Section1.643(a)-3(b)(2), (3).

11. Uniform Principal and Income Act (UPAIA) Section103(a)(1).

allocated to trust income, because to do so could result in a level of current distributions to the trust beneficiary that the grantor neither contemplated nor desired. Rather, some sort of discretionary allocation would be preferable in these situations. Fortunately, as alluded to above, the IRS permits capital gains to be characterized as part of DNI if the allocation is made "pursuant to a reasonable and impartial exercise of a discretionary power granted to the fiduciary by applicable local law or by the governing instrument, if not prohibited by applicable local law."[12]

UPAIA Section 103(b) permits a discretionary allocation of capital gains to income if the allocation is made "impartially, based on what is fair and reasonable to all of the beneficiaries" or if the terms of the trust "clearly manifest an intention that the fiduciary shall or may favor one or more of the beneficiaries."[13] The IRS regulations effectively eliminate the second UPAIA alternative from the DNI equation by providing that the only discretionary allocations of capital gains to income that the IRS will respect for DNI purposes are ones that are reasonably and impartially made by the trustee.

Thus, for a trust that's required to distribute all of its income currently, the UPAIA, as further limited by the IRS regulations, permits no more than a "reasonable and impartial" portion of the capital gains allocated to income to be included in the trust's DNI. What's considered a "reasonable and impartial" portion will depend on individual facts and

---

12. Treas. Regs Sections 1.643(a)-3(b), 1.643(b)-1.

13. UPAIA Section103(b).

circumstances, but, generally, the trustee may not completely favor the trust income beneficiaries at the expense of the remaindermen. Requiring that the trustee adhere to this limitation in exercising his discretionary power to allocate capital gains to trust accounting income could also help avoid any potential adverse gift or other transfer tax consequences when the trustee is also the current income beneficiary of the trust.[14]

For a trust that's not required to distribute all of its income currently, on the other hand, a discretionary allocation of capital gains to trust accounting income shouldn't be viewed as partial towards any beneficiary for purposes of the UPAIA as well as the IRS regulations. The allocation should, therefore, be respected for DNI purposes, and a discretionary distribution of the capital gains in excess of the 5 percent Section 2514(e)(3) limitation should, likewise, be respected for purposes of IRC Sections 661 and 662.

Regardless of the income distribution terms of the trust, for discretionary allocations of capital gains to trust income to be effective for purposes of determining the trust's DNI, it remains essential that the applicable state law first be examined to ensure that it satisfies the IRS' above-referenced regulatory requirement that discretionary allocations of capital gains to trust accounting income be "pursuant to a reasonable and impartial exercise of discretion by the fiduciary (in accordance

---

14. The alternative would be only to authorize a disinterested trustee or co-trustee to allocate capital gains to trust accounting income when the trust instrument requires that all or a portion of the trust's income be distributed currently.

with a power granted to the fiduciary by applicable local law or by the governing instrument if not prohibited by applicable local law)."[15]

Sample Forms

Capital gains may be distributed to the beneficiary through a combination of these trust forms, the first of which is merely an addition to the basic bypass or credit shelter trust form set forth above:

    1.3   The trustee may, in the trustee's sole discretion, distribute, use or apply so much of the income and principal of the trust estate (which is not withdrawable by the surviving grantor or by the surviving grantor's legal representative pursuant to the provisions of subsections 1.1 and 1.2, above) as the trustee may deem necessary to provide for the maintenance, support and health care of the surviving grantor, in the surviving grantor's accustomed manner of living. In addition, the trustee may, in such trustee's sole discretion, distribute, use or apply the income and principal of the trust estate (which is not withdrawable by the surviving grantor or by the surviving grantor's legal representative pursuant to the provisions of subsections 1.1 and 1.2, above) as the trustee may deem necessary for the maintenance, support, health care and education of any descendant of the grantors; [PROVIDED, HOWEVER, that (i) the needs of the

---

15. Treas.Regs. Section 1.643(a)-3(b).

surviving grantor as specified above shall be the primary concern of the trustee, and (ii) neither the income nor principal of the trust may be used to limit, relieve or otherwise discharge, in whole or in part, the legal obligation of any individual to support and maintain any other individual; PROVIDED FURTHER, HOWEVER, that if (i) the surviving grantor is serving as a trustee of the trust, (ii) any assets passed to the trust as a result of a disclaimer by the surviving grantor, or by the surviving grantor's legal representative, and (iii) the surviving grantor's ability to participate in the exercise of any discretion under the preceding provisions of this sentence would cause the surviving grantor's disclaimer not to be "qualified" within the meaning of Section 2518 of the Internal Revenue Code, or any successor section thereto, then the surviving grantor shall not be permitted to participate in the exercise of said discretion, and any discretion under the preceding provisions of this sentence may only be exercised by the co-trustee(s) other than the surviving grantor. In determining the amounts to be distributed, used or applied for the grantors' descendants, the trustee shall not be required to treat each of such persons equally but shall be governed more by the particular needs and interests of each of them.] **[PROVISOS NOT NEEDED IF TRUST ONLY FBO SPOUSE.]** The trustee other than the surviving grantor and other than a trustee designated by the surviving grantor who is "related or subordinate" to the surviving grantor within the meaning of current Section 672(c) of the Internal Revenue Code (substituting "the surviving grantor" for "the grantor" in said Section), may, in such trustee's sole discretion, utilize the income and principal of the trust estate (which is not withdrawable by the surviving grantor or by the surviving grantor's legal representative pursuant to the provisions of subsections 1.1 and 1.2, above) for the purpose of reimbursing the surviving grantor for any income tax liability accruing to the surviving grantor as a result of the surviving grantor's power of withdrawal under subsections 1.1 and 1.2, above; PROVIDED, HOWEVER, that the trustee shall not possess the discretionary power described in this sentence if, as a consequence of possessing said power, the surviving grantor is deemed to possess the same power for federal or state estate tax, gift tax, generation-skipping transfer tax, inheritance tax or other transfer tax purposes. The trustee shall be entitled to rely on the advice of legal counsel with respect to any matter under this subsection 1.3; PROVIDED, HOWEVER, that if said legal counsel's opinion is subsequently determined to be invalid as applied to this subsection, either as a result of a subsequently passed Internal Revenue Code provision or a subsequently promulgated Department of Treasury regulation or published ruling, or as a result of judicial decision, the trustee's limitations under this subsection, if any, shall be determined based on such subsequent development and not in accordance with said legal counsel's opinion.

Trustee Powers Article

In the administration of each trust hereunder the trustee shall have the power to determine what is principal and what is income of the trust estate; PROVIDED, HOWEVER, that: (a) in the case of securities purchased at a discount, the entire subsequent sale price or maturity value shall be credited to principal; (b) in the case of securities purchased at a premium, the premium shall be charged against principal without amortizing the same; (c) dividends on shares of stock payable in the stock of any class of the corporation declaring or authorizing the same shall be treated as principal, except that any such dividends paid in lieu of periodic cash dividends or in lieu of recoupment of dividends defaulted or accumulated while the shares of stock are held in the trust estate shall be income; (d) rents, royalties and cash dividends received from wasting assets (including, without limitation, cash dividends paid by oil, coal, lumber or mining companies), extraordinary cash dividends other than liquidating dividends, and dividends payable in the stock of a corporation other than the corporation declaring or authorizing the same shall be income; (e) the proceeds of the sale of unproductive or underproductive property, liquidating dividends, and rights to subscribe to stock or bonds shall be principal; and (f) all other capital gains and losses shall (I) if the trust does not require that all income be distributed currently to any beneficiary or beneficiaries, be automatically allocated to income, and (II) if the trust requires that all income be distributed currently to one or more beneficiaries, be allocated between income and principal by the trustee, in the trustee's sole discretion, provided that such allocation must be made by the trustee in a reasonable and impartial manner.

The trustee(s) of any trust hereunder, other than (i) either of the grantors, (ii) the primary current beneficiary of the trust, (iii) the spouse of the primary current beneficiary of the trust, (iv) any descendant of either of the grantors, (v) any descendant of the primary current beneficiary of the trust, and (vi) any other person or entity "related or subordinate," within the meaning of current Section 672(c) of the Internal Revenue Code, to the surviving grantor (substituting "the surviving grantor" for "the grantor" in said Section), to the primary current beneficiary of the trust (substituting "the primary current beneficiary of the trust" for "the grantor" in said Section) or to any descendant of the primary current beneficiary of the trust (substituting "descendant of the primary current beneficiary of the trust" for "the grantor" in said Section), may, in such trustee's or trustees' sole discretion, terminate the trust, in whole or in part (including, in such trustee's or trustees' sole discretion, for the purpose of paying the primary current beneficiary's income taxes attributable to any income of the trust, including capital gains), and distribute all or any portion of the remaining principal and accumulated and undistributed income of the trust (other than principal and accumulated and undistributed income of the trust which is then withdrawable by any individual) to or for the benefit of the primary current beneficiary of the trust and/or any descendant or descendants of the primary current beneficiary of the trust, in equal or unequal portions; PROVIDED, HOWEVER, the preceding provisions of this subsection ___ shall not apply if the primary current beneficiary of the trust is less than ___ years of age, and PROVIDED FURTHER, HOWEVER, the aforedescribed power to terminate the trust, in whole or in part, under this subsection ___ shall not apply (a) if an individual appointed the trustee who or which possesses the aforedescribed power to terminate the trust, in whole or in part, and if as a consequence thereof said individual is deemed to possess the same power for federal or state estate tax, gift tax, generation-skipping transfer tax, inheritance tax or other transfer tax purposes, or (b) to the extent the power or its exercise or nonexercise would (i) cause imposition of the federal generation-skipping transfer tax or any other transfer tax, or (ii) cause any person to make a taxable gift for federal or state gift tax purposes. The trustee shall have broad discretionary power pursuant to this subsection __, but in exercising said discretion the trustee shall focus primarily on the needs and general welfare of the primary current beneficiary of the trust, and secondarily on the needs and general welfare of the descendants of the primary current beneficiary of the trust. The trustee shall be entitled to rely on the advice of legal counsel with respect to any matter under this subsection __; PROVIDED, HOWEVER, that if said legal counsel's opinion is subsequently determined to be invalid as applied to this subsection either as a result of a subsequently passed Internal Revenue Code provision or a subsequently promulgated Department of Treasury regulation or published ruling, or as a result of judicial decision, the trustee's limitations under this subsection, if any, shall be determined based on such subsequent development and not in accordance with said legal counsel's opinion. **[MAY NEED TO CHANGE FROM DESCENDANTS TO RELEVANT REMAINDERMEN; REMEMBER TO EXCLUDE ANY TRUSTS THAT THE GRANTOR WOULD NOT WANT TERMINATED, SUCH AS A SPECIAL NEEDS TRUST OR A TRUST FOR A SECOND SPOUSE.]**

New Income Tax Basis at Death

The objective here is to achieve a new income tax basis at the surviving spouse's death. Traditionally this was always thought to be impossible for a bypass or credit shelter trust, but with a federal estate tax exemption of $5.45 million in 2016, the impossible has magically now become possible, at least for 99 percent of clients. This is accomplished by proper application of the estate tax portion rules discussed in Chapter 2. This objective may become even more important to achieve as result of the Presidential, Senate and House elections of 2016, and the prospect of federal estate tax repeal in the near future.

As already emphasized, outright distributions to a surviving spouse and reliance on the spousal portability election in order to obtain income tax basis step-up at the survivor's death is fraught with a myriad of unnecessary risks and uncertainties, in the vast majority of situations. A proper understanding of the *estate tax* portion rules described in Chapter 2 allows married couple clients to now have their cake and eat it too when it comes to income tax basis step-up at the surviving spouse's death. It is not necessary to subject the couple to all of the inherent disadvantages of outright ownership in the hands of the surviving spouse, in order to obtain basis step-up at his or her death.

Achieving new income tax basis if any beneficiary (including a surviving spouse beneficiary under a bypass, credit shelter or hybrid trust) should die during the term of the trust involves granting the beneficiary a conditional testamentary general POA (typically limited to the creditors of the beneficiary's estate) over the trust assets, to the extent the same won't result in any federal or state estate or inheritance tax liability to the beneficiary's estate.[16]   If an individual is a beneficiary of more than one trust, the conditional testamentary general POA is allocated among the relevant trusts, based on the fair market value of the respective trust assets at the beneficiary's death.

In order to preserve the full availability of the federal spousal portability election, an exception to this automatic rule is typically included in the conditional general power when the beneficiary is survived by a spouse. Instead of utilizing an automatic testamentary general POA, an independent trustee can be granted the discretionary ability to add the power, to the extent it's deemed beneficial, as well as the discretionary ability to remove it.[17] Another alternative in these situations would be to grant the beneficiary a testamentary limited POA over the trust assets, and then allow the beneficiary to intentionally violate IRC Section 2041(a)(3) (the so-called "Delaware tax trap"), to the extent it won't cause estate or inheritance taxes to be payable at the beneficiary's death, under still another application of the estate tax portion rules.[18]   Employing the

---

16.   The independent trustee's removal of the POA shouldn't be considered a taxable"lapse" of the power under Internal Revenue Code Section 2041(b)(2) because the beneficiary wouldn't have possessed an exercisable POA immediately prior to the removal.

17.   Treas. Regs. Section 20.2041-3(e)(2) includes an example that clarifies that a partial violation of IRC Section2041(a)(3) is possible.

18.   *See also* James G. Blase and Mimi G. Sharamitaro, "Consider the MAT,"Trusts & Estates (February2010), at p. 38.

latter alternative will be difficult in statutory or common law rule against perpetuities jurisdictions and may be impossible in jurisdictions that have passed special legislation aimed at preventing inadvertent violations of IRC Section 2041(a)(3).

Regardless of how the conditional testamentary general POA is included in the trust document, it's important to fashion the testamentary general POA in a manner that applies to the most appreciated assets of the trust first, to wipe out the most potential capital gains tax possible in the event a testamentary general POA over the entire trust would generate estate or inheritance taxes. It may also be advisable to structure the testamentary general POA so that it doesn't apply to any trust assets that have depreciated in value over their historical income tax basis. Finally, especially in light of the potential for repeal of the federal estate tax as a consequence of the 2016 Presidential, Senate and House election, the testamentary general POA should be carefully structured to avoid the surviving spouse's estate or the trust being automatically subject to income tax on any built-in gain attributable to any portion of the remaining trust assets.

Sample Form

This sample bypass or credit shelter trust assumes the trust is exempt for GST purposes, and that the primary remaindermen of the trust in turn are GST-exempt trusts for the couple's children. The exceptions to the testamentary powers of appointment in the form are for situations where qualified plan, IRA or nonqualified annuities are made payable to the trust (since income tax basis step-up is not possible here), as will be discussed in Chapter 5, and for situations where the independent trustee or trust protector may have altered the power.

Section 2. Distribution of Principal at Death of Surviving Grantor

2.1 Upon the death of the surviving grantor, unless assets have passed to the trust as a result of disclaimer by the surviving grantor, or by the surviving grantor's legal representative, after the death of the first of the grantors to die, and except as otherwise provided in Section __ of ARTICLE __ hereof [RELATING TO RETIREMENT BENEFITS], the trustee shall distribute all of the assets remaining in the trust estate, if any, including both principal and accumulated and undistributed income, to or among any of the grantors' descendants, in trust or otherwise, and in such proportions, as shall be designated by the surviving grantor in his or her Last Will and Testament (having the most recent date of execution by the surviving grantor) and which is filed with the probate court of the relevant jurisdiction within six (6) months following the surviving grantor's death, but if such Last Will and Testament shall be contested within the aforementioned six (6) month period, then as shall be designated in the surviving grantor's Last Will and Testament which is finally admitted to probate after the period for contesting the surviving grantor's Last Will and Testament has expired, and referring specifically to this provision, excluding, however, the surviving grantor, the surviving grantor's estate, the surviving grantor's creditors and the creditors of the surviving grantor's estate. In addition, unless assets have passed to the trust as a result of disclaimer by the surviving grantor, or by the surviving grantor's legal representative, after the death of the first of the grantors to die, and except as otherwise provided in Sections __ and __ of ARTICLE __ hereof, if the surviving grantor is not survived by a surviving spouse (as that term is defined for purposes of Section 2056 of the Internal Revenue Code, or any successor section thereto), then to the extent it will not result in (i) the surviving grantor's estate being liable for any federal or state estate or inheritance taxes, (ii) the surviving grantor's estate being liable to reimburse any government for any assistance or other benefits provided the surviving grantor during the surviving grantor's lifetime, (iii) the surviving grantor's estate or the trust being automatically subject to income tax on any gain attributable to any portion of the remaining trust assets, or (iv) a reduction in the federal income tax basis of any asset over its historical federal income tax basis, the surviving grantor shall also have the power to appoint those remaining trust assets, if any, beginning with the asset or assets having the greatest amount of built-in appreciation (calculated by subtracting the trust's income tax basis from the fair market value on the date of death of the surviving spouse), as a percentage of the fair market value of such asset or assets on the date of death of the surviving grantor, to the creditors of the surviving grantor's estate (or to the surviving grantor's estate if the power to distribute such assets to the creditors of the surviving grantor's estate is not sufficient to include such assets in the surviving grantor's estate for federal estate tax purposes), utilizing the same appointment procedure described immediately above; PROVIDED, HOWEVER, that if this trust has been or will be divided into two separate trusts for federal generation-skipping transfer tax purposes, the surviving grantor's foregoing additional power of appointment shall apply (i) first to the trust having an inclusion ratio, as defined in Section 2642(a) of the Internal Revenue Code, or any successor section thereto, of other than zero, but only to the extent such trust is not otherwise already includible in the surviving grantor's estate for federal estate tax purposes, pursuant to the other provisions of this trust instrument, and (ii) next to the trust having an inclusion ratio, as defined in Section 2642(a) of the Internal Revenue Code, or any successor section thereto, of zero; PROVIDED FURTHER, HOWEVER, that if the surviving grantor is the beneficiary of more than one trust which includes a provision similar to this sentence, the extent of the surviving grantor's foregoing additional power of appointment shall be reduced by multiplying the value of the assets otherwise subject to the surviving grantor's foregoing additional power of appointment by a fraction the numerator of which shall equal the value of the assets otherwise subject to the surviving grantor's foregoing additional power of appointment and the denominator of which shall equal the value of all assets otherwise subject to the surviving grantor's foregoing and similar additional power(s) of appointment, the intent being that under no circumstance shall the surviving grantor's estate be liable for any federal or state estate or inheritance tax as a consequence of the surviving grantor's foregoing additional power of appointment. If the surviving grantor is survived by a surviving spouse (as that term is defined for purposes of Section 2056 of the Internal Revenue Code, or any successor section thereto), the surviving grantor shall only possess the surviving grantor's foregoing additional power of appointment to the same or lesser extent that the trustee (other than the surviving grantor and other than a trustee who is "related or subordinate" to the surviving grantor within the meaning of current Section 672(c) of the Internal Revenue Code (substituting "the surviving grantor" for "the grantor" in said Section)) shall direct by instrument in writing filed with the trust during the surviving grantor's lifetime and not revoked by said trustee prior to the surviving grantor's death; PROVIDED, HOWEVER, that the trustee shall not possess the aforedescribed power to direct if the surviving grantor appointed the trustee who or which possesses the aforedescribed power to direct, and if as a consequence the surviving grantor is deemed to possess the aforedescribed power to direct for federal or state estate tax, gift tax, generation-skipping transfer tax, inheritance tax or other transfer tax purposes. In exercising said trustee's broad discretionary power in determining whether and to what extent the surviving grantor shall possess the aforesaid power of appointment if the surviving grantor is survived by a surviving spouse, said trustee shall be primarily concerned with minimizing overall income and transfer taxes to the surviving grantor's estate and to recipients of the trust assets after the surviving grantor's death, and with minimizing the liability of the surviving grantor's estate to reimburse any government for any assistance or other benefits provided the surviving grantor during the surviving grantor's lifetime. The trustee shall be entitled to rely on the advice of legal counsel with respect to any matter under this subsection 2.1; PROVIDED, HOWEVER, that if said legal counsel's opinion is subsequently determined to be invalid as applied to this subsection, either as a result of a subsequently passed Internal Revenue Code provision or a subsequently promulgated Department of Treasury regulation or published ruling, or as a result of judicial decision, the trustee's limitations under this subsection, if any, shall be determined based on such subsequent development and not in accordance with said legal counsel's opinion.

2.2   Upon the death of the surviving grantor, all remaining trust assets which are not effectively appointed by the surviving grantor pursuant to the provisions of subsection 2.1, above, shall be distributed, per stirpes, to the grantors' descendants who survive the surviving grantor; PROVIDED, HOWEVER, that the share of any child of the grantors shall be held in trust for the benefit of such child with income and principal administered and distributed pursuant to the provisions of ARTICLE __ hereof, and the share of any grandchild or more remote descendant of the grantors who is then less than thirty-five (35) years of age shall be held in trust for the benefit of such grandchild or more remote descendant with income and principal administered and distributed pursuant to the provisions of ARTICLE __ hereof.

Handling Existing Bypass Trusts

Estate planners are often faced with a surviving spouse who is a beneficiary of a traditional bypass or credit shelter trust which does not include a conditional testamentary general power of appointment designed to achieve an income tax basis step-up, but the combination of the bypass trust assets and the surviving spouse's independent assets are substantially below the current federal estate tax exemption level. Assuming the trust was not drafted in a flexible manner so that, for example, an independent trustee or trust protector is permitted to terminate the trust in favor of the surviving spouse, are there any other options available to the surviving spouse to achieve income tax basis step-up at his or her death for appreciated assets owned by the trust?

If the trust instrument includes standard maintenance, support and health care encroachment language, one argument for terminating the trust is that doing so will, in the long run, provide assistance in each of these three areas, because significant income taxes and trust administration expenses will be saved. In other words, standard maintenance, support and health care language is rarely limited to the beneficiary's *current* needs only. Provided the trustee can justify making the encroachment (e.g., to the remaindermen of the trust), and there are no longer any significant liability, remarriage, etc. concerns to the surviving spouse, the encroachment and termination of the bypass trust should be considered.

If the trust instrument includes a limited testamentary power of appointment in the surviving spouse, an alternative which may work even better, because it would not expose the trust assets to lawsuits, etc., would be for the surviving spouse to exercise the testamentary power in a manner which intentionally violates Section 2041(a)(3) of the Code. This would necessitate that the surviving spouse exercise the power in a manner which establishes additional powers of appointment in the children, which latter powers may be exercised by the children without reference to the date of the establishment of the surviving spouse's limited power. Note, however, that sometimes this alternative may be foreclosed by state law or by the manner in which the initial power of appointment was drafted.

Medium Size Estates

If the couple's estate falls into the "medium" category (e.g., $1 million to $4 million, including life insurance), the concern is that although there likely will be no federal estate tax at the surviving spouse's death, there definitely could be. Depending on the couple's state of residence, there could also be state estate or inheritance taxes to concern us.

A relatively common plan in the medium estate situation is to keep the home (say $500,000) joint, for a variety of reasons, among which include:

- In tenancy by entirety states which have not passed QST legislation, this helps insulate the home from lawsuits during the couple's joint lifetime;

- • The surviving spouse will automatically receive a 50 percent increase in income tax basis step-up, thus minimizing or eliminating capital gains taxes if the house is later sold; and

- • Because the entire home would be owned by the surviving spouse, the entire home will be eligible for the $250,000 capital gain exclusion available to a single individual.

Another common planning technique in medium size estate situations is to leave all benefits under IRAs, qualified plans and non-qualified annuities (say $1.5 million, total) outright to the surviving spouse, in order to qualify for the greatest level of income tax deferral. At best IRAs and qualified plan benefit made payable to a bypass or credit shelter trust must be distributed over the life expectancy of the surviving spouse, and non-qualified annuities will typically need to be distributed over five years.

Outright payments of IRAs and qualified retirement plan benefits to a surviving spouse, on the other hand, qualify for tax-free rollover treatment, meaning nothing need be distributed until the spouse reaches age 70-1/2, and at that point deferral is over the life expectancy of the spouse plus a fictional individual 10 years younger. Outright payments of non-qualified annuities may typically be deferred over the spouse's life expectancy, rather than only five years.

What about the balance of the couple's assets - say $2 million, including life insurance? While it is easy to fall into the trap of just relying on the federal portability election in these cases, and therefore leave everything joint or otherwise outright to the surviving spouse, the biggest concern would be if the surviving spouse were to remarry and the new spouse also predeceased. In this situation, the portability amount from the first spouse to die would no longer be available.

It is also possible that the inherited amounts could appreciate substantially in value, with the portability election amount only applying to the date of death value of the assets when the first spouse died. Thus, it will arguably be malpractice for the advisor to have relied on the portability election to eliminate estate taxes, when another, "risk-free option," was available, especially since the portability election option also exposes all of the assets to creditors of the surviving spouse as well as to the potential reach of a new spouse.

The risk-free option would be to divide the $2 million between the spouses, approximately $1 million each, and then at the first spouse to die's death have his or her $1 million pass to a bypass or credit shelter for the benefit of the surviving spouse and/or children. As we have seen, it is possible to solve the high income tax bracket concerns of the bypass trust without unnecessarily forcing compound income amounts into the surviving spouse's bank or brokerage account, and it is also possible to resolve the lost income tax basis step-up at the surviving spouse's death concerns without exposing the trust assets to estate taxes, creditors, or the rights of a new spouse.

With the principal income tax disadvantages of a bypass trust now negated, we are left only with the traditional estate tax savings, asset protection and "remarriage" protection benefits afforded by a bypass trust, all while allowing the surviving spouse control over the trust. Optimum estate planning has been achieved.

If the couple lives in a tenancy by the entirety state, such that owning property in joint names can create a layer of asset protection, they will always need to be mindful that this protection can be lost when a portion of their assets are divided into two shares rather than held as tenants by the entirety. If the couple is fortunate enough to reside in a two-share QST state, such as Delaware or Missouri, tenancy by the entirety type asset protection can easily be retained through funding the two shares with the $1 million in assets each.

It is very important to follow all of the statutory formalities of the particular state's QST statute (especially the funding formalities), however, since these can vary from state to state. Note too that the Missouri statute, at least, arguably contains issues of constitutional law by permitting separately-owned property to be transferred directly to separate shares of a QST, and receive tenancy by the entirety type creditor protection.[19]

If the couple resides in a state which does not have tenancy by the entirety for all types of property, property which is not tenancy by the entirety property can be divided between

---

19. James G. Blase, "Missouri Makes Dramatic Change to Asset Protection Law for Married Couples," Trusts & Estates (online edition - July 22, 2015).

the two shares freely, since asset protection is not available for the property anyway. As to any tenancy by the entirety property (i.e., in addition to the home), on the other hand, the couple would need to decide what is more important to them - asset protection while they are married, or estate tax and asset protection after the first spouse dies.

The purchase of additional liability insurance protection is another available option, and should be considered regardless, i.e., in order to protect future income. Further, some states offer irrevocable asset protection trusts even for property which is not tenancy by the entirety property. Working with other advisors to pass a two-share QST statute in the couple's state of residence would also be prudent, since this may be the trend of the future.

Large Estates

For large estates (e.g., in excess of $4 million), obtaining income tax basis step-up at the surviving spouse's death is largely just an extension of the planning which we do for medium-sized estates. The major difference is that we may not always have the income tax luxury of keeping the marital home joint and designating the surviving spouse as outright beneficiary of all qualified plan, IRA and non-qualified annuity benefits.

Assume, for example, a couple with $8 million of assets, consisting of a $2 million jointly-owned home, a $4 million rollover IRA, all owned by the wife with the husband as outright beneficiary, and $2 million worth of other jointly-owned assets. Assume also that the federal estate tax exemption is $5.5 million at all points. If we retained title to the home in joint names, the IRA with the husband as beneficiary, and divided the remaining $2 million equally between the two spouses (utilizing a separate share QST statute, where available, and a bypass trust), the survivor would have a taxable estate of $7 million in today's dollars, assuming no growth, with an available estate tax exemption (including the portability amount) of $9.8 million. If the surviving spouse were to remarry, however, and his or her new spouse also predeceases the surviving spouse, the survivor's available estate tax exemption would be only $5.5 million, with an estate tax burden for his or her children to pay of up to 40 percent (in 2017) on the $1.5 million excess amount over $5.5 million. This is better than potentially incurring estate taxes on the full $8 million, but unacceptable nonetheless.

The challenging question is: can we do better than to accept all of the estate tax and other risks inherent in relying on the spousal portability election? One solution would be to move all of the non-qualified assets other than the home into the husband's name, divide the home equally between the two spouses (which can also achieve a fractional interest estate tax discount at each spouse's death), and designate the bypass trust for the husband as beneficiary of one-half of the wife's rollover IRA (and incorporating the special income tax deferral required language which will be discussed in Chapter 5). How will this math work out, at the surviving spouse's death?

If the wife dies second, her taxable estate will consist of the $4 rollover IRA plus the $1 million value of the home, or $5 million. If the husband dies second, his taxable estate will consist of a $2 million rollover IRA, the $1 million portion of the home, and the $2 million in investments which were transferred to him initially, or $5 million. We are now below the $5.45 million estate tax exemption level, without taking on all of the estate tax and other non-task risks associated with relying exclusively on the spousal portability rule to achieve income tax basis step-up at the survivor's death.

Income Tax Consequences During the Survivor's Lifetime

One potential income tax disadvantage to this plan, however, is that there will be less income tax deferral on the one-half of the IRA which passes to the bypass trust. Of course, if the couple tells you the surviving spouse will be spending a lot of the IRA anyway, e.g., on retirement and long-term care, this asserted disadvantage is largely moot. Further, if, when asked by you, the couple tells you there is "no chance" that the survivor will remarry, this will be hugely relevant to you, and argue in favor of utilizing the spousal portability election over potential unnecessary acceleration of income taxes on IRA distributions when a portion of the IRA is made payable to the bypass trust. In this situation relying on the spousal portability election and a full outright distribution of the IRA to the surviving spouse actually makes perfect sense!

Another potential disadvantage to this plan is that the surviving spouse may incur a larger taxable capital gain if the home is sold during his or her lifetime, due to the loss of the $250,000 capital gains exclusion on any appreciation in the portion of the home owned by the bypass trust which occurs

82

subsequent to the first spouse's death. If this is a concern to the surviving spouse, it is a simple matter to have him or her purchase the one-half interest in the home from the bypass trust shortly after the first spouse to die's death, utilizing an installment promissory note payable using distributions from the IRA. Secure the promissory note with the home, so that residential interest tax deductions may be achieved. All or a portion of the interest payments may be ignored for federal income tax purposes regardless, as a result of the survivor's Section 678 power of withdrawal over income of the bypass trust and the income tax portion rules described in Chapter 2.

Income and Estate Tax Consequences at the Survivor's Death

It is at the second spouse's death where optimum estate planning becomes the most important. Remember that most of the income taxes payable on the income generated by the bypass trust will be paid by the surviving spouse, and not by the bypass trust. As a result, and because we all advise our clients to provide for their retirements and long-term care needs out of their own assets, first, and only second out of the bypass trust assets, a likely scenario under this example is that, when the surviving spouse dies, his or her taxable estate will be no larger than the original $5 million amount, while the bypass trust will have continued to appreciate, largely unreduced by income taxes as a consequence of the optimum estate plan. Personally paying a large portion of the income taxes attributable to the bypass trust's income has reduced the size of the surviving spouse's taxable estate.[20]

Assume, for example, that at the time of the survivor's death the federal estate tax exemption has grown to $6 million, while the survivor's taxable estate has remained at $5 million. Assume also that the bypass trust has appreciated in value to $6 million. What optimum estate planning and the estate tax portion rules described in Chapter 2 then do is intentionally include at least $1 million worth of assets from the bypass trust in the gross estate of the survivor. And which $1 million worth of assets? The $1 million in assets containing the most built-in appreciation, because this will lead to the greatest income tax basis step-up at the survivor's death.

If the bypass trust will own an undivided interest in the couple's marital home or other real estate along with the surviving spouse, consider broadening the surviving spouse's conditional testamentary general power of appointment to include not only the creditors of his or her estate, but also his or her estate itself. The reason for this is that a power to appoint to the creditors of the surviving spouse's estate may not be sufficient to eliminate the fractional interest estate tax discount on the home, thus potentially causing the family up to 20 percent in unnecessary capital gains taxes on the sale of the home after the surviving spouse's death. [See, in this regard, the related discussion in Chapter 6.]

---

20. This also eliminates all of the complexity and the lifetime QTIP Trust required as part of the "Supercharged Credit Shelter Trust" described later in this Chapter 3.

Once again, optimum estate tax planning has been attained, even with the larger estate. Income taxes payable during the survivor's lifetime are minimized, while income tax basis step-up at the survivor's death is maximized. Further, the significant estate tax risks at the survivor's death, inherent with relying on the spousal portability election, have been minimized, and assets have been protected from lawsuits and from the potential grasp of a new spouse. The surviving spouse's taxable estate has also been reduced by paying a large portion of the income taxes attributable to the income of the bypass trust.

Compare: "Unnecessary" QTIP Election

An unnecessary QTIP election involves a plan applicable in situations where, due to the existence of the spousal portability election, it is unlikely estate taxes will be payable at the surviving spouse's death. Rather than establish a traditional bypass trust at the first spouse's to die's death in such situations, the couple establishes an "unnecessary" QTIP Trust, and makes the normal QTIP election. The hope is that, at the surviving spouse's death, the assets of the unnecessary QTIP Trust will receive an income tax basis step-up, along with the surviving spouse's own assets, and thus as a consequence of also making a spousal portability election at the first spouse's death, there are no estate taxes payable at the survivor's death, and all of the assets receive an income tax basis step-up. The assumed advantage of the arrangement over just leaving all assets outright to the surviving spouse is the added creditor and remarriage protection afforded by the QTIP Trust.

One problem with this approach is that it is not yet clear whether it will work. In the Preamble to final portability regulations, the IRS announced that it will issue guidance regarding the potential application of Revenue Procedure 2001-38 in this area, and the potential that the QTIP election (and therefore the Section 1014/2044 basis adjustment) will be disregarded at the surviving spouse's death.[21]

As compared to the optimum estate planning approach to creating income tax basis step-up at the surviving spouse's death, the problem with an unnecessary QTIP Trust is that it also forces "unnecessary" income distributions into the surviving spouse's estate each year, which compounded deposits are then of course subject to potential federal or state estate taxes at the surviving spouse's death, creditors of the surviving spouse, and attachment by a new spouse. None of these potential disadvantages exist with optimum estate planning. As described above, optimum estate planning would also cause capital gains, which are potentially taxed to the trust at an additional 8.8 percent federal income tax rate, to instead be taxed to a surviving spouse, who may not be subject to all or some of these additional taxes.

Obtaining Income Tax Basis Step-Up at the First Spouse to Die's Death

Here the income tax basis step-up focus shifts to achieving the same at the first spouse to die's death, as opposed to at the survivor's death. The same techniques can apply in

---

21. Treasury Decision 9725, IRB 2015-26 (June 29, 2015).

small, medium and large estate situations, depending upon all the circumstances.

Under the most basic plan, a joint revocable trust agreement (or joint share of a three-share trust, including separate shares for the husband and wife already funded with the exemption amount) is prepared that grants each spouse the unfettered lifetime right to withdraw, without the consent of the trustee or other spouse and without the need to account for the same to the other spouse, distributions of income and principal from the entire trust for his "welfare and happiness." Because this right of withdrawal isn't limited by an ascertainable standard, doesn't require the consent of the other spouse to be exercised, and doesn't leave the other spouse with any rights in the withdrawn property, full inclusion of the trust corpus in each spouse's gross estate is achieved, under a combination of IRC Sections 2036, 2038 and 2041.[22] Even if a decedent has only a lifetime general POA that can't be exercised by will, he's treated as having the power at death for Section 2041 federal estate tax inclusion purposes.[23] As a result, and pursuant to Section 1014(b)(9) of the Code, the property is deemed to have been acquired from or to have passed from the decedent spouse.

The suggested income and principal withdrawal right not

---

22. Note that this requisite unrestricted nature of each spouse's unilateral power of withdrawal may not be appropriate for or acceptable to all married couples, and clients should, therefore, be cautioned of the obvious risks involved prior to funding the joint trust.

23. *See, e.g.*, Snyder v. United States, 203 F. Supp. 195 (W.D. Ky. 1962); Jenkins v. U.S., 428 F.2d 538 (5th Cir. 1970). *See also* Private Letter Ruling 200210051 (Dec. 10, 2001).

only causes complete gross estate inclusion for the first spouse to die for federal estate tax purposes, but it does so in a fashion that doesn't violate the IRC Section 1014(e) exception to new income tax basis for gifts to the decedent within one year of the decedent's death. The Section 1014(e) exception is avoided because the surviving spouse never makes a completed gift to the decedent spouse under this arrangement, as demonstrated by Treasury Regulations Section 25.2511-1(h)(4):

> If A creates a joint bank account for himself and B *(or a similar type of ownership by which A can regain the entire fund without B's consent)*, there is a gift to B when B draws upon the account for his own benefit, to the extent of the amount drawn without any obligation to account for a part of the proceeds to A.[24]

Because the trust document provides that either spouse can demand the entire trust income and corpus for his own individual welfare and happiness, a right that's not limited by a fixed or ascertainable standard, each spouse can, effectively, regain his or her own contributed share of the trust corpus and, as a result, hasn't made a completed gift.[25] The trust document

---

24. Emphasis added. *See also* Treas. Regs. Section 25.2511-2(b), (c). This position is supported in PLR200210051 (Dec. 10, 2001). Under the facts of that particular PLR, however, there was a completed gift by the surviving spouse at the death of the first spouse to die because, at that point, the surviving spouse no longer retained the power to revest the beneficial title to the property in himself. The type of joint revocable trust contemplated in this text is thus distinguishable from the one described in the PLR.

25. Treas.Regs. Section 25.2511-2(g).

88

is also drafted to allow each spouse the unrestricted ability to revoke his or her contributions to the trust during the couple's joint lifetimes (and the entire trust after the first spouse dies), thus lending further support for the absence of a completed gift.

This joint trust arrangement should be compared to PLR 200210051 (Dec. 10,2001), where, on similar facts, the IRS agreed there was no gift by either spouse during their joint lifetime, but there was a gift at the death of the first spouse to die because (unlike the joint trust arrangement contemplated here), at that point, the surviving spouse's ability to revoke the surviving spouse's portion of the trust terminated. For some reason (probably because it wasn't material to the outcome of the ruling), the IRS didn't attempt to argue the applicability of IRC Section 2514(e) when the surviving spouse's lifetime general POA over the first spouse to die's share of the joint trust lapsed at the first spouse to die's death.

It might be argued that only one-half of the value of the trust should be includible in the gross estate of the first spouse to die, as a "qualified joint interest" pursuant to IRC Section 2040(b); therefore, only only-half of the trust should receive a new income tax basis at the death of the first spouse to die. In cases involving joint trusts that applied the IRC of 1939, courts have so ruled.[26] Significantly, however, whereas the 1939 IRC (and the Revenue Act of 1926, which preceded it) employed the term "joint tenants," the 1954 IRC added the words, "with right of survivorship," presumably, in an effort to clarify that one of the two joint tenants can't simply take the entire joint interest

26. *See, e.g.*, Derby v. Commissioner, 20 T.C. 164 (1953); Hornor's Estate v. Commissioner, 130F.2d 649 (3d Cir. 1942).

as his own, thereby effectively eliminating the other joint tenant's right of survivorship.

More importantly, in the cases involving joint trusts decided under the 1939 IRC, there was no ability for one of the trust beneficiaries to receive a greater share than the other during their joint lifetime, which would have been a violation of the "unity of possession" requirement of a joint tenancy. The type of joint revocable trust agreement which is suggested above is distinguishable from the cases decided under the 1939 IRC and, as such, wouldn't constitute a qualified joint interest under Section 2040(b). The interests of the first spouse to die should therefore be fully includible in his gross estate, under a combination of Sections 2036, 2038 and 2041.[27]

Notwithstanding this rather clear statutory path to achieving income tax basis step-up at the first spouse's to die's death, it must be noted that, on substantially similar facts, the IRS issued a Technical Advice Memorandum declaring that the stepped up income tax basis for the surviving spouse's half interest in the trust account will not be honored, despite the fact that the interest was included in the first spouse to die's gross estate, because in the Service's opinion "the property was not

---

27. The trust interest would also not be includible under the general IRC Section 2040(a) because it doesn't amount to a deposit "with any person carrying on the banking business, in their joint names and payable to either or the survivor." See *also* PLRs 200101021 (Oct. 2, 2000) and 200210051 (Dec. 10, 2001), in which, on similar facts, the IRS made no effort to argue IRC Section 2040 applied. The IRS also didn't attempt to argue that IRC Section 2041 was inapplicable because the consent of the other spouse was required to exercise the general POA, the fact that either spouse could revoke the trust apparently not being relevant to the IRS.

acquired from the decedent under section 1014(a) and (e)."
According to the Service, taxpayer's position would produce
the "unintended and inappropriate tax benefit Congress
expressly eliminated in enacting section 1014(e)."[28]   The
Service thus appeared to make its decision based on policy
grounds, rather than on the express wording of the Code and its
own gift tax regulations.

For large estates a combination "joint share" and
"separate share" joint revocable trust can achieve a new income
tax basis to the maximum extent. Here's how the trust drafting
and funding would look:

- The revocable trust document would divide the
  initial trust corpus into three shares. The first
  share would be the joint share. The other two
  shares would be separate revocable shares for the
  husband and wife, which, for our purposes, will be
  labeled Share H and Share W.

- The revocable share of the first spouse to die
  would essentially become a bypass trust
  (including spendthrift provisions) for the benefit
  of the surviving spouse.

- Each revocable share would be funded with at
  least the minimum level of assets needed to
  minimize the federal estate tax exposure at the

---

28. TAM 9308002.

surviving spouse's death, after factoring in the potential availability of the spousal portability election. Thus, for example, if a couple owns a combined estate of $6 million, including $2 million worth of appreciated assets, they could place the $2 million of appreciated assets in the joint share and transfer $2 million of other assets each into Shares H and W, thus minimizing their exposure to federal estate tax at the surviving spouse's death.

- The joint share would be funded with the most highly appreciated assets to ensure a full income tax basis step-up for all of these highly appreciated assets at the first death. Assets that have depreciated in value should typically not be transferred to the joint share, in order to preserve the deductible income tax loss in such assets. It's also generally not advisable to transfer assets to the joint share that have neither appreciated nor depreciated in value, because transferring these assets to either Share H or Share W may help insulate the same from lawsuits after the first spouse's death, and may help ensure that no estate or inheritance taxes are payable at the surviving spouse's death. The income tax capital gains exclusion, which a surviving spouse may receive on the sale of his principal residence, should also be factored in when funding the joint share.

- For even larger estates, the couple would fund each of the revocable trust shares with at least the federal estate tax exemption amount (after factoring in adjusted taxable gifts and assets passing outside of the trust to third parties) and would fund the joint share with all or a portion of their assets that have appreciated in value. Thus, for example, a couple with a $20 million net worth (including $5 million of appreciated assets) might elect to place approximately $7.5 million worth of the nonappreciated assets in each of Share H and Share W and place the $5 million worth of appreciated assets in the joint share. In this fashion, all of the couple's appreciated assets will receive a new income tax basis at the first spouse's death, while the separate revocable share of the first spouse to die will be protected from lawsuits as against the surviving spouse and from estate taxes at the surviving spouse's death.[29]

• The trust instrument would obviously be drafted to allow for the movement of trust assets among the three shares, to account for changes in the tax law and the size of the couple's estate, as well as for future appreciation or depreciation in the couple's assets.

---

29. Note, however, that for non-tax reasons (e.g., asset protection, or marital righ issues), maximum funding of the joint share may not always be appropriate or advisable. Note also that the Share H or Share W of the first spouse in this fact pattern would break into separate bypass trust and qualified terminable interest property trust shares after the first spouse's to die's death.

Risks Associated with the Joint Share

It must be emphasized that, because the consent of the other spouse isn't required for either spouse to withdraw the entire trust corpus of the joint share with impunity, for non-tax reasons the joint trust strategy may not be appropriate or advisable in many instances, including recent second marriages or other situations in which the couple isn't comfortable with granting each spouse a basically unrestricted unilateral power of withdrawal over the trust corpus.

Also, transferring tenancy by the entirety property to the joint share generally will terminate the asset protection characteristic of that property because the requisite "unity of possession" of the tenancy will have been destroyed. Achieving a new income tax basis while preserving tenancy by entirety type asset protection may be possible under a statute similar to the recently enacted Missouri Qualified Spousal Trust (MQST)[30] statute or a similar statute in Delaware[31] and other states, which specifically allows married couples to preserve tenancy by the entirety type protection when they transfer the property in trust. The question is whether non-resident married couples owning tenancy by the entirety property may use a Missouri or Delaware type trust to achieve a new income tax basis at the first spouse's death, while still preserving their tenancy by the entirety asset protection during their joint lifetime.

---

30. RS Mo Section 456.950.

31. 12 Del. Code Sec. 3334. *See also* Md. Est. & Tr. Code Sec. 14-113; T.C.A. Sec. 35-15-510; W.S. 4-10-402(c)-(e).

Missouri law, for example, provides that the meaning and effect of the terms of a trust may be governed by Missouri law provided: (1) the trust terms provide for the same, and (2) the designation isn't contrary to a strong public policy of the jurisdiction having the most significant relationship to the matter at issue.[32] A recent federal bankruptcy case illustrates that one shouldn't count on a strong public policy argument turning in favor of the debtor, unless the preponderance of the contacts are located in the governing law state. Because the non-resident married couple would only be transferring previously protected tenancy by the entirety property to the MQST, however, there's actually a good chance that the court of the forum state may not view Missouri's law as contrary to its state's strong public policy, and may therefore uphold the protections afforded by the Missouri law.

Note also that it would be a relatively easy matter, in any state that recognizes tenancy by the entirety in personal property, to structure an agreement between a married couple that grants each spouse a unilateral and unrestricted power to freely withdraw assets from a joint brokerage account, thus achieving a full income tax basis step-up at the first spouse's death. The requisite unity of possession of the joint brokerage account would then be destroyed, however, and as a consequence, so too would the tenancy by entirety creditor protection of the account. For a similar reason, half of the joint account, even a joint account that doesn't qualify as a tenancy by the entirety, may actually be subject to probate at the first spouse's death because without the requisite unity of possession, a tenancy in common is typically created.

---

32. RS Mo Section 456.1-107(1).

Clients should always be cautioned of the non-tax risks involved prior to using any type of joint plan designed to achieve a new income tax basis at the first spouse's death. Estate-planning advisors should also be mindful of any state estate or inheritance tax laws that may, for example, provide exemptions which are smaller than the current federal estate tax exemption amount, and adjust the estate plan accordingly.

Compare: Supercharged Credit Shelter Trust

The so-called "supercharged credit shelter trust" shares one of the same goals as optimum estate planning, that is, tax the surviving spouse, rather than the bypass trust, on the income of the bypass or credit shelter trust, so that the entire bypass trust is preserved from both income and estate taxes. The supercharged credit shelter trust also allows the surviving spouse to purchase appreciated assets of the bypass trust, income tax-free, and therefore obtain income tax basis step-up for these assets at the surviving spouse's death. This is all accomplished by having the would be surviving spouse (the "transferor spouse") establish a lifetime QTIP Trust (structured as a complete grantor trust to the transferor spouse) for his or her spouse (the "transferee spouse"), funded with approximately the $5 million exemption amount, which trust then becomes a bypass trust for the transferor spouse when the transferee spouse predeceases.

There are significant admitted drawbacks to the supercharged credit shelter trust, however. For example, what if the transferor and transferee spouses divorce? The QTIP trust must continue for the benefit of the transferee spouse for his or her remaining lifetime, regardless of the divorce. If, at the death of the transferee spouse survived by the transferor spouse, the trust has grown to, say, $7.5 million in value at a time when the federal estate tax exemption amount is $6 million, there would be no estate tax marital deduction available to apply against the $1.5 million in growth.

What if the couple stays married but the transferee spouse survives the transferor spouse? Assume, for example, that in 2016 the transferor spouse has a $10 million estate and funds the supercharged credit shelter trust with $5 million. Now assume the transferor spouse predeceases the transferee spouse at a time when the supercharged credit shelter trust (which is still a lifetime QTIP Trust at this point) is worth $7.5 million, the transferor's spouse's remaining estate is worth $7.5 million, and the estate tax exemption has grown to $6 million. Under this scenario, an additional $1.5 million will be added to the QTIP Trust at the transferor's spouse's death (in order to eliminate estate taxes), leaving a total of $9 million in the QTIP Trust and therefore in the transferee spouse's taxable estate. Of this amount, however, only $1.5 million received a stepped-up income tax basis at the transferor spouse's death; assets having a value of $7.5 million received a gift tax carryover income tax basis.

Had the transferor instead waited until death to fund a typical bypass trust arrangement, the surviving spouse would still be looking at the same $9 million taxable estate, but the entire $15 million of assets passing to the bypass trust and to the QTIP Trust would have received a stepped-up income tax basis at the transferor's spouse's death.

Thus, although the supercharged credit shelter trust can achieve income tax savings goals in the marital context somewhat similar to the goals of optimum estate planning, it does so at the expense of significant risk, as well as added complexity. Note also that the supercharged credit shelter trust does not automatically achieve any income tax basis step-up for the credit shelter trust assets at the transferor spouse's death. Only the credit shelter trust assets which are actually purchased by the transferor spouse prior to his or her death, receive the step-up. Obviously the transferor spouse also loses control over the assets which he or she transfers to the lifetime QTIP Trust, and even the transferee spouse's hands are somewhat tied during the transferor spouse's lifetime, by the manner in which the lifetime QTIP Trust must be structured in order to achieve it's tax goals. Lastly, significant reciprocal trust doctrine issues are associated with the supercharged credit shelter trust when it is used by both spouses, which would normally be the desired goal.

Planning for Second Marriages

Optimum estate planning principles become vital in second marriage situations. This is because couples with children from previous marriages are typically concerned about protecting their assets for eventual distribution to their respective children. Thus, although obviously an estate plan which passes everything outright to the surviving spouse will accomplish all of the couple's income tax goals, it will do so at the potential expense of the children of the first spouse to die. Holding assets in trust for the surviving spouse, on the other hand, avoids this major concern, and allows the first spouse to die some control over the ultimate disposition of the trust assets.

Most second marriage couples are not adverse to allowing the surviving spouse to share in the income of the bypass trust, especially when limited to no more than five percent per year. In fact, most couples actually prefer an arrangement like this, so that the surviving spouse is not required to justify the use of every penny he or she receives from the bypass trust. The corpus of the bypass trust can then be protected in any fashion the couple chooses, i.e., from least restrictive to most restrictive. Because the surviving spouse would only possess a testamentary power to appoint to the creditors of his or her estate, the principal of the trust is preserved for the children of the first spouse to die, and with its income tax basis normally at least partially stepped up to its value as of the date of the surviving spouse's death.

If either or both spouses own substantial IRA or qualified plan benefits, optimum estate planning allows these benefits to be paid to a trust for the surviving spouse, without granting the latter full control over the same. Income tax deferral for the surviving spouse is achieved in the manner to be described in Chapter 5, without mandating that any required minimum distributions be distributed outright to the surviving spouse (except to the extent withdrawable, along with other trust income, under the five percent ceiling of the bypass trust, and except to the extent considered trust income under a QTIP trust), thereby protecting the unused required minimum distributions, and more importantly the balance of the IRA or qualified plan account at the surviving spouse's death, for the children of the first spouse to die.

Basis Planning with a Terminally Ill Spouse

In addition to joint share planning in order to achieve full income tax basis step-up at the death of the first spouse, on occasion one of two spouses is diagnosed as being terminally ill - or at least it is apparent that one spouse will likely predecease the other. In this potentially traumatic time for the family, it will be difficult for the advisor to raise with the family the subject of income tax basis planning in light of the circumstances; but, if possible, this discussion should be had.

The issue, of course, concerns transferring highly appreciated assets to the spouse with the shorter life expectancy, and then structuring the latter's estate plan in an effort to avoid the one-year rule of Code Section 1014(e). The clearest path to a successful outcome in this situation can be found by studying Private Letter Ruling 9026036. There the IRS applied another type of income tax portion rule when it determined that a Family Trust which provided a lifetime income interest in the donor/wife fell within the grasp of Section 1014(e), and as a consequence "the basis of a portion of the assets of the husband's trust would be the same as the adjusted basis of the assets at the time of husband's death." The basis of the rest of the trust, the remainder interest which did not revert to the wife, received a step-up.

It follows that a key in this type of basis step-up planning is to minimize the value of the surviving spouse's interest in the transferred assets after the deceased spouse's death. Of course this is easy to do if the surviving spouse is willing to have these assets pass to his or her children. But it would also seem that assets passing to a true sprinkle-discretionary trust (as to income and principal) for the benefit of both the surviving spouse and the couple's children should mitigate the effects of Section 1014(e). This should especially be the situation if the trustee is not the surviving spouse, is given absolute discretion over trust distributions of income and principal, and is permitted to take into consideration the surviving spouse's other resources (including any qualified plan or IRA benefits passing to her at the deceased spouse's death) before making any distributions to or for the benefit of the surviving spouse.

Chapter 4

Optimum Planning for Children and Other Non-Spouse Beneficiaries

Optimum estate planning also applies in the planning which we do for children and other non-spouse beneficiaries. The principles of this chapter relate equally to married couples planning for their children and grandchildren, as well as to any single individual planning for his or her children, grandchildren, parents, siblings, nephews, nieces, unmarried partner, etc.

For obvious reasons clients want to protect their younger children, but they oftentimes also want to protect their older children, e.g., against lawsuits, the rights of a divorced spouse, potential estate taxes at the children's subsequent deaths, spendthrift older children, special needs children, etc. Trusts, oftentimes even to the extent of lifetime trusts for children, are therefore frequently the vehicle of choice for planners.

The problem, again, is Congress and the IRS. In a manner similar to how bypass or credit shelter trusts are taxed for income tax purposes, Congress has chosen to impose its maximum income tax rates on trusts having as little as $12,500 in taxable income (in 2017). That's right. Because the clients are good parents and want to be sure their younger children, especially, are protected, the "penalty" will be that the trusts for the children are taxed at income tax rates of as high as 50% or more, including state income taxes, on taxable incomes of as little as $12,500. Other reasons typically offered as arguments for not using trusts for children are the potential loss of income tax deferral on IRAs and other qualified plan benefits (which will be addressed in Chapter 5), and the loss of income tax basis step-up at the children's deaths.

As already alluded to in Chapter 3, estate planners should ensure that no provision of the trust document will infringe on the power holder's Section 678 "sole power to vest" the trust income for the current tax year (including, if desired, capital gains) in himself. For example, a disinterested trustee may possess the power to suspend the beneficiary's withdrawal power (for example, if the beneficiary is exercising his withdrawal power in an unwise or immature manner, or if the beneficiary becomes divorced or the subject of a lawsuit), but only if the suspension power is not effective until the beginning of the trust's next tax year.

The suspension power referred to in the preceding paragraph will be important in situations involving younger children, where the clients may not want their children to have uncontrolled power over income before they have attained a certain age, e.g., 30 or 35, for fear this might create a disincentive for the children to work hard early in life, etc. The disinterested trustee would retain the ability to warn children who are "misbehaving" that their income withdrawal rights will be suspended beginning January 1 of the following year, if they do not correct their misbehavior before then, e.g., by enrolling in college full-time, getting a full-time job, etc. If a child's income withdrawal rights are suspended, the child will eventually obtain access to the accumulated income (i.e., when the suspension is eventually lifted), but by that time there will be a lot less accumulated income available to the child, i.e., due to the higher trust tax rates imposed on the income during the suspension period.

The sample forms below illustrate various trusts for children in a "traditional" sprinkle trust form, and in the alternative "minimum income tax" ("MIT") trust form. The MIT also works to achieve the already-described (in the Chapter 3 discussion on bypass trusts) optimum income tax basis step-up in the event a child dies during the term of the trust.

Sample Form for Single Trust for Children Until Youngest Attains Age 23

The assets to be held in the trust estate with the income and principal administered and distributed pursuant to the provisions of this ARTICLE shall be held by the trustee as a separate trust estate with the income and principal administered and distributed as follows:

[[Section 1. Distribution and Use of Income and Principal Prior to Termination - TRADITIONAL SPRINKLE TRUST FORM

The trustee may, in the trustee's sole discretion, distribute, use or apply so much of the income and principal of the trust estate as the trustee may deem necessary to provide for the maintenance, support, health care and education of any descendant of the grantor; PROVIDED, HOWEVER, that neither the income nor principal of the trust may be used to limit, relieve or otherwise discharge, in whole or in part, the legal obligation of any individual to support and maintain any other individual. In determining the amounts to be distributed, used or applied for the grantor's descendants, the trustee shall not be required to treat each of such persons equally but shall be governed more by the particular needs and interests of each of them.]]

[1.2   In order to adequately house the grantor's child or children along with the guardian's or guardians' own child or children, if any, the trustee(s)(other than a trustee or trustees who is/are acting as guardian(s) of the grantor's minor child or children and who is/are "related or subordinate," within the meaning of current Section 672(c) of the Internal Revenue Code, to the guardian(s) (substituting "the guardian(s)" for "the grantor" in said Section)) may, in such trustee's or trustees' sole discretion, use or apply the income and principal of the trust estate (excluding, however, the income and principal of "Share A" of the trust, as defined in Section __ of ARTICLE __ hereof) [RELATING TO RETIREMENT BENEFITS] for the purpose of improving the home of the guardian(s) of the grantor's minor child or children or for the purpose of assisting in the purchase of a new home to be occupied by the grantor's child or children, said guardian(s), and the child or children of said guardian(s). The guardian(s) shall not be required to reimburse the trust for any portion of the cost of such improvement or new home. **USE THIS OPTION WHEN THERE IS A GUARDIAN AND MINOR CHILD.**]

Section 1. Distribution and Use of Income and Principal Prior to Termination - MIT TRUST FORM

1.1   The grantor's then living children (including the legal representative acting on behalf of any child) shall each have the annual noncumulative power to withdraw, on or before December 31 of the calendar year, so much of the trust accounting income as is equal to all of the trust accounting income divided by the number of the grantor's children living at the beginning of such calendar year; PROVIDED, HOWEVER, that (i) the foregoing power(s) of withdrawal shall not extend to the portion of the trust accounting income which, for the calendar year, would be either exempt from federal income tax or subject to federal income tax to the trust, after all deductions and exemptions (but determined as though the trustee made no other income or principal distributions or encroachments during the year other than for trust expenses and taxes), at less than the general maximum federal income tax rate applicable to trusts (and for this purpose said excluded portion (I) shall begin with any dividends, capital gains or other items of trust accounting income which are subject to a maximum federal income tax rate which is lower than the general maximum federal income tax rate applicable to trusts, (II) shall next include any items of trust accounting income filling out the lower income tax brackets of the trust which do not constitute "net investment income" as defined in Section 1411(c) of the Internal Revenue Code, or any successor section thereto, (III) shall next include any additional items of trust accounting income filling out the lower income tax brackets of the trust which constitute "net investment income" as defined in Section 1411(c) of the Internal Revenue Code, or any successor section thereto, and (IV) shall assume that all items of federal gross income of the trust which do not constitute trust accounting income and which are not subject to a maximum federal income tax rate which is lower than the general maximum federal income tax rate applicable to trusts, are using up the lower income tax brackets of the trust first, before the aforesaid items of trust accounting income) and (ii) if Section 2514(e) of the Internal Revenue Code, or any successor section thereto, is in effect during the calendar year, the amount of trust accounting income subject to each such child of the grantor's foregoing power of withdrawal during the calendar year shall not exceed five percent (5%) (or such other percentage as shall be provided for in Section 2514(e)(2) of the Internal Revenue Code, or any successor section thereto) of the combined value of the principal and income of the trust on December 31 of the calendar year (or on the date of death of such child of the grantors, if earlier). If more than one item of trust accounting income is withdrawable by the grantor's children pursuant to the foregoing provisions of this subsection 1.1 (for example, taxable interest from corporate bonds and distributions from retirement assets (as defined in ARTICLE __, below)), but the above-described limitation of Section 2514(e) of the Internal Revenue Code, or any successor section thereto, shall apply, each child's foregoing power of withdrawal shall extend to a pro rata portion of each of such items based upon the ratio in which the total amount of each of such items bears to the total amount of all of such items (assuming the above-described limitation of Section 2514(e) of the Internal Revenue Code, or any successor section thereto, does not apply). Any such withdrawable trust accounting income which is not withdrawn by a child of the grantor (or by a legal representative acting on behalf of such child) by the end of any calendar year (or by the time of death of such child of the grantor, if earlier) shall be added to the principal of the trust estate, and the power of withdrawal of such child for such calendar year shall lapse. For purposes of this subsection 1.1, the term "trust accounting income" shall include all retirement assets (as defined in ARTICLE __, below, but ignoring the last proviso of the definition) paid to the trust during the year regardless of whether all of said retirement assets paid to the trust during the year are otherwise considered to be trust accounting income, and the principal of the trust shall include the underlying value of all retirement assets (as defined in ARTICLE

__, below, but ignoring the last proviso of the definition) and other assets which are payable to the trust over time and not yet paid to the trust. The trustee other than a trustee having any beneficial interest in the trust (other than solely as a contingent taker under ARTICLE __, below) may, in the sole and absolute discretion of said trustee, suspend the withdrawal power of any of the grantor's children under this subsection 1.1, in whole or part, by instrument in writing executed by said trustee before January 1 of the calendar year in which such withdrawal power would otherwise exist. Reasons for such suspension may include, but shall not be limited to, overall tax savings for the trust and its beneficiaries (including remainder beneficiaries), creditor protection for such child of the grantor, and unwise or immature use of withdrawn funds by such child of the grantor. During any period of time when one or more children of the grantor shall have his, her or their aforesaid power(s) of withdrawal suspended, said child or children shall be treated as deceased for purposes of determining the child or children of the grantor who retain said withdrawal power(s). In the event one or more of the grantor's children shall have his, her or their aforesaid power(s) of withdrawal suspended, in whole or in part, the trustee other than a trustee having any beneficial interest in the trust (other than solely as a contingent taker under ARTICLE __, below) may also, in the sole and absolute discretion of said trustee, restore his, her or their withdrawal power(s) under this subsection 1.1, in whole or part, at any time, by instrument in writing executed by said trustee.

     1.2   The grantor's then living children (including the legal representative acting on behalf of any child) shall each also have the annual noncumulative power to withdraw, on or before December 31 of the calendar year, so much of the "net investment income" of the trust (as defined in Section 1411(c) of the Internal Revenue Code, or any successor section thereto) which is not already withdrawable pursuant to the provisions of subsection 1.1, above, and which is not described in clause (III) of subsection 1.1, above (hereinafter "the excess net investment income"), as is equal to all of the excess net investment income divided by the number of the grantor's children living at the beginning of such calendar year; PROVIDED, HOWEVER, that (i) the foregoing power(s) of withdrawal shall not extend to the portion of the excess net investment income of the trust which, for the calendar year, is less than the dollar amount at which the highest tax bracket in section 1(e) of the Internal Revenue Code, or any successor section thereto, begins for such calendar year (but with said dollar amount being reduced, but not below zero, by (A) any net investment income, as defined in Section 1411(c) of the Internal Revenue Code, or any successor section thereto, which is not withdrawable by the grantor's the living children pursuant to the provisions of clause (III) of paragraph 1.1, above, and (B) an amount equal to the total of any costs which are deductible for purposes of determining the taxable income of the trust but not for purposes of determining the adjusted gross income of the trust, after the application of Section 67(e) of the Internal Revenue Code, or any successor section thereto), and (ii) if Section 2514(e) of the Internal Revenue Code, or any successor section thereto, is in effect during the calendar year, the amount of the excess net investment income subject to each such child of the grantors' foregoing power of withdrawal during the calendar year shall not exceed (A) five percent (5%) (or such other percentage as shall be provided for in Section 2514(e)(2) of the Internal Revenue Code, or any successor section thereto) of the combined value of the principal and income of the trust on December 31 of the calendar year (or on the date of death of such child of the grantor, if earlier), less (B) any amount which is withdrawable by such child of the grantor during the calendar year pursuant to the provisions of subsection 1.1, above. If more than one item of trust accounting income is withdrawable by the grantor's children pursuant to the foregoing provisions of this subsection 1.2 (for example, capital gains from the sale of various corporate stocks and dividend distributions on various corporate stocks), but the above-described limitation of Section 2514(e) of the Internal Revenue Code, or any successor section thereto, shall apply, each child's foregoing power of withdrawal shall extend to a pro rata portion of each of such items based upon the ratio in which the total amount of each of such items bears to the total amount of all of such items (assuming the above-described limitation of Section 2514(e) of the Internal Revenue Code, or any successor section thereto, does not apply). Any such withdrawable excess net investment income which is not withdrawn by a child of the grantor (or by a legal representative acting on behalf of such child) by the end of any calendar year (or by the time of death of such child of the grantor, if earlier) shall not be withdrawable by such child of the grantor in any subsequent calendar year. For purposes of this subsection 1.2, the principal of the trust shall include the underlying value of all retirement assets (as defined in ARTICLE __, below, but ignoring the last proviso of the definition) and other assets which are payable to the trust over time and not yet paid to the trust. The trustee other than a trustee having any beneficial interest in the trust (other than solely as a contingent taker under ARTICLE __, below) may, in the sole and absolute discretion of said trustee, suspend the withdrawal power of any of the grantor's children under this subsection 1.2, in whole or part, by instrument in writing executed by said trustee before January 1 of the calendar year in which such withdrawal power would otherwise exist. Reasons for such suspension may include, but shall not be limited to, overall tax savings for the trust and its beneficiaries (including remainder beneficiaries), creditor protection for such child of the grantor, and unwise or immature use of withdrawn funds by such child of the grantor. During any period of time when one or more children of the grantor shall have his, her or their aforesaid power(s) of withdrawal suspended, said child or children shall be treated as deceased for purposes of determining the child or children of the grantor who retain said withdrawal power(s). In the event one or more of the grantor's children shall have his, her or their aforesaid power(s) of withdrawal suspended, in whole or in part, the trustee other than a trustee having any beneficial interest in the trust (other than solely as a contingent taker under ARTICLE __, below) may also, in the sole and absolute discretion of said trustee, restore his, her or their withdrawal power(s) under this subsection 1.2, in whole or part, at any time, by instrument in writing executed by said trustee.

1.3 The trustee may, in such trustee's sole discretion, distribute, use or apply the income and principal of the trust estate (which is not withdrawable by the grantor's children or their legal representatives, as the case may be, pursuant to the provisions of subsections 1.1 and 1.2, above) as the trustee may deem necessary for the maintenance, support, health care and education of any descendant of the grantor; PROVIDED, HOWEVER, that neither the income nor principal of the trust may be used to limit, relieve or otherwise discharge, in whole or in part, the legal obligation of any individual to support and maintain any other individual. In determining the amounts to be distributed, used or applied for the grantor's descendants, the trustee shall not be required to treat each of such persons equally but shall be governed more by the particular needs and interests of each of them. The trustee other than a child of the grantor and other than a trustee designated by any of the grantor's children who is "related or subordinate" to any of the grantor's children within the meaning of current Section 672(c) of the Internal Revenue Code (substituting "any of the grantor's children" for "the grantor" in said Section), may, in such trustee's sole discretion, utilize the income and principal of the trust estate (which is not withdrawable by any child of the grantor or by the legal representative of any child of the grantor pursuant to the provisions of subsections 1.1 and 1.2, above) for the purpose of reimbursing the grantor's children for any income tax liability accruing to the grantor's children as a result of their powers of withdrawal under subsections 1.1 and 1.2, above; PROVIDED, HOWEVER, that the trustee shall not possess the discretionary power described in this sentence if, as a consequence of possessing said power, said child or children of the grantor is/are deemed to possess the same power for federal or state estate tax, gift tax, generation-skipping transfer tax, inheritance tax or other transfer tax purposes. The trustee shall be entitled to rely on the advice of legal counsel with respect to any matter under this subsection 1.3; PROVIDED, HOWEVER, that if said legal counsel's opinion is subsequently determined to be invalid as applied to this subsection 1.3, either as a result of a subsequently passed Internal Revenue Code provision or a subsequently promulgated Department of Treasury regulation or published ruling, or as a result of judicial decision, the trustee's limitations under this paragraph, if any, shall be determined based on such subsequent development and not in accordance with said legal counsel's opinion.

[USE THE FOLLOWING PROVISION IF MINOR CHILDREN AND GUARDIAN]

1.4   In order to adequately house the grantor's child or children along with the guardian's or guardians' own child or children, if any, the trustee(s) (other than a trustee or trustees acting as guardian(s) of the grantor's minor child or children) may, in such trustee's or trustees' sole discretion, use or apply the income and principal of the trust estate (which is not withdrawable by any child of the grantor or by the legal representative of any child of the grantor pursuant to the provisions of subsections 1.1 and 1.2, above) (excluding, however, the income and principal of "Share A" of the trust, as defined in Section 12 of ARTICLE __ hereof [RELATING TO

RETIREMENT BENEFITS]) for the purpose of improving the home of the guardian(s) of the grantor's minor child or children or for the purpose of assisting in the purchase of a new home to be occupied by the grantor's child or children, said guardian(s), and the child or children of said guardian(s). The guardian(s) shall not be required to reimburse the trust for any portion of the cost of such improvement or new home.

Section 2.   Distribution of Principal

This trust shall terminate at such time as all of the grantor's children have either attained the age of twenty-three (23) years or have died before or after attaining said age.   Upon such termination, the trustee shall distribute all of the assets remaining in the trust estate, including both principal and accrued and undistributed income, to the grantor's descendants who survive the termination of the trust, per stirpes; PROVIDED, HOWEVER, that the share of any child or more remote descendant of the grantor who is then less than thirty-five (35) years of age shall be held in trust for the benefit of such child or more remote descendant with income and principal administered and distributed pursuant to the provisions of ARTICLE __ hereof.

Sample Form for "Age 35" Trust for Children and More Remote Descendants

The assets to be held in a trust estate for the benefit of any child or more remote descendant of the grantor pursuant to the provisions of this ARTICLE shall be held by the trustee as a separate trust estate for the benefit of such child or more remote descendant (hereinafter in this ARTICLE referred to as "the beneficiary") with income and principal used, applied and distributed as follows:

[Section 1. Distribution of Income - TRADITIONAL USE AND APPLY INCOME FORM]

The trustee may distribute, use, apply and expend so much of the income of the trust estate as the trustee, in the trustee's sole discretion, shall deem reasonably necessary to provide for the maintenance, support, health care and education of the beneficiary.

Section 2. Encroachment on Principal

The trustee may encroach upon the principal of the trust estate for the maintenance, support, health care and education of the beneficiary in the beneficiary's accustomed manner of living. In addition, the trustee may encroach upon the principal of the trust estate for the maintenance, support, health care and education of [the beneficiary's spouse and] any descendant of the beneficiary; PROVIDED, HOWEVER, that the principal of the trust may not be used to discharge, relieve or limit, wholly or partially, the legal obligation of any individual to support and maintain any other individual.]

Section 1. Distribution of Income and Principal During Lifetime of Beneficiary - MIT TRUST FORM

1.1 During the beneficiary's lifetime the beneficiary (including any legal representative acting on behalf of any beneficiary under a legal incapacity) shall have the annual noncumulative power to withdraw all or any portion of the trust accounting income on or before December 31 of the calendar year; PROVIDED, HOWEVER, that (i) the foregoing power of withdrawal shall not extend to the portion of the trust accounting income which, for the calendar year, would be either exempt from federal income tax or subject to federal income tax to the trust, after all deductions and exemptions (but determined as though the trustee made no other income or principal distributions or encroachments during the year other than for trust expenses and taxes), at less than the general maximum federal income tax rate applicable to trusts (and for this purpose said excluded portion (I) shall begin with any dividends, capital gains or other items of trust accounting income which are subject to a maximum federal income tax rate which is lower than the general maximum federal income tax rate applicable to trusts, (II) shall next include any items of trust accounting income filling out the lower income tax brackets of the trust which do not constitute "net investment income" as defined in Section 1411(c) of the Internal Revenue Code, or any successor section thereto, (III) shall next include any additional items of trust accounting income filling out the lower income tax brackets of the trust which constitute "net investment income" as defined in Section 1411(c) of the Internal Revenue Code, or any successor section thereto, and (IV) shall assume that all items of federal gross income of the trust which do not constitute trust accounting income and which are not subject to a maximum federal income tax rate which is lower than the general maximum federal income tax rate applicable to trusts, are using up the lower income tax brackets of the trust first, before the aforesaid items of trust accounting income) and (ii) if Section 2514(e) of the Internal Revenue Code, or any successor section thereto, is in effect during the calendar year, the amount of trust accounting income subject to the foregoing power of withdrawal during the calendar year shall not exceed five percent (5%) (or such other percentage as shall be provided for in Section 2514(e)(2) of the Internal Revenue Code, or any successor section thereto) of the combined value of the principal and income of the trust on December 31 of the calendar year (or on the date of the beneficiary's death, if earlier). If more than one item of trust accounting income is withdrawable by the beneficiary pursuant to the foregoing provisions of this subsection 1.1 (for example, taxable interest from corporate bonds and distributions from retirement assets (as defined in ARTICLE __, below)), but the above-described limitation of Section 2514(e) of the Internal Revenue Code, or any successor section thereto, shall apply, the beneficiary's power of withdrawal shall extend to a pro rata portion of each of such items based upon the ratio in which the total amount of each of such items bears to the total amount of all of such items (assuming the above-described limitation of Section

2514(e) of the Internal Revenue Code, or any successor section thereto, does not apply). Any such withdrawable trust accounting income which is not withdrawn by the beneficiary or by the beneficiary's legal representative by the end of any calendar year (or by the time of the beneficiary's death, if earlier) shall be added to the principal of the trust estate, and the beneficiary's power of withdrawal for such calendar year shall lapse. For purposes of this subsection 1.1, the term "trust accounting income" shall include all retirement assets (as defined in ARTICLE __, below, but ignoring the last proviso of the definition) paid to the trust during the year regardless of whether all of said retirement assets paid to the trust during the year are otherwise considered to be trust accounting income, and the principal of the trust shall include the underlying value of all retirement assets (as defined in ARTICLE __, below, but ignoring the last proviso of the definition) and other assets which are payable to the trust over time and not yet paid to the trust. The trustee other than a trustee having any beneficial interest in the trust (other than solely as a contingent taker under ARTICLE __, below) may, in the sole and absolute discretion of said trustee, suspend the beneficiary's withdrawal power under this subsection 1.1, in whole or part, by instrument in writing executed by said trustee before January 1 of the calendar year in which such withdrawal power would otherwise exist. Reasons for such suspension may include, but shall not be limited to, overall tax savings for the trust and its beneficiaries (including remainder beneficiaries), creditor protection for the beneficiary, and unwise or immature use of withdrawn funds by the beneficiary. In the event the beneficiary shall have the beneficiary's aforesaid power of withdrawal suspended, in whole or in part, the trustee other than a trustee having any beneficial interest in the trust (other than solely as a contingent taker under ARTICLE ___, below) may also, in the sole and absolute discretion of said trustee, restore the beneficiary's withdrawal power under this subsection 1.1, in whole or part, at any time, by instrument in writing executed by said trustee. **[MAY NOT WANT TO USE 5% WITHDRAWAL WHEN 1) SECOND SPOUSE, 2) SPENDTHRIFT CHILD, OR 3) HIGH NET WORTH CLIENT AND NO TAX BENEFIT FOR SUCH POWER OVER NON-GST TAX-EXEMPT TRUST]**

1.2 During the beneficiary's lifetime the beneficiary (including any legal representative acting on behalf of any beneficiary under a legal incapacity) shall also have the annual noncumulative power to withdraw all or any portion of the "net investment income" of the trust (as defined in Section 1411(c) of the Internal Revenue Code, or any successor section thereto) which is not already withdrawable pursuant to the provisions of subsection 1.1, above, and which is not described in clause (III) of subsection 1.1, above (hereinafter "the excess net investment income"), on or before December 31 of the calendar year; PROVIDED, HOWEVER, that (i) the foregoing power of withdrawal shall not extend to the portion of the excess net investment income of the trust which, for the calendar year, is less than the dollar amount at which the highest tax bracket in section 1(e) of the Internal Revenue Code, or any successor section thereto, begins for such calendar year (but with said dollar amount being reduced, but not below zero, by (A) any net investment income, as defined in Section 1411(c) of the Internal Revenue Code, or any successor section thereto, which is not withdrawable by the beneficiary pursuant to the provisions of clause (III) of paragraph 1.1, above, and (B) an amount equal to the total of any costs which are deductible for purposes of determining the taxable income of the trust but not for purposes of determining the adjusted gross income of the trust, after the application of Section 67(e) of the Internal Revenue Code, or any successor section thereto), and (ii) if Section 2514(e) of the Internal Revenue Code, or any successor section thereto, is in effect during the calendar year, the amount of the excess net investment income subject to the foregoing power of withdrawal during the calendar year shall not exceed (A) five percent (5%) (or such other percentage as shall be provided for in Section 2514(e)(2) of the Internal Revenue Code, or any successor section thereto) of the combined value of the principal and income of the trust on December 31 of the calendar year (or on the date of the beneficiary's death, if earlier), less (B) any amount which is withdrawable by the beneficiary during the calendar year pursuant to the provisions of subsection 1.1, above. If more than one item of excess net investment income is withdrawable by the beneficiary pursuant to the foregoing provisions of this subsection 1.2 (for example, capital gains from the sale of various corporate stocks and dividend distributions on various corporate stocks), but the above-described limitation of Section 2514(e) of the Internal Revenue Code, or any successor section thereto, shall apply, the beneficiary's power of withdrawal shall extend to a pro rata portion of each of such items based upon the ratio in which the total amount of each of such items bears to the total amount of all of such items (assuming the above-described limitation of Section 2514(e) of the Internal Revenue Code, or any successor section thereto, does not apply). Any such withdrawable excess net investment income which is not withdrawn by the beneficiary or by the beneficiary's legal representative by the end of any calendar year (or by the time of the beneficiary's death, if earlier) shall not be withdrawable by the beneficiary in any subsequent calendar year. For purposes of this subsection 1.2, the principal of the trust shall include the underlying value of all retirement assets (as defined in ARTICLE __, below, but ignoring the last proviso of the definition) and other assets which are payable to the trust over time and not yet paid to the trust. The trustee other than a trustee having any beneficial interest in the trust (other than solely as a contingent taker under ARTICLE __, below) may, in the sole and absolute discretion of said trustee, suspend the beneficiary's withdrawal power under this subsection 1.2, in whole or part, by instrument in writing executed by said trustee before January 1 of the calendar year in which such withdrawal power would otherwise exist. Reasons for such suspension may include, but shall not be limited to, overall tax savings for the trust and its beneficiaries (including remainder beneficiaries), creditor protection for the beneficiary, and unwise or immature use of withdrawn funds by the beneficiary. In the event the beneficiary shall have the beneficiary's aforesaid power of withdrawal suspended, in whole or in part, the trustee other than a trustee having any beneficial interest in the trust (other than solely as a contingent taker under ARTICLE __, below) may also, in the sole and absolute discretion of said trustee, restore the beneficiary's withdrawal power under this subsection 1.2, in whole or part, at any time, by instrument in writing executed by said trustee. **[MAY NOT WANT TO USE 5% WITHDRAWAL WHEN 1) SECOND SPOUSE, 2) SPENDTHRIFT CHILD, OR 3) HIGH NET WORTH AND NO TAX BENEFIT FOR SUCH POWER OVER NON-GST TAX-EXEMPT TRUST]**

1.3 The trustee may, in the trustee's sole discretion, distribute, use or apply so much of the income and principal of the trust estate (which is not withdrawable by the beneficiary or by the beneficiary's legal representative pursuant to the provisions of subsections 1.1 and 1.2, above) as the trustee may deem necessary to provide for the maintenance, support, health care and education of the beneficiary, in the beneficiary's accustomed manner of living. In addition, the trustee may, in the trustee's sole discretion, distribute, use or apply the income and principal of the trust estate (which is not withdrawable by the beneficiary or by the beneficiary's legal representative pursuant to the provisions of subsections 1.1 and 1.2, above) as the trustee may deem necessary for the maintenance, support, health care and education of any descendant of the beneficiary; PROVIDED, HOWEVER, that (i) the needs of the beneficiary as specified above shall be the primary concern of the trustee, and (ii) neither the income nor principal of the trust may be used to limit, relieve or otherwise discharge, in whole or in part, the legal obligation of any individual to support and maintain any other individual. In determining the amounts to be distributed, used or applied for the beneficiary's descendants, the trustee shall not be required to treat each of such persons equally but shall be governed more by the particular needs and interests of each of them. The trustee other than the beneficiary and other than a trustee designated by the beneficiary who is "related or subordinate" to the beneficiary within the meaning of current Section 672(c) of the Internal Revenue Code (substituting "the beneficiary" for "the grantor" in said Section), may, in such trustee's sole discretion, utilize the income and principal of the trust estate (which is not withdrawable by the beneficiary or by the beneficiary's legal representative pursuant to the provisions of subsections 1.1 and 1.2, above) for the purpose of reimbursing the beneficiary for any income tax liability accruing to the beneficiary as a result of the beneficiary's power of withdrawal under subsections 1.1 and 1.2, above; PROVIDED, HOWEVER, that the trustee shall not possess the discretionary power described in this sentence if, as a consequence of possessing said power, the beneficiary is deemed to possess the same power for federal or state estate tax, gift tax, generation-skipping transfer tax, inheritance tax or other transfer tax purposes. The trustee shall be entitled to rely on the advice of legal counsel with respect to any matter under this subsection 1.3; PROVIDED, HOWEVER, that if said legal counsel's opinion is subsequently determined to be invalid as applied to this subsection 1.3, either as a result of a subsequently passed Internal Revenue Code provision or a subsequently promulgated Department of Treasury regulation or published ruling, or as a result of judicial decision, the trustee's limitations under this paragraph, if any, shall be

124

determined based on such subsequent development and not in accordance with said legal counsel's opinion.

Section 2.   Distribution of Principal

2.1   When the beneficiary attains twenty-five (25) years of age, the trustee shall distribute to the beneficiary one-third (⅓) of the then remaining assets in the trust estate. When the beneficiary attains thirty (30) years of age, the trustee shall distribute to the beneficiary one-half (½) of the then remaining assets in the trust estate. When the beneficiary attains thirty-five (35) years of age, the trustee shall distribute to the beneficiary all of the assets remaining in the trust estate, and the trust for such beneficiary shall terminate. If the beneficiary is twenty-five (25) years of age or older at the time this trust is established, the trustee shall forthwith distribute to the beneficiary, outright and free from trust, that portion of the trust estate which the beneficiary is entitled to pursuant to the foregoing distribution schedule on account of the beneficiary's age. [Notwithstanding the previous provisions of this subsection 2.1, no distributions under this subsection 2.1 shall be made before the beneficiary has attained thirty-five (35) years of age, unless the beneficiary first (i) is enlisted to serve in a branch of the United States Military, or (ii) has been, for a minimum of one year prior to the date of a scheduled distribution under this subsection, (a) gainfully employed full-time, including self-employment, in the sole and absolute discretion of the trustee, (b) enrolled and attending classes full-time in a college, university or trade school, (c) a full-time

125

"homemaker" (i.e. staying at home to raise his/her minor children), or (d) occupied full-time with any combination of the activities listed in (a), (b), or (c), above (e.g. working part-time while also being enrolled and attending college classes part-time); PROVIDED, HOWEVER, that the aforesaid stipulations shall not apply if the trustee, in the trustee's sole and absolute discretion, shall determine that the beneficiary is unable to satisfy any one of the aforesaid stipulations because of a mental or physical disability not brought on by the beneficiary's own voluntary action(s), including but not limited to voluntary action leading to the abuse of drugs or alcohol; PROVIDED FURTHER, HOWEVER, that, if a scheduled distribution is not distributed as a result of the beneficiary failing to satisfy any one of the stipulations in clause (ii), above, the beneficiary shall be allowed to receive such undistributed scheduled distribution upon the beneficiary's satisfaction of any one of the stipulations in clause (ii), above, if such satisfaction occurs prior to the date of the next scheduled distribution. In exercising the sole and absolute discretion provided for in this subsection 2.1, the trustee shall be entitled to act unreasonably, and no court or other person shall be entitled to substitute its or their judgment for the discretionary decision or decisions made by the trustee.]

2.2   If the beneficiary shall die before receiving all of the remaining assets of the trust estate, then, [except as otherwise provided in Sections __ and __ of ARTICLE __ hereof ___ [RELATING TO RETIREMENT ASSETS] **MAY NOT BE**

126

NECESSARY; DEPENDS ON WHO PERMISSIBLE APPOINTEES ARE], all of such remaining assets, including both principal and accumulated and undistributed income, shall be distributed to or among [the beneficiary's surviving spouse and] the grantor's descendants (other than the beneficiary), in trust or otherwise, and in such proportions, as shall be designated by the beneficiary by and in the beneficiary's Last Will and Testament (having the most recent date of execution by the beneficiary) and which is filed with the probate court of the relevant jurisdiction within six (6) months following the beneficiary's death, but if such Last Will and Testament shall be contested within the aforementioned six (6) month period, then as shall be designated in the beneficiary's Last Will and Testament which is finally admitted to probate after the period for contesting the beneficiary's Last Will and Testament has expired, and referring specifically to this provision, excluding, however, the beneficiary, the beneficiary's estate, the beneficiary's creditors and the creditors of the beneficiary's estate. [; PROVIDED, HOWEVER, if the beneficiary is survived by one or more descendants, no more than fifty percent (50%) of such remaining trust assets may be appointed to or in trust for the benefit of the beneficiary's surviving spouse.] In addition, except as otherwise provided in Sections __ and __ of ARTICLE __ hereof [RELATING TO RETIREMENT ASSETS], if the beneficiary is not survived by a surviving spouse (as that term is defined for purposes of Section 2056 of the Internal Revenue Code, or any successor section thereto, or for purposes of the law of the state or other jurisdiction in which the beneficiary was domiciled at the time of his or her death, if said state or other jurisdiction has an estate or inheritance tax in effect at the time of the beneficiary's death), then to the extent it will not result in (i) the beneficiary's estate being liable for any federal or state estate or inheritance taxes, (ii) the beneficiary's estate being liable to reimburse any government for any assistance or other benefits provided the beneficiary during the beneficiary's lifetime, (iii) the beneficiary's estate or the trust being automatically subject to income tax on any gain attributable to any portion of the remaining trust assets, or (iv) a reduction in the federal income tax basis of any asset over its historical federal income tax basis, the beneficiary shall also have the power to appoint those remaining trust assets, if any, beginning with the asset or assets having the greatest amount of built-in appreciation (calculated by subtracting the trust's income tax basis from the fair market value on the date of death of the beneficiary), as a percentage of the fair market value of such asset or assets on the date of death of the beneficiary, to the creditors of the beneficiary's estate (or to the beneficiary's estate if the power to distribute such assets to the creditors of the beneficiary's estate is not sufficient to include such assets in the beneficiary's estate for federal estate tax purposes), utilizing the same appointment procedure described immediately above; PROVIDED, HOWEVER, that if this trust has been or will be divided into two separate trusts for federal generation-skipping transfer tax purposes, the beneficiary's foregoing additional power of appointment shall apply (i) first to the trust having an inclusion ratio, as defined in Section 2642(a) of the Internal Revenue Code, or any successor section thereto, of other than zero, but only to the extent such trust is not otherwise already includible in the beneficiary's estate for federal estate tax purposes, pursuant to the other provisions of this trust instrument, and (ii) next to the trust having an inclusion ratio, as defined in Section 2642(a) of the Internal Revenue Code, or any successor section thereto, of zero; PROVIDED FURTHER, HOWEVER, that if the beneficiary is the beneficiary of more than one trust which includes a provision similar to this sentence, the extent of the beneficiary's foregoing additional power of appointment shall be reduced by multiplying the value of the assets otherwise subject to the beneficiary's foregoing additional power of appointment by a fraction the numerator of which shall equal the value of the assets otherwise subject to the beneficiary's foregoing additional power of appointment and the denominator of which shall equal the value of all assets otherwise subject to the beneficiary's foregoing and similar additional power(s) of appointment, the intent being that under no circumstance shall the beneficiary's estate be liable for any federal or state estate or inheritance tax as a consequence of the beneficiary's foregoing additional power of appointment. If the beneficiary is survived by a surviving spouse (as that term is defined for purposes of Section 2056 of the Internal Revenue Code, or any successor section thereto, or for purposes of the law of the state or other jurisdiction in which the beneficiary was domiciled at the time of his or her death, if said state or other jurisdiction has an estate or inheritance tax in effect at the time of the beneficiary's death), the beneficiary shall only possess the beneficiary's foregoing additional power of appointment to the same or lesser extent that the trustee (other than the beneficiary and other than a trustee who is "related or subordinate" to the beneficiary within the meaning of current Section 672(c) of the Internal Revenue Code (substituting "the beneficiary" for "the grantor" in said Section)) shall direct by instrument in writing filed with the trust during the beneficiary's lifetime and not revoked by said trustee prior to the beneficiary's death; PROVIDED, HOWEVER, that the trustee shall not possess the foregoing power to direct if the beneficiary appointed the trustee who or which possesses the foregoing power to direct, and if as a consequence the beneficiary is deemed to possess the foregoing power to direct for federal or state estate tax or inheritance tax purposes. In exercising said trustee's broad discretionary power in determining whether and to what extent the beneficiary shall possess the beneficiary's foregoing power of appointment if the beneficiary is survived by a surviving spouse, said trustee shall be primarily concerned with minimizing overall income and transfer taxes to the beneficiary's estate, to the beneficiary's surviving spouse's estate, and to recipients of the trust assets after the beneficiary's death, and with minimizing the liability of the beneficiary's estate to reimburse any government for any assistance or other benefits provided the beneficiary during the beneficiary's lifetime. The trustee shall be entitled to rely on the advice of legal counsel with respect to any matter under this subsection 2.2; PROVIDED, HOWEVER, that if said legal counsel's opinion is subsequently determined to be invalid as applied to this subsection, either as a result of a subsequently passed Internal Revenue Code provision or a subsequently promulgated Department of Treasury regulation or published ruling, or as a result of judicial decision, the trustee's limitations under this subsection, if any, shall be determined based on such subsequent development and not in accordance with said legal counsel's opinion.

2.3   If the beneficiary shall die before receiving all of the remaining assets of the trust estate, all of the remaining assets of the trust estate which are not effectively appointed by the beneficiary pursuant to the provisions of subsection 2.2, above, shall be distributed, per stirpes, to the descendants of the beneficiary who survive the beneficiary, or, if the beneficiary is not survived by one or more descendants, to the descendants who survive the beneficiary of the least remote ancestor of the beneficiary who is either the grantor or a descendant of the grantor and who has descendants who survive the beneficiary; PROVIDED, HOWEVER, that the share of any child or more remote descendant of the grantor who is then less than thirty-five (35) years of age shall be held in trust for the benefit of such child or more remote descendant with income and principal administered and distributed pursuant to the provisions of this ARTICLE.

Sample Form for "Lifetime" Trust for Child

The assets to be held in a trust estate for the benefit of any child of the grantor pursuant to the provisions of this ARTICLE shall be held by the trustee as a separate trust estate for the primary benefit of such child of the grantor (hereinafter in this ARTICLE referred to as "the beneficiary") with income and principal used, applied and distributed as follows:

[Section 1. Distribution of Income - TRADITIONAL USE AND APPLY INCOME FORM

The trustee may distribute, use, apply and expend so much of the income of the trust estate as the trustee shall, in the trustee's sole discretion, deem reasonably necessary to provide for the maintenance, support, health care and education of the beneficiary, in the beneficiary's accustomed manner of living.

Section 2. Encroachment on Principal

The trustee may encroach upon the principal of the trust estate for the maintenance, support, health care and education of the beneficiary in the beneficiary's accustomed manner of living. In addition, the trustee may encroach upon the principal of the trust estate for the maintenance, support, health care and education of the [beneficiary's spouse and] any descendant of the beneficiary; PROVIDED, HOWEVER, that the principal of the trust may not be used to discharge, relieve or limit, wholly or partially, the legal obligation of any individual to support and maintain any other individual.]

Section 1. Distribution of Income and Principal During Lifetime of Beneficiary - MIT TRUST FORM

1.1   During the beneficiary's lifetime the beneficiary (including any legal representative acting on behalf of any beneficiary under a legal incapacity) shall have the annual noncumulative power to withdraw all or any portion of the trust accounting income on or before December 31 of the calendar year; PROVIDED, HOWEVER, that (i) the foregoing power of withdrawal shall not extend to the portion of the trust accounting income which, for the calendar year, would be either exempt from federal income tax or subject to federal income tax to the trust, after all deductions and exemptions (but determined as though the trustee made no other income or principal distributions or encroachments during the year other than for trust expenses and taxes), at less than the general maximum federal income tax rate applicable to trusts (and for this purpose said excluded portion (I) shall begin with any dividends, capital gains or other items of trust accounting income which are subject to a maximum federal income tax rate which is lower than the general maximum federal income tax rate applicable to trusts, (II) shall next include any items of trust accounting income filling out the lower income tax brackets of the trust which do not constitute "net investment income" as defined in Section 1411(c) of the Internal Revenue Code, or any successor section thereto, (III) shall next include any additional items of trust accounting income filling out the lower income tax brackets of the trust which constitute "net investment income" as defined in Section 1411(c) of the Internal Revenue Code, or any successor section thereto, and (IV) shall assume that all items of federal gross income of the trust which do not constitute trust accounting income and which are not subject to a maximum federal income tax rate which is lower than the general maximum federal income tax rate applicable to trusts, are using up the lower income tax brackets of the trust first, before the aforesaid items of trust accounting income) and (ii) if Section 2514(e) of the Internal Revenue Code, or any successor section thereto, is in effect during the calendar year, the amount of trust accounting income subject to the foregoing power of withdrawal during the calendar year shall not exceed five percent (5%) (or such other percentage as shall be provided for in Section 2514(e)(2) of the Internal Revenue Code, or any successor section thereto) of the combined value of the principal and income of the trust on December 31 of the calendar year (or on the date of the beneficiary's death, if earlier). If more than one item of trust accounting income is withdrawable by the beneficiary pursuant to the foregoing provisions of this subsection 1.1 (for example, taxable interest from corporate bonds and distributions from retirement assets (as defined in ARTICLE __, below)), but the above-described limitation of Section 2514(e) of the Internal Revenue Code, or any successor section thereto, shall apply, the beneficiary's power of withdrawal shall extend to a pro rata portion of each of such items based upon the ratio in which the total amount of each of such items bears to the total amount of all of such items (assuming the above-described limitation of Section 2514(e) of the Internal Revenue Code, or any successor section thereto, does not apply). Any such withdrawable trust accounting income which is not withdrawn by the beneficiary or by the beneficiary's legal representative by the end of any calendar year (or by the time of the beneficiary's death, if earlier) shall be added to the principal of the trust estate, and the beneficiary's power of withdrawal for such calendar year shall lapse. For purposes of this subsection 1.1, the term "trust accounting income" shall include all retirement assets (as defined in ARTICLE __, below, but ignoring the last proviso of the definition) paid to the trust during the year regardless of whether all of said retirement assets paid to the trust during the year are otherwise considered to be trust accounting income, and the principal of the trust shall include the underlying value of all retirement assets (as defined in ARTICLE __, below, but ignoring the last proviso of the definition) and other assets which are payable to the trust over time and not yet paid to the trust. The trustee other than a trustee having any beneficial interest in the trust (other than solely as a contingent taker under ARTICLE __, below) may, in the sole and absolute discretion of said trustee, suspend the beneficiary's withdrawal power under this subsection 1.1, in whole or part, by instrument in writing executed by said trustee before January 1 of the calendar year in which such withdrawal power would otherwise exist. Reasons for such suspension may include, but shall not be limited to, overall tax savings for the trust and its beneficiaries (including remainder beneficiaries), creditor protection for the beneficiary, and unwise or immature use of withdrawn funds by the beneficiary. In the event the beneficiary shall have the beneficiary's aforesaid power of withdrawal suspended, in whole or in part, the trustee other than a trustee having any beneficial interest in the trust (other than solely as a contingent taker under ARTICLE __, below) may also, in the sole and absolute discretion of said trustee, restore the beneficiary's withdrawal power under this subsection 1.1, in whole or part, at any time, by instrument in writing executed by said trustee. **[MAY NOT WANT TO USE 5% WITHDRAWAL WHEN 1) SECOND SPOUSE, 2) SPENDTHRIFT CHILD, OR 3) HIGH NET WORTH CLIENT AND NO TAX BENEFIT FOR SUCH POWER OVER NON-GST TAX-EXEMPT TRUST]**

1.2 During the beneficiary's lifetime the beneficiary (including any legal representative acting on behalf of any beneficiary under a legal incapacity) shall also have the annual noncumulative power to withdraw all or any portion of the "net investment income" of the trust (as defined in Section 1411(c) of the Internal Revenue Code, or any successor section thereto) which is not already withdrawable pursuant to the provisions of subsection 1.1, above, and which is not described in clause (III) of subsection 1.1, above (hereinafter "the excess net investment income"), on or before December 31 of the calendar year; PROVIDED, HOWEVER, that (i) the foregoing power of withdrawal shall not extend to the portion of the excess net investment income of the trust which, for the calendar year, is less than the dollar amount at which the highest tax bracket in section 1(e) of the Internal Revenue Code, or any successor section thereto, begins for such calendar year (but with said dollar amount being reduced, but not below zero, by (A) any net investment income, as defined in Section 1411(c) of the Internal Revenue Code, or any successor section thereto, which is not withdrawable by the beneficiary pursuant to the provisions of clause (III) of paragraph 1.1, above, and (B) an amount equal to the total of any costs which are deductible for purposes of determining the taxable income of the trust but not for purposes of determining the adjusted gross income of the trust, after the application of Section 67(e) of the Internal Revenue Code, or any successor section thereto), and (ii) if Section 2514(e) of the Internal Revenue Code, or any successor section thereto, is in effect during the calendar year, the amount of the excess net investment income subject to the foregoing power of withdrawal during the calendar year shall not exceed (A) five percent (5%) (or such other percentage as shall be provided for in Section 2514(e)(2) of the Internal Revenue Code, or any successor section thereto) of the combined value of the principal and income of the trust on December 31 of the calendar year (or on the date of the beneficiary's death, if earlier), less (B) any amount which is withdrawable by the beneficiary during the calendar year pursuant to the provisions of subsection 1.1, above. If more than one item of excess net investment income is withdrawable by the beneficiary pursuant to the foregoing provisions of this subsection 1.2 (for example, capital gains from the sale of various corporate stocks and dividend distributions on various corporate stocks), but the above-described limitation of Section 2514(e) of the Internal Revenue Code, or any successor section thereto, shall apply, the beneficiary's power of withdrawal shall extend to a pro rata portion of each of such items based upon the ratio in which the total amount of each of such items bears to the total amount of all of such items (assuming the above-described limitation of Section 2514(e) of the Internal Revenue Code, or any successor section thereto, does not apply). Any such withdrawable excess net investment income which is not withdrawn by the beneficiary or by the beneficiary's legal representative by the end of any calendar year (or by the time of the beneficiary's death, if earlier) shall not be withdrawable by the beneficiary in any subsequent calendar year. For purposes of this subsection 1.2, the principal of the trust shall include the underlying value of all retirement assets (as defined in ARTICLE ___, below, but ignoring the last proviso of the definition) and other assets which are payable to the trust over time and not yet paid to the trust. The trustee other than a trustee having any beneficial interest in the trust (other than solely as a contingent taker under ARTICLE ___, below) may, in the sole and absolute discretion of said trustee, suspend the beneficiary's withdrawal power under this subsection 1.2, in whole or part, by instrument in writing executed by said trustee before January 1 of the calendar year in which such withdrawal power would otherwise exist. Reasons for such suspension may include, but shall not be limited to, overall tax savings for the trust and its beneficiaries (including remainder beneficiaries), creditor protection for the beneficiary, and unwise or immature use of withdrawn funds by the beneficiary. In the event the beneficiary shall have the beneficiary's aforesaid power of withdrawal suspended, in whole or in part, the trustee other than a trustee having any beneficial interest in the trust (other than solely as a contingent taker under ARTICLE ___, below) may also, in the sole and absolute discretion of said trustee, restore the beneficiary's withdrawal power under this subsection 1.1, in whole or part, at any time, by instrument in writing executed by said trustee. **[MAY NOT WANT TO USE 5% WITHDRAWAL WHEN 1) SECOND SPOUSE, 2) SPENDTHRIFT CHILD, OR 3) HIGH NET WORTH AND NO TAX BENEFIT FOR SUCH POWER OVER NON-GST TAX-EXEMPT TRUST]**

1.3   The trustee may, in the trustee's sole discretion, distribute, use or apply so much of the income and principal of the trust estate (which is not withdrawable by the beneficiary or by the beneficiary's legal representative pursuant to the provisions of subsections 1.1 and 1.2, above) as the trustee may deem necessary to provide for the maintenance, support, health care and education of the beneficiary, in the beneficiary's accustomed manner of living. In addition, the trustee may, in the trustee's sole discretion, distribute, use or apply the income and principal of the trust estate (which is not withdrawable by the beneficiary or by the beneficiary's legal representative pursuant to the provisions of subsections 1.1 and 1.2, above) as the trustee may deem necessary for the maintenance, support, health care and education of any descendant of the beneficiary; PROVIDED, HOWEVER, that (i) the needs of the beneficiary as specified above shall be the primary concern of the trustee, and (ii) neither the income nor principal of the trust may be used to limit, relieve or otherwise discharge, in whole or in part, the legal obligation of any individual to support and maintain any other individual. In determining the amounts to be distributed, used or applied for the beneficiary's descendants, the trustee shall not be required to treat each of such persons equally but shall be governed more by the particular needs and interests of each of them. The trustee other than the beneficiary and other than a trustee designated by the beneficiary who is "related or subordinate" to the beneficiary within the meaning of current Section 672(c) of the Internal Revenue Code (substituting "the beneficiary" for "the grantor" in said Section), may, in such trustee's sole discretion, utilize the income and principal of the trust estate (which is not withdrawable by the beneficiary or by the beneficiary's legal representative pursuant to the provisions of subsections 1.1 and 1.2, above) for the purpose of reimbursing the beneficiary for any income tax liability accruing to the beneficiary as a result of the beneficiary's power of withdrawal under subsections 1.1 and 1.2, above; PROVIDED, HOWEVER, that the trustee shall not possess the discretionary power described in this sentence if, as a consequence of possessing said power, the beneficiary is deemed to possess the same power for federal or state estate tax, gift tax, generation-skipping transfer tax, inheritance tax or other transfer tax purposes. The trustee shall be entitled to rely on the advice of legal counsel with respect to any matter under this subsection 1.3; PROVIDED, HOWEVER, that if said legal counsel's opinion is subsequently determined to be invalid as applied to this subsection, either as a result of a subsequently passed Internal Revenue Code provision or a subsequently promulgated Department of Treasury regulation or published ruling, or as a result of judicial decision, the trustee's limitations under this subsection, if any, shall be determined based on such subsequent development and

140

not in accordance with said legal counsel's opinion.

Section 2.   Investment in Business of Beneficiary

The trustee may, in the trustee's sole discretion, apply the principal of the trust (which is not withdrawable by the beneficiary or by the beneficiary's legal representative pursuant to the provisions of subsections 1.1 and 1.2, above) for the purpose of investing in a business or profession operated by, or to be operated by, the beneficiary or the beneficiary's spouse and owned or to be owned by the trust and/or may make secured or unsecured loans of principal (which is not withdrawable by the beneficiary or by the beneficiary's legal representative pursuant to the provisions of subsections 1.1 and 1.2, above) to the beneficiary for the purpose of enabling the beneficiary to purchase, start up or invest in a business or profession operated by, or to be operated by, the beneficiary or the beneficiary's spouse and owned or to be owned by the beneficiary. The trustee's aforesaid powers shall be limited to the extent necessary to avoid any adverse estate or gift tax consequences to the beneficiary or to the beneficiary's estate under Section 2036, 2038, 2041, 2501 or 2514 of the Internal Revenue Code, including any successor sections thereto, and the trustee shall be entitled to rely on the advice of legal counsel as to what limitations, if any, shall be required in this respect; PROVIDED, HOWEVER, that if said legal counsel's opinion is subsequently determined to be invalid as applied to this Section 2, either as a result of a subsequently enacted Internal Revenue Code provision or a subsequently promulgated Department of the Treasury regulation or published ruling, or as a result of judicial decision, the trustee's limitations, if any, shall be determined based on such subsequent development and not in accordance with said legal counsel's opinion.

Section 3. Acquisition of Residence for Beneficiary

The trustee may, in the trustee's sole discretion, apply the principal of the trust (which is not withdrawable by the beneficiary or by the beneficiary's legal representative pursuant to the provisions of subsections 1.1 and 1.2, above) for the purpose of purchasing a home to be owned by the trust and used and occupied by the beneficiary and/or may make secured or unsecured loans of principal (which is not withdrawable by the beneficiary or by the beneficiary's legal representative pursuant to the provisions of subsections 1.1 and 1.2, above) to the beneficiary for the purpose of enabling the beneficiary to purchase a home to be used and occupied by the beneficiary. In the case of a home owned by the trust, the trustee may pay and charge to the income or principal account, or partly to each, in the trustee's sole discretion, the taxes, insurance payments, maintenance costs and other expenses required in order to keep such residence in proper repair and free of liens. The trustee's aforesaid powers shall be limited to the extent necessary to avoid any adverse estate or gift tax consequences to the beneficiary or to the beneficiary's estate under Section 2036, 2038, 2041, 2501 or 2514 of

142

the Internal Revenue Code, including any successor sections thereto, and the trustee shall be entitled to rely on the advice of legal counsel as to what limitations, if any, shall be required in this respect; PROVIDED, HOWEVER, that if said legal counsel's opinion is subsequently determined to be invalid as applied to this Section 3, either as a result of a subsequently enacted Internal Revenue Code provision or a subsequently promulgated Department of the Treasury regulation or published ruling, or as a result of judicial decision, the trustee's limitations, if any, shall be determined based on such subsequent development and not in accordance with said legal counsel's opinion.

Section 4. Distribution of Principal at Death of Beneficiary

4.1   Upon the death of the beneficiary, [and except as otherwise provided in Sections __ and __ of ARTICLE __ hereof – [RELATING TO RETIREMENT ASSETS] **MAY NOT BE NECESSARY; DEPENDS ON WHO ARE THE PERMISSIBLE APPOINTEES]** , all of the remaining assets of the trust estate, including both principal and accumulated and undistributed income, shall be distributed to or among [the beneficiary's surviving spouse and] the grantor's descendants (other than the beneficiary), in trust or otherwise, and in such proportions, as shall be designated by the beneficiary by and in the beneficiary's Last Will and Testament (having the most recent date of execution by the beneficiary) and which is filed with the probate court of the relevant jurisdiction within six (6) months following the beneficiary's death, but if such Last Will and Testament shall be contested within the aforementioned six (6) month period, then as shall be designated in the beneficiary's Last Will and Testament which is finally admitted to probate after the period for contesting the beneficiary's Last Will and Testament has expired, and referring specifically to this provision, excluding, however, the beneficiary, the beneficiary's estate, the beneficiary's creditors and the creditors of the beneficiary's estate. [; PROVIDED, HOWEVER, if the beneficiary is survived by one or more descendants, no more than fifty percent (50%) of such remaining trust assets may be appointed to or in trust for the benefit of the beneficiary's surviving spouse.] In addition, except as otherwise provided in Sections __ and __ of ARTICLE __ hereof [RELATING TO RETIREMENT ASSETS], if the beneficiary is not survived by a surviving spouse (as that term is defined for purposes of Section 2056 of the Internal Revenue Code, or any successor section thereto, or for purposes of the law of the state or other jurisdiction in which the beneficiary was domiciled at the time of his or her death, if said state or other jurisdiction has an estate or inheritance tax in effect at the time of the beneficiary's death), then to the extent it will not result in (i) the beneficiary's estate being liable for any federal or state estate or inheritance taxes, (ii) the beneficiary's estate being liable to reimburse any government for any assistance or other benefits provided the beneficiary during the beneficiary's lifetime, (iii) the beneficiary's estate or the trust being automatically subject to income tax on any gain attributable to any portion of the remaining trust assets, or (iv) a reduction in the federal income tax basis of any asset over its historical federal income tax basis, the beneficiary shall also have the power to appoint those remaining trust assets, if any, beginning with the asset or assets having the greatest amount of built-in appreciation (calculated by subtracting the trust's income tax basis from the fair market value on the date of death of the beneficiary), as a percentage of the fair market value of such asset or assets on the date of death of the beneficiary, to the creditors of the beneficiary's estate (or to the beneficiary's estate if the power to distribute such assets to the creditors of the beneficiary's estate is not sufficient to include such assets in the beneficiary's estate for federal estate tax purposes), utilizing the same appointment procedure described immediately above; PROVIDED, HOWEVER, that if this trust has been or will be divided into two separate trusts for federal generation-skipping transfer tax purposes, the beneficiary's foregoing additional power of appointment shall apply (i) first to the trust having an inclusion ratio, as defined in Section 2642(a) of the Internal Revenue Code, or any successor section thereto, of other than zero, but only to the extent such trust is not otherwise already includible in the beneficiary's estate for federal estate tax purposes, pursuant to the other provisions of this trust instrument, and (ii) next to the trust having an inclusion ratio, as defined in Section 2642(a) of the Internal Revenue Code, or any successor section thereto, of zero; **[ALTERNATIVE PROVISO IF THERE IS ALSO A NON-GST ARTICLE FOR KIDS --** PROVIDED, HOWEVER, that the beneficiary's foregoing additional power of appointment shall only apply if all of the assets held in all trusts for the primary benefit of the beneficiary having an inclusion ratio, as defined in Section 2642(a) of the Internal Revenue Code, or any successor section thereto, of other than zero, if any, are already includible in the beneficiary's estate for federal estate tax purposes;] PROVIDED FURTHER, HOWEVER, that if the beneficiary is the beneficiary of more than one trust which includes a provision similar to this sentence, the extent of the beneficiary's foregoing additional power of appointment shall be reduced by multiplying the value of the assets otherwise subject to the beneficiary's foregoing additional power of appointment by a fraction the numerator of which shall equal the value of the assets otherwise subject to the beneficiary's foregoing additional power of appointment and the denominator of which shall equal the value of all assets otherwise subject to the beneficiary's foregoing and similar additional power(s) of appointment, the intent being that under no circumstance shall the beneficiary's estate be liable for any federal or state estate or inheritance tax as a consequence of the beneficiary's foregoing additional power of appointment. If the beneficiary is survived by a surviving spouse (as that term is defined for purposes of Section 2056 of the Internal Revenue Code, or any successor section thereto, or for purposes of the law of the state or other jurisdiction in which the beneficiary was domiciled at the time of his or her death, if said state or other jurisdiction has an estate or inheritance tax in effect at the time of the beneficiary's death), the beneficiary shall only possess the beneficiary's foregoing additional power of appointment to the same or lesser extent that the trustee (other than the beneficiary and other than a trustee who is "related or subordinate" to the beneficiary within the meaning of current Section 672(c) of the Internal

Revenue Code (substituting "the beneficiary" for "the grantor" in said Section)) shall direct by instrument in writing filed with the trust during the beneficiary's lifetime and not revoked by said trustee prior to the beneficiary's death; PROVIDED, HOWEVER, that the trustee shall not possess the foregoing power to direct if the beneficiary appointed the trustee who or which possesses the foregoing power to direct, and if as a consequence the beneficiary is deemed to possess the foregoing power to direct for federal or state estate tax or inheritance tax purposes. In exercising said trustee's broad discretionary power in determining whether and to what extent the beneficiary shall possess the beneficiary's foregoing power of appointment if the beneficiary is survived by a surviving spouse, said trustee shall be primarily concerned with minimizing overall income and transfer taxes to the beneficiary's estate, to the beneficiary's surviving spouse's estate, and to recipients of the trust assets after the beneficiary's death, and with minimizing the liability of the beneficiary's estate to reimburse any government for any assistance or other benefits provided the beneficiary during the beneficiary's lifetime. The trustee shall be entitled to rely on the advice of legal counsel with respect to any matter under this subsection 4.1; PROVIDED, HOWEVER, that if said legal counsel's opinion is subsequently determined to be invalid as applied to this subsection, either as a result of a subsequently passed Internal Revenue Code provision or a subsequently promulgated Department of Treasury regulation or published ruling, or as a result of judicial decision, the trustee's limitations under this subsection, if any, shall be determined based on such subsequent development and not in accordance with said legal counsel's opinion.

4.2   Upon the death of the beneficiary, all of the remaining assets of the trust estate which are not effectively appointed by the beneficiary pursuant to the provisions of subsection 4.1, above, shall be distributed, per stirpes, to the descendants of the beneficiary who survive the beneficiary, or if the beneficiary is not survived by one or more descendants, to the grantor's descendants who survive the beneficiary, per stirpes; PROVIDED, HOWEVER, that the share of any child of the grantor shall be held in trust for the primary benefit of such child with income and principal administered and distributed pursuant to the provisions of this ARTICLE, and the share of any grandchild or more remote descendant of the grantor who is then less than thirty-five (35) years of age shall be held in trust for the primary benefit of such grandchild or more remote descendant with income and principal administered and distributed pursuant to the provisions of ARTICLE __ hereof.

Special Needs Beneficiaries

If the beneficiary has special needs, consider granting someone other than the beneficiary (for example, a sibling or siblings) the Section 678 withdrawal power over trust income, to minimize overall income taxes. Having the special needs beneficiary possess the full withdrawal power would reduce the amount of government aid available to the beneficiary. The "substitute" withdrawal power holder's rights would, again, naturally include the ability to withdraw any trust income necessary to pay his additional income taxes, or an independent trustee could reimburse the power holder for these amounts. The special needs beneficiary (or his or her legal representative) should be granted the power to suspend the withdrawal rights of the power holder, for example, in the event of abuse of the withdrawal right by the power holder or a lawsuit against the power holder, or otherwise for the welfare of the special needs beneficiary.[33] Remember that the suspension may not be effective until the beginning of the next tax year, however.

Note that this particular strategy won't work with a supplemental needs payback trust established pursuant to 42 U.S.C. Section 1396p(d)(4)(A), because these types of trusts must be for the sole benefit of the special needs beneficiary. Further, in situations in which the withdrawal power in a third party is granted, an independent trustee should be given the power to suspend the third party's Section 678 power when the tax benefits of Section 642(b)(2)(C)'s higher exemption for a trust that qualifies as a "qualified disability trust" outweigh the tax benefits of having the trust income taxed to the lower income tax bracket third party or parties.

---

33. The ability of the special needs beneficiary to permit or suspend the power holder's rights shouldn't present any adverse gift tax consequences because, by definition, a special needs beneficiary has no legal rights in the trust.

Sample Special Needs Trust Form

The assets to be held in a trust estate for the benefit of _____, pursuant to the provisions of this ARTICLE shall be held by the trustee as a separate trust estate for the primary benefit of _____ (hereinafter in this ARTICLE referred to as "the beneficiary") with income and principal used, applied and distributed as follows:

Section 1. Distribution and Use of Income and Principal

1.1 During the beneficiary's lifetime, _____ (hereinafter in this ARTICLE referred to as "the second beneficiary"), including any legal representative acting on behalf of the second beneficiary, shall have the annual noncumulative power to withdraw all or any portion of the trust accounting income on or before December 31 of the calendar year; PROVIDED, HOWEVER, that (i) the foregoing power of withdrawal shall not extend to the portion of the trust accounting income which, for the calendar year, would be either exempt from federal income tax or subject to federal income tax to the trust, after all deductions and exemptions (but determined as though the trustee made no other income or principal distributions or encroachments during the year other than for trust expenses and taxes), at less than the general maximum federal income tax rate applicable to trusts (and for this purpose said excluded portion (I) shall begin with any dividends, capital gains or other items of trust accounting income which are subject to a maximum federal income tax rate which is lower than the general maximum federal income tax rate applicable to trusts, (II) shall next include any items of trust accounting income filling out the lower income tax brackets of the trust which do not constitute "net investment income" as defined in Section 1411(c) of the Internal Revenue Code, or any successor section thereto, (III) shall next include any additional items of trust accounting income filling out the lower income tax brackets of the trust which constitute "net investment income" as defined in Section 1411(c) of the Internal Revenue Code, or any successor section thereto, and (IV) shall assume that all items of federal gross income of the trust which do not constitute trust accounting income and which are not subject to a maximum federal income tax rate which is lower than the general maximum federal income tax rate applicable to trusts, are using up the lower income tax brackets of the trust first, before the aforesaid items of trust accounting income) and (ii) if Section 2514(e) of the Internal Revenue Code, or any successor section thereto, is in effect during the calendar year, the amount of trust accounting income subject to the foregoing power of withdrawal during the calendar year shall not exceed five percent (5%) (or such other percentage as shall be provided for in Section 2514(e)(2) of the Internal Revenue Code, or any successor section thereto) of the combined value of the principal and income of the trust on December 31 of the calendar year (or on the date of the second beneficiary's death, if earlier). If more than one item of trust accounting income is withdrawable by the second beneficiary pursuant to the foregoing provisions of this subsection 1.1 (for example, taxable interest from corporate bonds and distributions from retirement assets (as defined in ARTICLE __ below)), but the above-described limitation of Section 2514(e) of the Internal Revenue Code, or any successor section thereto, shall apply, the second beneficiary's power of withdrawal shall extend to a pro rata portion of each of such items based upon the ratio in which the total amount of each of such items bears to the total amount of all of such items (assuming the above-described limitation of Section 2514(e) of the Internal Revenue Code, or any successor section thereto, does not apply). Any such withdrawable trust accounting income which is not withdrawn by the second beneficiary or by the second beneficiary's legal representative by the end of any calendar year (or by the time of the second beneficiary's death, if earlier) shall be added to the principal of the trust estate, and the second beneficiary's power of withdrawal for such calendar year shall lapse. For purposes of this subsection 1.1, the term "trust accounting income" shall include all retirement assets (as defined in ARTICLE __, below, but ignoring the last proviso of the definition) paid to the trust during the year regardless of whether all of said retirement assets paid to the trust during the year are otherwise considered to be trust accounting income, and the principal of the trust shall include the underlying value of all retirement assets (as defined in ARTICLE __, below, but ignoring the last proviso of the definition) and other assets which are payable to the trust over time and not yet paid to the trust. The beneficiary (including any legal representative acting on his behalf) may suspend the second beneficiary's withdrawal power under this subsection 1.1, in whole or part, by instrument in writing executed by the beneficiary (including any legal representative acting on behalf of the beneficiary) before January 1 of the calendar year in which such withdrawal power would otherwise exist; PROVIDED, HOWEVER, that if the second beneficiary shall be the legal representative of the beneficiary, then the trustee (other than the second beneficiary and other than a trustee having any beneficial interest in the trust (other than solely as a contingent taker under ARTICLE __, below)) may also, in the sole and absolute discretion of said trustee, suspend the second beneficiary's withdrawal power under this subsection 1.1, in whole or part, by instrument in writing executed by said trustee before January 1 of the calendar year in which such withdrawal power would otherwise exist. Reasons for such suspension may include, but shall not be limited to, creditor protection for the second beneficiary, unwise or immature use of withdrawn funds by the second beneficiary, overall tax savings for the trust and its beneficiaries (including remainder beneficiaries) [such as the situation where the overall income tax benefits from a higher income tax exemption for a trust which qualifies as a "qualified disability trust" under Section 642(b)(2)(C) of the Internal Revenue Code, or any successor section thereto, outweighs the overall income tax benefits of the second beneficiary having the aforesaid withdrawal power under this subsection 1.1], and the general welfare of the beneficiary.

1.2   During the beneficiary's lifetime, the second beneficiary (including any legal representative acting on behalf of the second beneficiary) shall also have the annual noncumulative power to withdraw all or any portion of the "net investment income" of the trust (as defined in Section 1411(c) of the Internal Revenue Code, or any successor section thereto) which is not already withdrawable pursuant to the provisions of subsection 1.1, above, and which is not described in clause (III) of subsection 1.1, above (hereinafter "the excess net investment income"), on or before December 31 of the calendar year; PROVIDED, HOWEVER, that (i) the foregoing power of withdrawal shall not extend to the portion of the excess net investment income of the trust which, for the calendar year, is less than the dollar amount at which the highest tax bracket in section 1(e) of the Internal Revenue Code, or any successor section thereto, begins for such calendar year (but with said dollar amount being reduced, but not below zero, by (A) any net investment income, as defined in Section 1411(c) of the Internal Revenue Code, or any successor section thereto, which is not withdrawable by the secondary beneficiary pursuant to the provisions of clause (III) of paragraph 1.1, above, and (B) an amount equal to the total of any costs which are deductible for purposes of determining the taxable income of the trust but not for purposes of determining the adjusted gross income of the trust, after the application of Section 67(e) of the Internal Revenue Code, or any successor section thereto), and (ii) if Section 2514(e) of the Internal Revenue Code, or any successor section thereto, is in effect during the calendar year, the amount of the excess net investment income subject to the foregoing power of withdrawal during the calendar year shall not exceed (A) five percent (5%) (or such other percentage as shall be provided for in Section 2514(e)(2) of the Internal Revenue Code, or any successor section thereto) of the combined value of the principal and income of the trust on December 31 of the calendar year (or on the date of the second beneficiary's death, if earlier), less (B) any amount which is withdrawable by the second beneficiary during the calendar year pursuant to the provisions of subsection 1.1, above. If more than one item of excess net investment income is withdrawable by the second beneficiary pursuant to the foregoing provisions of this subsection 1.2 (for example, capital gains from the sale of various corporate stocks and dividend distributions on various corporate stocks), but the above-described limitation of Section 2514(e) of the Internal Revenue Code, or any successor section thereto, shall apply, the second beneficiary's power of withdrawal shall extend to a pro rata portion of each of such items based upon the ratio in which the total amount of each of such items bears to the total amount of all of such items (assuming the above-described limitation of Section 2514(e) of the Internal Revenue Code, or any successor section thereto, does not apply). Any such withdrawable excess net investment income which is not withdrawn by the second beneficiary or by the second beneficiary's legal representative by the end of any calendar year (or by the time of the second beneficiary's death, if earlier) shall not be withdrawable by the second beneficiary in any subsequent calendar year. For purposes of this subsection 1.2, the principal of the trust shall include the underlying value of all retirement assets (as defined in ARTICLE __, below, but ignoring the last proviso of the definition) and other assets which are payable to the trust over time and not yet paid to the trust. The beneficiary (including any legal representative acting on his behalf) may suspend the second beneficiary's withdrawal power under this subsection 1.2, in whole or part, by instrument in writing executed by the beneficiary (including any legal representative acting on behalf of the beneficiary) before January 1 of the calendar year in which such withdrawal power would otherwise exist; PROVIDED, HOWEVER, that if the second beneficiary shall be the legal representative of the beneficiary, then the trustee (other than the second beneficiary and other than a trustee having any beneficial interest in the trust (other than solely as a contingent taker under ARTICLE __, below)) may also, in the sole and absolute discretion of said trustee, suspend the second beneficiary's withdrawal power under this subsection 1.2, in whole or part, by instrument in writing executed by said trustee before January 1 of the calendar year in which such withdrawal power would otherwise exist. Reasons for such suspension may include, but shall not be limited to, creditor protection for the second beneficiary, unwise or immature use of withdrawn funds by the second beneficiary, and overall tax savings for the trust and its beneficiaries (including remainder beneficiaries) [such as the situation where the overall income tax benefits from a higher income tax exemption for a trust which qualifies as a "qualified disability trust" under Section 642(b)(2)(C) of the Internal Revenue Code, or any successor section thereto, outweighs the overall income tax benefits of the second beneficiary having the aforesaid withdrawal power under this subsection 1.2] and the general welfare of the beneficiary.

1.3   The trustee may, in the trustee's sole and absolute discretion, distribute, use, apply and expend so much of the income and principal of the trust estate (which is not withdrawable by the second beneficiary or by the second beneficiary's legal representative pursuant to the provisions of subsections 1.1 and 1.2, above) as the trustee may, in the trustee's sole and absolute discretion, deem reasonably necessary to provide for the supplemental needs of the beneficiary which are not being met by federal or state programs; PROVIDED, HOWEVER, that under no circumstance shall the trustee be under an obligation to distribute, use, apply or expend the income or principal for the aforesaid needs of the beneficiary. In making the aforesaid distributions to or for the benefit of the beneficiary, the trustee shall take into consideration the amounts which the beneficiary shall be entitled to from any government agency, including, but not by way of limitation, Social Security Administration benefits, Veterans Administration benefits, Medicaid benefits and Supplemental Security Income benefits. The individual trustee(s), if any, otherwise the corporate trustee, shall assist the beneficiary in obtaining the full benefit of these programs, and shall collect, expend and account for separately all such governmental assistance benefits, but shall not commingle them with these trust funds. It is the grantors' intent that any distributions to or for the benefit of the beneficiary from the assets of this trust estate supplement rather than supplant any governmental assistance which may be available to the beneficiary.

1.4   The trustee may also, in the trustee's sole discretion, distribute, use, apply and expend so much of the income and principal of the trust estate (which is not withdrawable by the second beneficiary or by the second beneficiary's legal representative pursuant to the provisions of subsections 1.1 and 1.2, above) as the trustee may deem reasonably necessary to provide for the maintenance, support, health care and education of the beneficiary's descendants; PROVIDED, HOWEVER, that neither the income nor the principal of the trust may be used to discharge, relieve or limit, wholly or partially, the legal obligation of any individual to support and maintain any other individual. **[NOTE: Do not use this clause if may attempt to qualify the trust for the larger IRS Section 642(b)(2)(C) exemption.]**

1.5   In addition, the trustee other than the second beneficiary and other than a trustee designated by the second beneficiary who is "related or subordinate" to The second beneficiary within the meaning of current Section 672(c) of the Internal Revenue Code (substituting " The second beneficiary" for "the grantor" in said Section), may, in such trustee's sole discretion, utilize the income and principal of the trust estate (which is not withdrawable by the second beneficiary or by the second beneficiary's legal representative pursuant to the provisions of subsections 1.1 and 1.2, above) for the purpose of reimbursing the second beneficiary for any income tax liability accruing to the second beneficiary as a result of the second beneficiary's power of withdrawal under subsections 1.1

and 1.2, above; PROVIDED, HOWEVER, that the trustee shall not possess the discretionary power described in this subsection if, as a consequence of possessing said power, the second beneficiary is deemed to possess the same power for federal or state estate tax or inheritance tax purposes.

1.6 In exercising the sole and absolute discretion provided for in this Section, the trustee shall be entitled to act unreasonably, and no court or other person shall be entitled to substitute its or their judgment for the discretionary decision or decisions made by the trustee.

Section 2. Acquisition of Residence for Beneficiary

The trustee may, in the trustee's sole and absolute discretion, apply the principal of the trust (which is not withdrawable by the second beneficiary or by the second beneficiary's legal representative pursuant to the provisions of subsections 1.1 and 1.2, above) for the purpose of purchasing a home to be owned by the trust and used and occupied by the beneficiary and/or may make secured or unsecured loans of principal (which is not withdrawable by the second beneficiary or by the second beneficiary's legal representative pursuant to the provisions of subsections 1.1 and 1.2, above) to the beneficiary for the purpose of enabling the beneficiary to purchase a home to be used and occupied by the beneficiary, but only to the extent that doing so will not disqualify the beneficiary from receiving any government assistance benefits. In the case of a home owned by the trust, the trustee may pay and charge to the income or principal account, or partly to each, in the trustee's sole discretion, the taxes, insurance payments, maintenance costs and other expenses required in order to keep such residence in proper repair and free of lien, but only to the extent that doing so will not disqualify the beneficiary from receiving any government assistance benefits. The trustee's aforesaid powers shall be limited to the extent necessary to avoid any adverse estate or gift tax consequences to the beneficiary or to the beneficiary's estate under Section 2036, 2038, 2041, 2501 or 2514 of the Internal Revenue Code, including any successor sections thereto. In exercising the sole and absolute discretion provided for in this Section, the trustee shall be entitled to act unreasonably, and no court or other person shall be entitled to substitute its or their judgment for the discretionary decision or decisions made by the trustee. The trustee shall be entitled to rely on the advice of legal counsel with respect to any matter under this Section; PROVIDED, HOWEVER, that if said legal counsel's opinion is subsequently determined to be invalid as applied to this subsection, either as a result of a subsequently passed federal law, state law, or Internal Revenue Code provision or a subsequently promulgated Department of Treasury regulation or published ruling, or as a result of judicial decision, the trustee's limitations under this paragraph, if any, shall be determined based on such subsequent development and not in accordance with said legal counsel's opinion.

Section 3.   Distribution of Principal at Death
of Beneficiary

3.1   Upon the death of the beneficiary, and except as otherwise provided in Section __ of ARTICLE __ hereof [RELATING TO RETIREMENT ASSETS], all of the remaining assets of the trust estate, including both principal and accumulated and undistributed income, shall be distributed to or among the beneficiary's surviving spouse and the grantors' descendants (other than the beneficiary), in trust or otherwise, and in such proportions, as shall be designated by the beneficiary by and in the beneficiary's Last Will and Testament (having the most recent date of execution by the beneficiary) and which is filed with the probate court of the relevant jurisdiction within six (6) months following the beneficiary's death, but if such Last Will and Testament shall be contested within the aforementioned six (6) month period, then as shall be designated in the beneficiary's Last Will and Testament which is finally admitted to probate after the period for contesting the beneficiary's Last Will and Testament has expired, and referring specifically to this provision, excluding, however, the beneficiary, the beneficiary's estate, the beneficiary's creditors and the creditors of the beneficiary's estate; PROVIDED, HOWEVER, if the beneficiary is survived by one or more descendants, no more than fifty percent (50%) of such remaining trust assets may be appointed to or in trust for the benefit of the beneficiary's surviving spouse. In addition, if the beneficiary is not survived by a surviving spouse (as that term is defined for purposes of Section 2056 of the Internal Revenue Code, or any successor section thereto, or for purposes of the law of the state or other jurisdiction in which the beneficiary was domiciled at the time of his or her death, if said state or other jurisdiction has an estate or inheritance tax in effect at the time of the beneficiary's death), then to the extent it will not result in (i) the beneficiary's estate being liable for any federal or state estate or inheritance taxes, (ii) the beneficiary's estate being liable to reimburse any government for any assistance or other benefits provided the beneficiary during the beneficiary's lifetime, (iii) the beneficiary's estate or the trust being automatically subject to income tax on any gain attributable to any portion of the remaining trust assets, or (iv) a reduction in the federal income tax basis of any asset over its historical federal income tax basis, the beneficiary shall also have the power to appoint those remaining trust assets, if any, beginning with the asset or assets having the greatest amount of built-in appreciation (calculated by subtracting the trust's income tax basis from the fair market value on the date of death of the beneficiary), as a percentage of the fair market value of such asset or assets on the date of death of the beneficiary, to the creditors of the beneficiary's estate (or to the beneficiary's estate if the power to distribute such assets to the creditors of the beneficiary's estate is not sufficient to include such assets in the beneficiary's estate for federal estate tax purposes), utilizing the same appointment procedure described immediately above; PROVIDED, HOWEVER, that if this trust has been or will be divided into two separate trusts for federal generation-skipping transfer tax purposes, the beneficiary's foregoing additional power of appointment shall apply (i) first to the trust having an inclusion ratio, as defined in Section 2642(a) of the Internal Revenue Code, or any successor section thereto, of other than zero, but only to the extent such trust is not otherwise already includible in the beneficiary's estate for federal estate tax purposes, pursuant to the other provisions of this trust instrument, and (ii) next to the trust having an inclusion ratio, as defined in Section 2642(a) of the Internal Revenue Code, or any successor section thereto, of zero; PROVIDED FURTHER, HOWEVER, that if the beneficiary is the beneficiary of more than one trust which includes a provision similar to this sentence, the extent of the beneficiary's foregoing additional power of appointment shall be reduced by multiplying the value of the assets otherwise subject to the beneficiary's foregoing additional power of appointment by a fraction the numerator of which shall equal the value of the assets otherwise subject to the beneficiary's foregoing additional power of appointment and the denominator of which shall equal the value of all assets otherwise subject to the beneficiary's foregoing and similar additional power(s) of appointment, the intent being that under no circumstance shall the beneficiary's estate be liable for any federal or state estate or inheritance tax as a consequence of the beneficiary's foregoing additional power of appointment. If the beneficiary is survived by a surviving spouse (as that term is defined for purposes of Section 2056 of the Internal Revenue Code, or any successor section thereto, or for purposes of the law of the state or other jurisdiction in which the beneficiary was domiciled at the time of his or her death, if said state or other jurisdiction has an estate or inheritance tax in effect at the time of the beneficiary's death), the beneficiary shall only possess the beneficiary's foregoing additional power of appointment to the same or lesser extent that the trustee (other than the beneficiary and other than a trustee who is "related or subordinate" to the beneficiary within the meaning of current Section 672(c) of the Internal Revenue Code (substituting "the beneficiary" for "the grantor" in said Section)) shall direct by instrument in writing filed with the trust during the beneficiary's lifetime and not revoked by said trustee prior to the beneficiary's death; PROVIDED, HOWEVER, that the trustee shall not possess the foregoing power to direct if the beneficiary appointed the trustee who or which possesses the foregoing power to direct, and if as a consequence the beneficiary is deemed to possess the foregoing power to direct for federal or state estate tax or inheritance tax purposes. In exercising said trustee's broad discretionary power in determining whether and to what extent the beneficiary shall possess the beneficiary's foregoing power of appointment if the beneficiary is survived by a surviving spouse, said trustee shall be primarily concerned with minimizing overall income and transfer taxes to the beneficiary's estate, to the beneficiary's surviving spouse's estate, and to recipients of the trust assets after the beneficiary's death, and with minimizing the liability of the beneficiary's estate to reimburse any government for any assistance or other benefits provided the beneficiary during the beneficiary's lifetime. The trustee shall be entitled to rely on the advice of legal counsel with respect to any matter under this subsection 3.1; PROVIDED,

HOWEVER, that if said legal counsel's opinion is subsequently determined to be invalid as applied to this subsection, either as a result of a subsequently passed Internal Revenue Code provision or a subsequently promulgated Department of Treasury regulation or published ruling, or as a result of judicial decision, the trustee's limitations under this subsection, if any, shall be determined based on such subsequent development and not in accordance with said legal counsel's opinion.

3.2   Upon the death of the beneficiary, all of the remaining assets of the trust estate which are not effectively appointed by the beneficiary pursuant to the provisions of subsection 3.1, above, shall be distributed, per stirpes, to the descendants of the beneficiary who survive the beneficiary, or, if the beneficiary is not survived by one or more descendants, to the grantors' descendants who survive the beneficiary; PROVIDED, HOWEVER, that the share of any child or more remote descendant of the grantors who is then less than thirty-five (35) years of age shall be held in trust for the benefit of such child or more remote descendant with income and principal administered and distributed pursuant to the provisions of ARTICLE __ hereof.

Dealing with Existing Irrevocable Trusts

Many clients are beneficiaries of existing irrevocable trusts that, typically, won't include any of the above-described MIT Trust provisions. In these situations, if the governing law of the trust is that of a state that has passed so-called "decanting trust" legislation,[34] it may be possible, depending on how the trust and the state's particular decanting trust statute each read, to prepare a new irrevocable trust that will include one or more of the MIT Trust provisions, and then transfer the assets from the existing irrevocable trust to the "decanting trust."

Although a complete discussion of state decanting trust legislation is beyond the scope of this book, in states that impose a fiduciary duty on the trustee previous to transferring assets to a decanting trust, ample benefit to all of the beneficiaries of the trust, both current beneficiaries and remaindermen, should be easy to demonstrate. The larger problem will be ensuring that the particular trust document and decanting trust statute permit the contemplated transfer.[35]

Another potential route for achieving MIT Trust income tax benefits for an existing irrevocable trust may arise if the existing trust instrument includes a so-called "trust protector" clause. Depending on how the particular clause is crafted, it may include within its scope permissible amendments to the trust to achieve income tax advantages for the trust and its beneficiaries. Some states may also have "trust modification"

---

34. *See, e.g.*, RSMo Section 456.4-419. For a discussion of whether a trustee located in a state that doesn't boast a decanting statute may successfully move the trust to another state that does, see Rashad Wareh and Eric Dorsch, "Decanting: A Statutory Cornucopia," Trusts & Estates (March 2012),at p. 22.

35. Note also that in some states where decanting trust legislation hasn't been passed, decanting trust-type transfers may, nevertheless, still be permitted, pursuant to the common law of the particular state.

statutes that permit revisions to irrevocable trust documents under specified circumstances, with or without court approval, including revisions to achieve tax advantages.

An estate-planning attorney must also be mindful of all the potential transfer tax issues that may attend transferring trust assets to a decanting trust,[36] exercising a trust protector power, or otherwise participating in a modification of an irrevocable trust. These potential transfer tax issues include generation-skipping transfer tax issues involving grandfathered and other currently exempt trusts, as well as other estate and gift tax questions. In most situations it should be possible to navigate these potential transfer tax issues, however, through careful analysis and planning.

If the existing irrevocable trust happens to include a testamentary limited POA in the beneficiary, another tool the beneficiary may have to at least achieve a new income tax basis for his heirs in the trust's most appreciated assets at his death, is to follow the plan (outlined in Chapter 3) of intentionally violating Section 2041(a)(3), at least to the extent of the most appreciated assets of the trust, but without causing estate or inheritance taxes to be payable at the beneficiary's death.[37] For this planning technique to succeed, however, it must first be determined that the strategy isn't already foreclosed by the provisions of the applicable trust document or by applicable

---

34. *See* IRS Notice 2011-101, 2011-2 C.B.932 (Dec. 27, 2011).

35.   Treas. Regs. Section 20.2041-3(e)(2) includes an example that makes it clear that   a partial violation of IRC Section 2041(a)(3) is possible.

state law.

Finally, if all else fails, and the client would still like to pursue achieving a basis step-up at death for all of some of the assets owned by an existing irrevocable trust, following a plan (similar to the plan outlined in Chapter 3) for terminating existing bypass trusts, in whole or in part, may be produce benefits.

Creating Stepped-up Basis When a Parent Dies

A possible opportunity exists today for a child to have the income tax basis of his or her *own* highly appreciated assets stepped-up when his or her parent dies. This possibility exists because of the current $5.5 federal estate and gift tax exemption, along with the estate tax portion rules outlined in Chapter 2.

The concept is to transfer the client's most appreciated assets to an irrevocable trust for the benefit of others (including a spouse and/or children), and grant the parent a general testamentary power of appointment over the trust's most appreciated assets, though capped so that adverse estate tax consequences cannot occur at the parent's death. At the parent's death, the portion of the trust subject to the parent's general testamentary power of appointment flows back into a trust for the benefit of the client and his or her family, and the parent's unused generation-skipping transfer tax exemption is applied to the trust.

Similar to the planning done for a terminally ill spouse, the trust should be drafted to minimize the possible effects of the Section 1014(e) one-year rule. Thus, *as to assets transferred to the trust by the client within one year of the parent's death only,* after the parent's death the trustee should not be the client, and the trustee should be given absolute discretion over trust distributions of income and principal. Further, as to this same portion the trustee should be permitted to take into consideration the client's other resources (including any other assets passing to or for the benefit of the client at the parent's death) before making any distributions to or for the benefit of the client.

In addition to achieving the stepped-up income tax basis goal, another desirable result of this planning technique is that all appreciation in the value of the trust corpus occurring from the date of the transfer until the client's death will escape estate taxes at the child's death, due to the lifetime use of the client's gift tax exemption and the allocation of the parent's generation-skipping transfer tax exemption to the trust. This is all despite the fact that the client will normally be able to serve as trustee and retain access to the economic benefits of the transferred assets after the parent's death.

Application of Step Transaction Doctrine

If the attorney is concerned that the IRS may attempt to assert step transaction doctrine type principles when the parent possesses only a testamentary general power of appointment and no other interest in the trust, the parent can be granted a beneficial interest in the trust. It may even be wise to make distributions to or for the parent's benefit, from time to time. It might also be prudent to have the parent actually exercise the testamentary power of appointment in favor of a trust for the benefit of the client and his or her family, rather than have the trust automatically established in the event of a default in the exercise of the power.

If the arrangement is structured so that the parent actually exercises the power of appointment, it will affect the income tax reporting for the trust after the parent's death. As originally structured the "retained" trust would have been treated as wholly owned by the client for Section 671 et al income tax purposes. If the trust is "created" by the parent, on the other hand, i.e., through the exercise of the testamentary general power of appointment, the normal Section 678 portion rules described in Chapter 2 would apply after the death of the parent, assuming the trust is structured in this fashion.

An actual exercise of the general power of appointment by the parent may also be recommended when dealing with the transfer of depreciated real estate. This is because there is a technical argument that a mere lapse of a general power of appointment may not be sufficient to achieve full income tax basis step-up in this situation, under a broad reading of the second sentence of IRC Section 1014(b)(9): "[I]f the property is acquired before the death of the decedent, the basis shall be the amount determined under subsection (a) reduced by the amount allowed to the taxpayer as deductions in computing taxable income under this subtitle or prior income tax laws for exhaustion, wear and tear, obsolescence, amortization, and depletion on such property before the death of the decedent."

Charitable Beneficiaries

Especially in light of the large federal estate tax exemption, the process for making charitable gifts at death also needs to be re-examined. For example, it obviously makes little tax sense to make a basic testamentary charitable gift if the client's estate is under the federal estate tax exemption amount. In this situation the charitable gift will normally generate neither an estate or income tax benefit, as the general rule is that a trust or estate will not receive a charitable income tax deduction for the devise. Charitable gifts that are specially designated to be made out of estate or trust gross income for federal income tax purposes can generate an income tax deduction to the estate or trust, provided the estate or trust has sufficient gross income to absorb the deduction. Special thought and careful drafting and administration of the estate or trust by the executor or trustee is necessary here, however.

Consideration should therefore be given to having the client's surviving spouse and/or children make the client's desired charitable gifts, so that at least these heirs will receive an income tax deduction for the gifts. Of course, if the client feels the family members will not actually make the desired charitable dispositions, this would not be a wise plan.

A similar rationale applies to charitable gifts of life insurance. Rather than donate the policy to the charity during the insured's lifetime, a better approach might be to leave the insurance proceeds to the insured's spouse and/or children, and allow them to contribute all or a portion of the proceeds to the charity. In this fashion not only has the client maintained control over the policy and its proceeds, in the event either the client or the client's family should end up needing to access the policy's cash value or its proceeds, but the family members now will receive an income tax charitable deduction for proceeds which they received income and estate tax free. If the client is in a taxable estate situation, identical control and tax benefits can be achieved by first transferring the policy to a WRAP Trust, and then allowing the family members to donate all or a portion of the proceeds which they receive from the trust to charity.

Another excellent option is to use the client's IRA or other qualified plan as the source of funding the charitable gifts after the client's death, and as long as the actual disposition of the funds is made within the required minimum distribution timelines after the client's demise. It is normally best to provide for the charitable gifts in the client's estate planning documents regardless, with a clause which offsets the gifts by any amounts passing directly to charity outside of the will or trust.

A Corporate Trustee is the W.I.S.E. Choice

Approximately one-third to one-half of each attorney-client estate planning conference today is devoted to the important topic of the choice of trustee or trustees of a revocable trust to serve during the client's lifetime and after the client's death. The considerations are vital and vast, which no doubt accounts for the considerable discussion. When all of the dialogue is complete, however, and the pros and cons of the various alternatives have all been discussed, the client will oftentimes determine that the utilization of a corporate trustee or co-trustee (i.e., along with an individual co-trustee or co-trustees) is the wisest choice, for four primary reasons, the first letters of which coincidentally spell out the word WISE.

Wisdom

The wisdom of a corporate trustee simply cannot be overstated. Individual trustees will rarely possess the level of experience required to handle the important substantive and procedural aspects of trust administration.

While outside investment advisors can and should definitely assist an individual trustee with the investments of the trust, a non-corporate trustee investment advisor's primary expertise lies in the area of investing and preserving assets for retirement, and not in area of investing for heirs after the client's death, when cash flow infusions have ceased. Although one may view this factor as a "distinction without a difference," corporate trustees know better. They know that, subsequent to the death of the client, their primary role should shift from planning to secure the client's retirement needs, to planning to invest the trust assets in a manner which will ensure that all beneficiaries of the trust have been provided for adequately, based upon the stated purposes of the client in the trust document.

Similarly, whereas an individual trustee lacking sufficient experience expending limited trust funds may have a difficult time gauging how much may be expended for the benefit of one or more beneficiaries at any particular stage or stages in life, without risking the exhaustion of the trust corpus before all trust purposes have been accomplished, a corporate trustee will have significant experience making these determinations.

A corporate trustee also possesses the wisdom to deal with an endless variety of beneficiary issues, from suspiciously scrutinizing the demands of a spendthrift child who feels an entitlement to all of the trust assets immediately, despite the client's stated purposes to the contrary in the trust document, at the one extreme, to carefully securing the requirements of a special needs child, at the other.

Independence

An individual trustee often faces outside pressures which a corporate trustee is normally impervious to. Difficult or conflicting circumstances include, but are not limited to, situations where the trustee is a relative of the trust beneficiary.

A common concern expressed by clients is that no one in their family possesses the requisite investment skills to preserve and grow the trusts assets for the clients' heirs. Although an individual trustee can and should employ outside investment counsel, one concern is that the individual trustee will feel pressured to use a friend or other acquaintance as the investment advisor, even though the latter would not have been the clients' first choice. Utilizing the services of a corporate trustee or co-trustee would eliminate this worrisome issue.

174

Few family members will want to serve as sole trustee-
for very long at least - when the clients' children begin making
encroachment and other demands which extend beyond the
clients' stated intentions in establishing the trust. Designating
a corporation as co-trustee may serve to alleviate this situation,
by allowing the family member co-trustee to pronounce the
corporate co-trustee as the "bad guy" in enforcing the terms of
the trust, thus preserving harmony in the extended family, yet
while still retaining an element of control over the situation.

The need for an independent corporate trustee is
especially acute in situations where disputes involving the trust
corpus may arise in the future. These situations include, but are
not limited to, situations involving a family business and
situations involving a blended family.

Service

In the context of the trustee relationship, the word
"service" encompasses not only the administration and
investment of the trust assets, but also the ability and
willingness to make oneself readily available to the many and
varied needs of the trust's beneficiaries. In most instances it is
simply not practical to expect an otherwise already too busy
individual trustee to have the time available to administer the
trust properly and to be fully attentive to all of the
beneficiaries' needs.

Recent changes to the trust laws have increased the
administrative duties of the trustee. These changes include
potentially greater obligations in investing trust assets, along

with much more onerous accounting and reporting responsibilities, including a duty to keep the trust beneficiaries informed about the administration of the trust. Of course, these added responsibilities are in addition to the ongoing requirement of the trustee to file tax returns and to calculate and prepare estimated payments for the trust. Assuming the individual trustee is even cognizant of all of the aforesaid requirements, the obvious question becomes whether the trustee will have sufficient extra time to perform all of these duties fully and properly. The situation becomes even more exasperating if the individual trustee is also serving as legal guardian to the clients' minor children.

The many and varied trustee duties and responsibilities, as well as the potential personal liability associated with not satisfying the same fully and properly, have caused many clients to opt to utilize the services of a corporate fiduciary either as the sole trustee or as co-trustee with an individual co-trustee (or co-trustees). The individual co-trustee's primary responsibility then becomes to direct or advise the corporate co-trustee on beneficiary distribution of income and encroachment on principal decisions, while the corporate co-trustee becomes primarily responsible for all of the other investment, administrative and reporting responsibilities of the trust. Especially if the corporate co-trustee has a significant local presence, this arrangement normally works out quite nicely.

The fact that a corporate trustee normally performs (or at least subcontracts) all of the above services "under one roof" has two primary benefits. First, it represents the principal

176

reason why it is normally much cheaper to utilize the services of a corporate trustee or co-trustee than to have the individual trustee employ outside agents to assist him or he in completing all of his or her required tasks.[38] Second, and perhaps more importantly, utilizing all of the available resources of the corporate trustee or co-trustee to complete the work of the trust, as opposed to having the trustee employ outside agents to assist with these duties, helps avoid the all too frequently observed "too many cooks" situation, with its potential damaging effects on the trust and its beneficiaries.

Expertise

Last but not least, a corporate trustee is obviously an expert in the areas of trust administration, investing and reporting, as this is all they do. Whereas concerns will normally arise whether an individual who has been designated to serve as trustee is "equal to the task," the client need not worry that the trustee will properly fulfill its multiple roles and responsibilities if the expert services of a corporate trustee are utilized.

The corporate trustee's expertise is beneficial not only in fulfilling its traditional administrative, investment and reporting roles and responsibilities, but also in ensuring the

---

38. Note that corporate trustees normally utilize a trustee fee schedule which they make readily available. Note also that corporate trustee fees are not payable unless and until the corporate trustee actually serves, not merely because it has been designated to serve as successor trustee in the future under an individual's trust document.

best possible tax positioning for the trust and its beneficiaries. Additionally, corporate trustees typically possess notable expertise in valuing, operating and liquidating closely-held businesses. They oftentimes also have social workers on staff, in order to assist elderly and other special needs clients and beneficiaries.

The corporate trustee's considerable expertise can also be very useful to the trust's beneficiaries and any individual co-trustees, who will oftentimes be in need of a sounding board in which to run by their ideas with respect to trust investments, sales, etc.

Finally, and arguably most importantly, with all of its expertise in trusts and estate planning, a trust company also makes excellent sense as an investment advisor during the lifetime of the client. Understanding how assets need to be titled and beneficiaries arranged, in order to best minimize taxes and avoid probate, enables the trust company to monitor the client's estate planning situation "in between meetings" with the estate planning attorney. With estate tax rates as high as 45 percent and probate fees as high as 5 percent, not to mention income tax rates and where they may be headed, many clients simply cannot afford to utilize an investment advisor who is not sensitive to their estate planning situation.

Wisdom, independence, service, expertise. This unique combination of qualities, which the corporate trustee or co-trustee possesses, should be considered by every estate planning client who is contemplating the utilization of a trustee as part of his or her estate plan.

Chapter 5

Optimum Planning for Retirement Benefits

From an overall tax perspective, there is perhaps no other area of estate planning requiring more of the attorney's attention than planning for retirement benefits, whether they be IRAs, 401ks, non-qualified annuities or any other form of qualified or non-qualified plan. The client's estate planning desires with respect to retirement benefits typically include: (1) to defer and minimize income taxes on the benefits, (2) to avoid or minimize estate taxes on the benefits, (3) to insulate the benefits from all potential claims against the recipient or recipients, and (4) to maintain a level of control over the ultimate use of the benefits. The aim of optimum estate planning is to achieve all of the client's goals. Especially in light of the Supreme Court's recent decision in *Clark v.*

Rameker,[39] that an inherited IRA of a non-spouse beneficiary is not shielded from creditors for federal bankruptcy purposes (at least in most states), the use of trusts to protect retirement funds after the owner's death has been pushed even further towards the front page.

Deferring Income Taxes While Maintaining Control and Protection

Private letter rulings issued by the Internal Revenue Service over the last decade[40] have created concern among estate-planning attorneys regarding the best way to draft trusts that are intended as potential receptacles of IRA or other qualified plan benefits upon the death of the participant. This concern flows from the fact that, unless the trust is properly drafted, it won't be possible to stretch out the payment of the retirement benefits over the trust beneficiary's lifetime.

One alternative to ensure the maximum possible income tax deferral for the retirement benefits is the so-called "conduit trust" described in the final IRS regulations. The problem is that conduit trusts have numerous problems for most estate-planning clients. Another approach, sometimes referred to as the "accumulation trust" approach, has its own set of potential problems.

---

39. 134 S.Ct. 2242 (1914).

40. *See, e.g.*, Private Letter Rulings 200610026 and 200843042. Note that I've deemed that earlier PLRs on a similar subject matter that were not applying the final Internal Revenue Service regulations, are not relevant to this discussion.

I suggest lawyers consider using what I call the "modified accumulation trust" or "MAT." Hopefully this trust alternative will provide clients with maximum deferral of income taxes on qualified retirement plan and IRA benefits after the participant's death—but without creating other significant estate-planning problems. A similar approach should apply to non-qualified annuities payable to trusts after the holder's death, provided the particular non-qualified annuity contract in question permits payments to a trust after the holder's death over the life expectancy of the trust beneficiary.

Background

On April 17, 2002, final regulations relating to the payment of plan benefits to trusts were published in the Federal Register applicable to calendar years beginning after Jan. 1, 2003.[41] These final regs specify that if a beneficiary's entitlement to the participant's benefit is contingent on an event other than the participant's death or the death of another beneficiary, the contingent beneficiary is considered in determining which designated beneficiary has the shortest life expectancy as well as whether any beneficiary is not an individual.[42]

---

41. 67 Federal Register 18987-19028 (April 17, 2002). In addition, the "final" regulations have been modified in part. See 2004-26 Internal Revenue Bulletin 1082, 1098 (June 28, 2004).

42. Treasury Regulations Section 1.401(a)(9)-5, Q&A-7(b).

The final regs also provide that a person will not be considered a beneficiary for purposes of determining (1) who is the beneficiary with the shortest life expectancy, or (2) whether a person who is not an individual is a beneficiary, merely because the person could become the successor to the interest of one of the beneficiaries after the beneficiary's death.[43] Instead, if the person has "any right (including a contingent right) to an employee's benefit beyond being a mere potential successor to the interest of one of the employee's beneficiary upon that beneficiary's death," the person will be considered a beneficiary for these purposes.[44]

Retirement expert Natalie B. Choate has an excellent summary of the IRS rules in her handbook, Life and Death Planning for Retirement Benefits: The Essential Handbook for Estate Planners.[45] "How does the mere potential successor rule apply to a trust?" she writes. "For purposes of testing trust beneficiaries for 'mere potential successor' status, the world can be divided into two types of trusts: 'conduit trusts' and 'accumulation trusts.'"

"Under a conduit trust, because the trustee is required, under the terms of the governing instrument, to distribute to the individual trust beneficiary any distribution the trustee receives from the retirement plan (1) after the participant's death and (2)

---

43. Treas. Regs. Section 1.401(a)(9)-5, Q&A-7(c)(1).

44. Treas. Regs. Section 1.401(a)(9)-5, Q&A-7(c)

45. Natalie B. Choate, Life and Death Planning for Retirement Benefits: The Essential Handbook for Estate Planners, Ataxplan Publications, (7th ed. 2011), at para. 6.3.

during the lifetime of such beneficiary. . . . The conduit trust for one individual beneficiary is a safe harbor. It is guaranteed to qualify as a see-through trust, and it is guaranteed that all remainder beneficiaries (even if they are charities, an estate, or older individuals) are disregarded under the MRD [minimum required distribution] trust rules."

"Any trust that is not a conduit trust is . . . an accumulation trust, . . . meaning that the trustee has the power to accumulate plan distributions in the trust. Under an accumulation trust . . . some or all of the potential remainder beneficiaries *do* count (i.e., they are not disregarded) for purposes of the MRD trust rules."

Problems with Conduit Trusts

The significant drawbacks inherent to the conduit trust approach are self-evident to the attorney practicing in the estate-planning area. Among the potential undesirable results are:

- forcing annual conduit trust payments onto a minor beneficiary;

- forcing annual conduit trust payment onto a younger (even though not a minor) beneficiary;

- forcing annual conduit trust payments onto a beneficiary who is older but a spendthrift;

- forcing annual conduit trust payments onto a special needs child;

- forcing annual payments onto a surviving spouse from a second marriage, when the desire is that the trust corpus pass to the descendants of the first spouse to die at the surviving spouse's death (which would normally be the case when a trust is used);

- subjecting conduit trust payments to potential creditors of the beneficiary;

- subjecting conduit trust payments to the potential rights of a divorced spouse; and

- subjecting conduit trust payments, compounded over the lifetime of the beneficiary, to estate tax at the life beneficiary's death as well as at the subsequent deaths of the beneficiary's descendants.

Practicing estate-planning attorneys, who have for years prided themselves on their ability to provide protection against all of these potential issues, naturally will want something better than a conduit trust approach to qualifying retirement benefits for the maximum potential income tax deferral.

Problems with Accumulation Trusts

Accumulation trusts designed to provide maximum income tax deferral for qualified plan and IRA benefits, while not suffering from any of the problems associated with conduit trusts, have their own set of estate-planning concerns, including:

- Contingent takers under the accumulation trust may not include individuals who are older than the lifetime beneficiary of the trust, because the IRS then might seek to include these older individuals for purposes of determining the shortest life expectancy of the trust.

- Contingent takers under the accumulation trust cannot include one or more charities or an undetermined surviving spouse, because the IRS then might argue that the trust has no designated oldest individual beneficiary.

- The accumulation trust may not include a limited testamentary power of appointment in favor of charities, surviving spouses, or older beneficiaries, because the IRS then might argue that there is either no designated oldest individual beneficiary of the trust (that is to say, when a charity or an undetermined surviving spouse is a permissible appointee), or at least that the trust

185

must use the oldest permissible individual appointee as the individual beneficiary with the shortest life expectancy.

A Possible Solution

Through PLRs interpreting the final regulations, the IRS has created a "rule" that Natalie Choate very succinctly and accurately identifies as: "Under the approach exemplified in [PLRs 200438044, 200522012 and 200610026], you test an accumulation trust by 'counting' all successive beneficiaries down the 'chain' of potential beneficiaries who could take under the trust, until you come to the beneficiary(ies) who or which will be entitled to receive the trust property *immediately* and *outright* upon the death of the prior beneficiary(ies). . . . Any beneficiary who might receive the benefits as a result of the death(s) of the immediate outright beneficiary(ies) is ignored as a 'mere successor beneficiary.'"[46]

Regardless of whether we agree that the approach the IRS has taken in its recent PLRs is supported by the final regulations themselves, the fact is that these PLRs nevertheless exist, and estate planners therefore need to know how best to deal with them in a manner that does not hamper their clients' other legitimate estate planning objectives.

Once all conduit and accumulation trusts' potential drawbacks are explained, very few clients who own interests in

---

46. *Ibid* at para. 6.3.08. See also PLR 200843042, to the same effect.

substantial qualified retirement plan benefits and/or IRAs are enamored by the possibility of establishing them, even to ensure maximum deferral of income taxes on qualified plan and IRA benefits. Yet clients often still want the principal advantage of these trusts—the ability for their beneficiaries to defer income tax on the retirement plan and IRA benefits.

One potential solution is the MAT. A MAT includes these seven provisions, some of which are mandatory; others of which are optional:

- A MAT must include a Share A and a Share B. Share A is the trust's right to receive the benefits under all qualified retirement plan benefits and IRAs, including Roth IRAs, and including the proceeds and reinvested proceeds therefrom. Share B is all other trust assets.

- Permissible testamentary appointees under Share A of the MAT may include only descendants of the primary current beneficiary of the trust's parents in the same or younger generation as the primary current beneficiary of the trust.

- If desired, permissible appointees under Share A of the MAT also may include a surviving spouse who is no older than a designated number of years older than the primary current beneficiary of the trust.

- In the event of the death of the MAT's primary current beneficiary before the trust terminates, all potential outright remaindermen of Share A (including contingent remaindermen) who are older than the oldest living descendant[47] of the grantor at the time of the grantor's death (assuming all such descendants were alive at the termination of the trust), and all non-individual remaindermen, should be deemed to be deceased or not in existence for purposes of construing the remaindermen provisions (including contingent provisions) that would otherwise apply. To ensure that contingent takers of the client's retirement benefits be as closely related to the grantor as possible, if the application of this rule will result in all otherwise then-living descendants of the grantor's (and, if applicable under the trust document, the grantor's spouse's) parents being deemed to be deceased, then the youngest living remainderman who is a descendant of either the grantor's (or the grantor's spouse's) parents should not be deemed to be deceased under such circumstances.

- Outright remaindermen (including contingent remaindermen) who were deemed to be deceased or not in existence for purposes of construing Share A of the MAT will receive a priority

---

43. If the trust is for the benefit of a grandchild, in order to allow for a greater deferral (or "stretch") period, then the word "grandchild" should be substituted for the word "descendant" here.

distribution of Share B assets until they have received an amount sufficient to "make them whole" with respect to what they would have received from Share A, had they not been deemed to be deceased or not in existence.

- To avoid a potential escheat situation, if the sole contingent taker under the trust document is a charity or charities, heirs-at-law must be added to take in the event one or more of the charities are not (or are deemed not) then in existence.

- If desired, an additional equitable adjustment to the above-described Share B priority distribution can be made for the fact that the priority takers may receive their priority shares at a different income tax cost than the takers under Share A.

Drafting attorneys opting to employ MAT features must be aware of the standard so-called "facilitation of payment" clause that is commonly included in most estate-planning attorneys' trust forms. These clauses authorize a trustee to retain assets that otherwise would be distributable outright to a beneficiary under a legal (or sometimes other) incapacity in further trust for the benefit of the beneficiary. The drafting attorney's standard facilitation of payment form therefore may need to be modified in light of the special MAT requirements.

For example, the clause cannot provide that the trust assets may be distributed in the trustee's discretion to another individual or entity to be held for the benefit of the beneficiary, other than to the beneficiary's legal guardian, conservator or custodian, or pass to the estate of the beneficiary at his death.

If a client is concerned that the MAT will generate more income tax (because of the compressed trust income tax brackets) than the standard conduit trust, it's a simple matter to mitigate this issue by granting the primary current beneficiary of the trust an IRC Section 678 withdrawal power over income of the trust that would otherwise be taxed in the maximum trust income tax bracket (subject to Section 2514's requisite 5 percent limitation to avoid annual taxable gifts), as described in Chapters 2 and 3. This system of taxing trust income to the primary current beneficiary of the trust, without actually requiring payment of the same to the beneficiary, also could result in a significant reduction in estate taxes at the beneficiary death.[48] Additionally, and as described in Chapter 3, in many states this approach provides a greater level of asset protection than afforded by the conduit trust, with its attendant required outright distribution of the annual retirement plan and IRA benefit payments.

Non-Qualified Annuities

Authorities and insurance companies differ regarding whether the rules applicable to qualified plans and IRAs payable to trusts also apply to non-qualified annuities payable to trusts. In a book titled simply, *The Annuity Advisor*, authors

---

48. *See* James G. Blase, "Recent Tax Acts Require Focus on Income Tax Aspects of Estate Planning," 30 Estate Planning, Vol. 12, at p. 617 (December 2003).

John Olsen and Michael E. Kitces argue that non-qualified annuities cannot be paid to a trust over the lifetime of the trust beneficiary, primarily because the IRS has not specifically ruled that they can, as the Service has done with qualified plans and IRAs.[49] According to these co-authors, because IRC Section 72(s)(2)(A) provides that stretched annuity payments after the death of the holder may only be paid "to (or for the benefit of) a designated beneficiary," and because Section 72(s)(4) in turn provides that, "[f]or purposes of this subsection, the term 'designated beneficiary' means any individual designated a beneficiary by the holder of a contract," currently only outright payments to individuals qualify for deferral under Section 72(s)(2)(A).

The problem with this narrow analysis is that the Internal Revenue Code section on which these qualified plan and IRA trust regulations are based [IRC Section 401(a)(9)(B)] employs language that is virtually identical to IRC Section 72(s). Both sections employ the phrase "payable to (or for the benefit of) a designated beneficiary." By choosing to narrowly define the circumstances under which non-qualified annuities payable to trusts can be deferred after the death of the holder, Olsen and Kitces are basically ascribing no meaning to the words "or for the benefit of," or to the fact that the overall structure of IRC Section 401(a)(9)(B) is virtually identical to Section 72(s).

Olsen and Kitces nevertheless rightly point out that, regardless of whether Section 72(s) permits stretched annuity payments to trusts, the issue is moot as to those insurance

---

49. John Olsen and Michael E. Kitces, *The Annuity Advisor* at pp. 135-142 (2d ed. 2009).

companies that do not allow payments to trusts to be stretched under their contracts, which appears to be the great majority of the companies.

So what does this discussion on non-qualified annuities mean for our drafting and our advice to clients relative to the payment of non-qualified annuities to trusts? The basic drafting rules should be the same as those for retirement benefits generally. But because not all insurance carriers permit the payment of non-qualified annuities to trusts on a deferred basis after the death of the holder, estate planners must study all relevant non-qualified annuity contracts of their clients to first ensure that payment of the non-qualified annuity to a trust after the death of the holder, on a deferred basis, will be permitted. If it is not, the planner must decide whether it's better to name outright beneficiaries (which may require the establishment of a court guardianship or conservatorship for minors or other beneficiaries under a legal incapacity) or pay the trust on a lump sum (oftentimes five-year) basis.

Regardless of the option chosen, the trust document should specify that annuity payments that may not be made to the trust on a deferred basis, pursuant to the annuity contract or otherwise (for example, under the tax law), should not be divided on the separate Share A and Share B MAT basis, because such division would not be necessary.

When is the Full MAT Unnecessary

There are certain situations in which the MAT (or at least the full version of the same) may not be best for particular retirement benefits or non-qualified annuities. For example:

- The MAT format is arguably unnecessary when the client owns little in the way of retirement benefits and non-qualified annuities. Of course, "little" is subject to individual interpretation. Just bear in mind that the MAT's only complexity is it must contain two separate accounts, which likely will necessitate two separate sets of annual income tax return filings for the trust. And separate filings may produce some income tax benefit that could grow to be significant in the future. Planners should be mindful of the fact that what may be only a small retirement benefit or non-qualified annuity today may of course grow to be significant in the future.

- The MAT separate share approach also may not be necessary or advisable when (a) a married individual already is beyond the required beginning date under a retirement plan or IRA or beyond the annuity starting date under the non-qualified annuity, and (b) the individual wants to pay the balance of his account after death to a trust for the benefit of his surviving spouse. Because the rules applicable to both retirement plans and non-qualified annuities permit the payments after the account owner's death to be made at least as rapidly as they were under the method of distribution being used as of the date of the account owner's death, and because in most situations the surviving spouse is close in age to the account owner, the MAT normally will generate very little additional tax benefit to the clients in such circumstances, and the separate Share A and Share B probably won't be helpful.

• The MAT typically will not be necessary or advisable if, assuming the lifetime beneficiary of the trust died immediately after the death of the grantor, (1) no outright remainderman of the trust would be a nonindividual (including a trust) or an individual older than the grantor's oldest living descendant at the time of his death; and (2) neither any individual other than a descendant of the grantor nor any non-individual (including a trust) would be a permissible appointee of all or a portion of the trust assets under a testamentary power of appointment in favor of the lifetime beneficiary of the trust. Even the IRS' recent narrow PLR posture would not create a problem under these circumstances.

Finally, a much simpler form of MAT may be all that is required when a client has numerous children and grandchildren. In these fairly frequent situations, the chances are negligible that the contingent gift to heirs-at-law under the client's estate-planning documents will actually take effect. Thus, it's typically unnecessary under such circumstances to protect potentially disinherited heirs through the full Share A/Share B form of MAT. The "oldest beneficiary" issue can easily be addressed by providing in the contingent gift clause that all heirs-at-law older than the client's oldest living descendant at the time of the client's death are deemed to be deceased. Note, however, that when a client wishes to bestow upon the trust beneficiaries a limited testamentary power to appoint to potentially older individuals (including a surviving spouse) and/or charity, the full Share A/Share B form of MAT still would be required.

Combining MAT with Life Insurance for Maximum Advantage

A technique which can produce superior overall tax results is to combine life insurance with IRA stretch planning and the MAT. The concept is to pay income tax-free life insurance (including survivorship life insurance) to one or more MATs for the owner's children, and pay all or a portion of the IRA benefits to one or more MATs for the owner's grandchildren. In this fashion maximum advantage is take of the income tax stretch potential for the IRA, but the owner is able to maintain control over the ultimate disposition of the IRA proceeds by designating his children as trustees of the trusts for the grandchildren.

Of particular relevance today is survivorship life insurance. Typically used as a vehicle for efficiently paying estate taxes when the surviving spouse dies, now the same can also be used as wealth replacement for the children when all or a portion of the owner's IRA is directed toward grandchildren, in order to maximize its deferral potential. In addition, oftentimes today it is actually possible to "re-purpose" an existing survivorship policy which was originally purchased to pay estate taxes, into a policy which is now utilized to create this maximum income tax deferral arrangement.

Sample MAT Form Language

Separate Accounting for Retirement Assets

Except as otherwise provided in paragraph 4, below, if (i) any retirement assets (as defined in ARTICLE __, below) shall become payable to any trust hereunder as a result of the surviving grantor's death, whether immediately or over time, and (ii) assuming the below described Share A/B arrangement is established, the aggregate present fair market value (as of the date of the surviving grantor's death, and as determined for federal estate tax purposes, if the federal estate tax is in existence at the time of the surviving grantor's death, otherwise as determined by the trustee, in the trustee's sole discretion) of all of said retirement assets (as so defined) payable to all trusts hereunder which are to be established as a result of the surviving grantor's death, divided by the total number of said trusts, shall exceed Fifty Thousand Dollars ($50,000), the trustee shall set aside and maintain as a separate share (hereinafter referred to as "Share A") from the remainder of the assets of each trust established hereunder (hereinafter referred to as "Share B"), said trust's right to receive all retirement assets (as so defined), together with the proceeds from the same, and with respect to any such separate shares created hereunder, the following rules shall apply notwithstanding any other provision of this instrument to the contrary:

1.   No testamentary power of appointment in Share A may be exercised in favor of the primary current beneficiary of the trust's surviving spouse (other than a surviving spouse who is no more than five (5) years older than the primary current beneficiary of the trust), any creditor of the primary current beneficiary of the trust's estate, the primary current beneficiary's estate or any charitable organization.   If, as a result of the application of the immediately preceding sentence, an otherwise permissible appointee or appointees in Share A has or have been eliminated, and if there is a percentage ceiling on the proportion of the original trust which the primary current beneficiary of the trust may appoint to said appointee or appointees, then said percentage ceiling shall be raised over the remaining principal and accumulated income of Share B to the extent necessary to allow the primary current beneficiary of the trust to exercise his or her testamentary power of appointment over Share B in favor of said appointee or appointees who or which were eliminated as a permissible appointee or appointees in Share A, to the full extent of the ceiling over the original trust, recognizing that it may not be possible to fully achieve the percentage ceiling over the original trust.

2.   For purposes of construing the provisions of the "CONTINGENT REMAINDER INTERESTS" under ARTICLE __ hereof which will potentially apply at the termination of Share A, all potential heirs-at-law of either of the grantors who are older than the oldest

living descendant of the grantors at the time of the surviving grantor's death (assuming all such descendants were alive at the termination of the trust) shall be deemed to be deceased, and all non-individual potential takers shall be deemed to be not then in existence; PROVIDED, HOWEVER, if one or more grandchildren or more remote descendants of either of the grantors' parents, other than the grantors' descendants, are living at the time of the surviving grantor's death, and if the application of the foregoing provisions of this paragraph 2 shall result in all such descendants being deemed to be deceased, then [the youngest such descendant of either of the grantors' parents who is living at the time of the surviving grantor's death, as well as at the time of the termination of the trust, shall not be deemed to be deceased pursuant to the foregoing provisions of this paragraph 2, but all other heirs-at-law of either of the grantors shall be deemed to be deceased. **[HERE THE ATTORNEY MAY INSERT LANGUAGE OVERRIDING THE GENERAL RULE THAT ALL SUCH DESCENDANTS ARE DEEMED TO BE DECEASED, E.G., BY NOT DEEMING ANY GRANDCHILD OR MORE REMOTE DESCENDANT OF THE GRANTORS' PARENTS TO BE DECEASED IN THIS SITUATION - SHOULD BE DISCUSSED WITH CLIENT IF ALL OR MOST NIECES/NEPHEWS ARE OLDER THAN GRANTORS' CHILDREN AND ALSO IF NO NEPHEWS/NIECES].** If, as a result of the application of the immediately preceding sentence, an individual or individuals and/or a non-individual or non-individuals who and/or which would have otherwise received a portion of Share A as a contingent taker or takers under ARTICLE __ hereof is or are deemed to be deceased or otherwise not then in existence, only these individual(s) and/or non-individual(s) (other than any ancestors of the individual takers in Share A pursuant to the immediately preceding sentence, who shall be deemed to be deceased) shall be deemed to be then living and/or designated for purposes of determining contingent takers of Share B under said ARTICLE __ hereof, until such time as said individual(s) and/or non-individual(s) receive the same share(s) in Share B which they would have received in Share A had they not have been deemed to be deceased or not then in existence pursuant to the application of the immediately preceding sentence, after which point the provisions of said ARTICLE __ hereof shall apply normally to the balance of Share B. **WARNING: MAY NEED TO MODIFY THE AGE RESTRICTION IF GRANTORS HAVE ONLY ONE CHILD IN ORDER TO CAPTURE ALL EXISTING NIECES AND NEPHEWS INSTEAD OF DEEMING ALL NIECES AND NEPHEWS DECEASED EXCEPT FOR ONE; GOOD EXAMPLE IS IN HESS WHERE ONE CHILD AND ALL OLDER NIECES AND NEPHEWS.**

3.   If the trust has an inclusion ratio, as defined in Section 2642(a) of the Internal Revenue Code or in any successor section thereto, of other than zero, and if, assuming the primary current beneficiary of the trust died immediately, a "taxable termination" as defined in Section 2612(a) of the Internal Revenue Code

or in any successor section thereto, would occur, then the primary current beneficiary of the trust shall have the power to withdraw all of the income and principal of Share A of the trust, but only with the consent of the then acting trustee or co-trustees of the trust (other than the primary current beneficiary of the trust or any institution in which the primary current beneficiary of the trust owns any interest) who and/or which is/are not adverse to the exercise by the primary current beneficiary of the trust of the aforesaid power of withdrawal (within the meaning of Internal Revenue Code Section 2041(b)(1)(C)(ii), or any successor section thereto, and Section 20.2041-3(c)(2) of the Treasury Regulations, or any successor section(s) thereto), or if all of the then acting trustees (other than the primary current beneficiary of the trust or any institution in which the primary current beneficiary of the trust owns any interest) are adverse to said exercise, then only with the consent of a nonadverse individual or institution (other than the primary current beneficiary of the trust or any institution in which the primary current beneficiary of the trust owns any interest) designated by the then acting trustee or co-trustees of the trust (other than the primary current beneficiary of the trust or any institution in which the primary current beneficiary of the trust owns any interest), or, if no such nonadverse individual or institution has been designated, only with the consent of the institution (or its successor) designated herein as the sole ultimate successor institutional trustee of the trust. (The previous provisions of this paragraph 3 shall not be construed as a limitation on any trust beneficiary who is already entitled to receive all of the income of the trust currently, pursuant to the terms of the trust, or who

200

already possesses a current right to withdraw all or any portion of the trust income or principal, pursuant to the terms of the trust.)

4.   The foregoing provisions of this Section shall not apply to the trust if, assuming the primary current beneficiary of the trust died immediately after the surviving grantor's death, (i) no heir-at-law of either of the grantors who is living on the date of the surviving grantor's death, as determined under ARTICLE __ hereof, would be older than the grantors' oldest living descendant at the time of the surviving grantor's death, (ii) no non-individual (including a trust) would be a taker under ARTICLE __ hereof (assuming ARTICLE __ applied), and (iii) neither any individual other than a descendant of the grantors nor any non-individual (including a trust) would be a permissible appointee over all or a portion of the trust assets under a testamentary power of appointment in favor of the primary current beneficiary of the trust.

5.   If the foregoing provisions of this Section apply to the trust, said provisions shall continue to apply to any other trust which is subsequently funded utilizing assets of the original trust, in whole or in part. **[WATCH FOR ANY GIFTS TO KIDS ETC. AT FIRST DEATH TO EXCLUDE SHARE A.] [WARNING: DON'T NEED SHARE A/B APPROACH IF DISPOSITION IS OUTRIGHT. ALSO EVEN IF DISPOSITION IS NOT OUTRIGHT, DISCUSS WITH CLIENTS, ESPECIALLY IF NOT MUCH IRA MONEY, THE**

BENEFITS OF PAYING IRA TO TRUST VS. PAYING OUTRIGHT TO BENEFICIARIES, AND THEN DEAL WITH ACCORDINGLY IN TITLING MEMO]

Trust Beneficiary Designation Wording

There are numerous competing interests when a client designates one or more trusts as beneficiary of qualified plan, IRA or non-qualified annuity benefits. The major goal, of course, is to enable the trustee to defer income taxes on the retirement benefits to the maximum extent possible. A subsidiary goal is simplicity. The problem is trying to satisfy the trustee, the retirement plan or IRA brokerage firm/broker dealer ("the IRA administrator"), and the IRS, all at the same time.

For example, if the client designates the "Doe Family Trust" as secondary beneficiary of his or her IRA (with the spouse as primary beneficiary), but the trust document itself includes one single trust for children until they have all attained age 23, with separate trusts afterwards, how will the IRA administrator dispose of the IRA after the surviving spouse's death? Unfortunately, there is no consistent answer to this question among IRA administrators. Some will continue to pay the IRA benefits to a single trust, even if the trust document itself has divided the trust into multiple shares, or subtrusts. Aside from switching IRA administrators (which understandably will not normally be the client's preference), what, if anything, can be done to solve this dilemma?

This suggested beneficiary designation approach we provide to clients adopts a type of "good," "better," and "best" car wash purchase system, complete with appropriate client warnings:

The **secondary** beneficiary designation for BOTH OF YOUR **non-qualified annuity benefits, qualified retirement plans and similar qualified benefits**, including benefits payable under IRAs, Roth IRAs, profit sharing plans, 401k plans, 403b plans, etc.,should be as follows:

ALTERNATIVE 1:   (**Best Alternative if accepted by plan administrator**.)

The descendants of the owner/participant who survive the owner/participant, per stirpes;   P R O V I D E D, HOWEVER, that (i) the share of either child of the owner/participant shall be held in trust for the benefit of such child with income and principal administered and distributed pursuant to the provisions of ARTICLE __ of the DOE FAMILY TRUST dated _____, 2017, as may be amended, and (ii) the share of any grandchild or more remote descendant of the owner/participant who is then less than thirty-five (35) years of age shall be held in trust for the benefit of such grandchild or more remote descendant with income and principal administered and distributed pursuant to the provisions of ARTICLE __ of the DOE FAMILY TRUST dated _____, 2017, as may be amended; PROVIDED FURTHER, HOWEVER, that, notwithstanding the immediately preceding proviso, if any child of the owner/participant is then living and less than twenty-three (23) years of age, all of such assets shall be held in trust with income and principal administered and distributed pursuant to the provisions of ARTICLE __ of the DOE FAMILY TRUST dated _____, 2017, as may be amended.

ALTERNATIVE 2: **(Next best alternative; it is more likely that this or similar language will be accepted by plan administrator than Alternative 1 language.)**

While your youngest child is less than age 23:

JOHN DOE, or his successors in trust, trustee of the DOE FAMILY TRUST dated _____, 2017, as may be amended, to be further divided and/or distributed if and as said trustee directs **(Note: Last two lines required.)**

When your youngest child has attained age 23:**

50% to JOHN DOE, or his successors in trust, trustee of the ARTICLE __ TRUST FBO JANE DOE UNDER THE DOE FAMILY TRUST dated _____,

2017, as may be amended.*

50% to JOHN DOE, or his successors in trust, trustee of the ARTICLE __ TRUST FBO MARY DOE UNDER THE DOE FAMILY TRUST dated _____, 2017, as may be amended.*

* When a child attains age 35, such child replaces John Doe as the sole trustee of such child's Article __ Trust, so you should revise the relevant beneficiary designation accordingly.

ALTERNATIVE 3: (**Use this Alternative when the plan administrator will not accept Alternative 1 or Alternative 2 language.**)

JOHN DOE, or his successors in trust, trustee of the DOE FAMILY TRUST dated _____, 2017, as may be amended, to be further divided and/or distributed if and as said trustee directs (**Note: Last two lines required.**)

**NOTE THAT IF YOU USE ALTERNATIVE 2, ABOVE, YOU (OR YOUR AGENT UNDER YOUR GENERAL DURABLE POWER OF ATTORNEY) WILL HAVE TO REVISE THIS BENEFICIARY DESIGNATION IN

THE EVENT EITHER OF YOUR CHILDREN SHOULD PREDECEASE YOU, SO THAT SUCH RETIREMENT PLAN BENEFITS PASS IN ACCORDANCE WITH THE INTENTIONS OF YOUR REVOCABLE TRUST PLAN.

***NOTE ALSO THAT PRIOR TO DESIGNATING YOUR TRUST AS A BENEFICIARY OF A NON-QUALIFIED ANNUITY, YOU SHOULD CHECK WITH THE ISSUER OF SUCH ANNUITY AS TO WHETHER IT WILL PERMIT AN EXTENDED PAYOUT OF THE ANNUITY TO THE TRUST AFTER YOUR DEATH.

Warnings aside, the obvious problem is that the client may not remember, or be mentally able, to change a beneficiary designation in the event of an unusual order of death, e.g., in the event a child predeceases a parent. We need to do the best we can here, too, to solve these potential problems.

With an ever aging population, the attorney needs to address the situation where a child may predecease a client after the latter has become mentally incapable of handling his or her financial affairs. Consider including a clause similar to the following in the client's financial power of attorney, assuming state law permits the same:

Power to Make or Change Beneficiary Designations. **To make and/or change beneficiary**

designations of any asset of mine (including, but not limited to, retirement plans, real estate, bank accounts, brokerage accounts, and life insurance policies); PROVIDED, HOWEVER, that my Agent may only make or change a beneficiary designation in such a manner so that such assets pass to the same beneficiary(ies), and in the same proportions, as my assets are directed to pass under my revocable trust agreement (or under my last will and testament if I have not executed a revocable trust agreement) at my death (or at the death of my spouse if I shall be survived by my spouse).

A further practical problem is making sure the financial agent is aware that he or she possesses the above-outlined power, and should exercise the power where appropriate. For this reason, we recommend a warning on the cover page of the financial power, similar to the following:

NOTICE TO AGENT

DESIGNATED UNDER GENERAL DURABLE POWER OF ATTORNEY

GIVEN BY JOHN DOE, AS PRINCIPAL

PLEASE READ THIS NOTICE CAREFULLY.

My Agent hereunder has the express authority under paragraph __ of ARTICLE __ of this General Durable Power of Attorney to make or change beneficiary designations of any asset of mine (e.g. retirement plan, real estate, brokerage account, bank account, life insurance policy, etc.) in the event that a currently designated beneficiary of any such asset should predecease me, but only so that said asset(s) pass to the same beneficiary(ies), and in the same proportions, as those assets passing under [THE PRINCIPAL'S MOST RECENTLY EXECUTED REVOCABLE TRUST OR, IF NONE, LAST WILL AND TESTAMENT].

I direct that my Agent hereunder shall exercise said aforesaid authority in the event a currently designated beneficiary of any asset of mine should predecease me, but my Agent shall not be held liable or otherwise accountable to anyone for failing to do so.

If you have any questions concerning this Notice or concerning this General Durable Power of Attorney, please contact an attorney at _____.

As a final "fallback" approach to address the situation where the client and/or agent fails to address a predeceased child situation, we recommend inserting language similar to the following in the child's trust article:

Notwithstanding the previous provisions of this ARTICLE, if the beneficiary has predeceased the surviving grantor, and if there are retirement assets (as defined in ARTICLE __, below) of either of the grantors that are payable directly to the trust under this ARTICLE for the benefit of the beneficiary as a result of the surviving grantor's death, the trust under this ARTICLE for the benefit of the beneficiary shall not be established, and such retirement assets shall instead be distributed, per stirpes, to the descendants of the beneficiary who survive the surviving grantor, or if none, then to the grantors' descendants who survive the surviving grantor, per stirpes; PROVIDED, HOWEVER, that the share of any child of the grantors shall be held in trust for the benefit of such child with income and principal administered and distributed pursuant to the provisions of this ARTICLE, and the share of any grandchild or more remote descendant of the grantors who is then less than thirty-five (35) years of age shall be held in trust for the benefit of such grandchild or more remote descendant with income and principal administered and distributed pursuant to the provisions of ARTICLE __ hereof.

Minimizing Income and Estate Taxes

When balanced against the income tax treatment of a non-qualified portfolio of investments, post-death distributions from qualified plans and individual retirement accounts (retirement benefits) will generally produce a significantly inferior result. There are many reasons for this, including: (1) retirement benefits receive no step-up in income tax basis at the participant's or owner's death, (2) retirement benefits must be distributed post-death according to an established set of required minimum distribution (RMD) rules, whereas a non-qualified portfolio of investments includes no such post-death mandatory distribution requirement, and (3) retirement benefit distributions are taxed at ordinary income tax rates, as opposed to the now as little as one-half as high capital gain or dividend tax rates on distributions from non-qualified portfolios.[50]

Let's explore options for minimizing this disparate post-death income tax treatment. For illustrative purposes, let's work with an example of a male account owner, age 60 and in excellent health. He owns a taxable IRA account in which he's invested $500,000 and that has a current appreciated value of $1 million. Assume the account owner lives to his approximate life expectancy of age 80 and that all investments grow at a 5 percent (principal plus income) compound rate. Also assume a combined 40 percent federal and state ordinary income tax rate and a 20 percent combined capital gains tax rate. Finally, for simplicity purposes, assume an RMD each year (beginning at age 70 1/2) of 5 percent, or the same as the assumed total return rate, because 5 percent approximates the average annual RMD for individuals ages 70 through 80.

---

50. In certain situations the alternative minimum tax (AMT) may come into play to alter this tax rate disparity somewhat. To simplify the comparative analysis contained in this article, the AMT will be ignored.

Alternative 1: Only Withdraw RMDs During Owner's Lifetime

This is probably the most prevalent retirement benefit withdrawal plan today, that is, to take only the RMDs during the owner's lifetime, at least for larger IRAs. But question: Is this the smartest financial plan? Assuming all after-tax RMDs beginning at age 70-1/2 (approximately $80,000 per year, gross and $48,000 per year, net of tax) are reinvested in a portfolio of securities producing no current taxable income but 5 percent overall growth, at age 80, the owner's original $1 million taxable IRA would look something like this:

Non-qualified portfolio	**$600,000 (tax basis = $480,000; any recognized gains taxes at capital gains rates; eligible for full basis step-up at death)**
Taxable IRA	**$1.6 million (all future distributions taxed at ordinary income tax rates; not eligible for basis step-up at death)**

As the above table indicates, approximately 73 percent of the of the owner's $2.2 million portfolio at age 80 would be growing at an eventual combined 40 percent federal and state income tax rate and wouldn't be eligible for basis step-up at death, while only 27 percent of his portfolio would be growing at the lower combined 20 percent federal and state capital gain tax rate and would be eligible for full basis step-up at death. There would be an income tax basis step-up of only $120,000 on the non-qualified portfolio if the owner were to die, while there would be no income tax basis step-up on the $1.6 million taxable IRA. RMDs would continue on the taxable IRA after the owner's death, but there would be no requirement to liquidate the smaller, nonqualified portion of the portfolio in the hands of the owner's spouse or other heirs.

Note that, under the above-described plan, the owner's original $500,000 investment in the IRA would have already been withdrawn, over ages 70 through 80, and appropriately taxed to him at ordinary income tax rates, because he received a deduction for a like amount off of ordinary income. An additional $300,000 would have also been withdrawn under the RMD rules, again all taxed at ordinary income rates, even though no prior income tax deduction was received for this amount and even though the IRA may have been invested entirely in the stock market. The after-tax reinvested sum (or $48,000 per year) would have grown, outside of the IRA, to $600,000 and would be properly eligible for income tax basis step-up at the owner's death.

The challenges presented are: (1) how can the IRA owner plan now to effectively avoid taxing all growth in his IRA at ordinary income tax rates as opposed to capital gain rates; (2) how can the IRA owner proceed at present to effectively achieve an income tax basis step-up for a portion of the IRA balance at his death; and (3) what actions can the IRA owner immediately take to effectively cause a portion of the

IRA balance to be taxed, if at all, at the more favorable capital gains income tax rates to his heirs?

Alternative 2: Convert All or a Portion of the IRA to a Roth IRA

Converting the $1 million IRA at age 60 will obviously mean that the entire amount will be taxed at a higher combined federal and state income tax rate, which for our purposes we'll assume is 45 percent. This leaves $550,000 to grow inside of the Roth IRA, which, after 20 years at 5 percent compounded, will equal approximately $1.459 million.[51]

Although this plan arguably solves all of challenges (1) through (3), described above, it does so in a manner that, at age 80, actually leaves the owner and his family with slightly less than the after-tax value they would have received under Alternative 1 ($1.48 million, assuming the IRA was liquidated at the same 45 percent combined federal and state income tax rate and a step-up in income tax basis for the nonqualified portfolio). Thus, it appears that a complete Roth conversion isn't the answer to the issues we have with the unfair manner in which post-death IRA distributions are taxed.

Smaller and annual partial IRA conversions may provide a slightly better result than a complete conversion at age 60,

---

51. Note that transferring less than the entire distributed amount to a Roth individual retirement account wouldn't be advisable prior to the owner's attaining the age of 59-1/2, due to the imposition of the 10 percent excise tax on the portion that's not rolled to the Roth IRA.

primarily because of the lower income tax rate on the smaller withdrawals. For example, if at age 60, the owner were to begin withdrawing $50,000 from the taxable IRA each year and convert the net amount after 40 percent ordinary income taxes, or $30,000, into a Roth, the Roth account would grow to approximately $1 million by the time the owner reached age 80. Added to the after 45 percent tax rate value of the approximately $1 million still remaining in the taxable IRA, at age 80, the after-tax value of the owner's portfolio would be approximately $1.55 million, $70,000 more than the original result in Alternative 1, above.

Alternative 3: Immediately Begin Taking Small Distributions from the IRA and Invest the After-Tax Amount into Life Insurance

This plan is similar to the annual Roth conversions option discussed under Alternative 2, but instead of transferring the $30,000 net amount into a Roth IRA each year, the net amount is used to purchase as much face value life insurance as possible. To preserve some of the IRA for the owner's lifetime needs, the premiums are intentionally kept smaller and only paid for 10 years.[52]

---

52. Note that although this plan will generally only be advisable if the owner has attained age 59 1/2 due to the 10 percent excise tax on early IRA distributions – it may be possible to use other funds to pay the life insurance premiums until the owner has attained age 59 1/2. It may also be possible to use the Internal Revenue Code Section 72(t) exception for a "series of equal payments." See IRC Section 72(t)(2)(A)(iv) and Natalie Choate, Life and Death Planning for Retirement Benefits ¶9.2 (7th ed. 2011).

Under the plan, at age 80, the owner's financial situation is projected as:[53]

Income Tax-Free Life
Insurance Death Benefit   **$1.1 million**

Non-qualified Portfolio   **$377,000**

Taxable IRA   **$1 million**

Assuming a 45 percent combined federal and state income tax rate if the taxable IRA were liquidated in full and a stepped-up income tax basis on the owner's non-qualified portfolio, the after-tax value of the owner's portfolio, if he were to die at age 80, would be approximately $2.027 million or $477,000 (approximately 31 percent) more than the best of the two Roth conversion options described in Alternative 2, above ($1.55 million) and $547,000 (approximately 37 percent) more than the original result in Alternative 1 ($1.48 million). What's potentially even more significant, under Alternative 3, the owner's family would have $1.477 million growing at capital gain tax rates (or at no tax, to the extent the assets are not sold during life), compared to only $600,000 growing in this favorable tax environment under Alternative 1.

---

53. Based on the guaranteed results under John Hancock's Protection UL policy; other companies' policies produce substantially similar results.

In taxable estate situations, Alternative 3 presents the additional possibility of having the income tax-exempt life insurance policy held inside an irrevocable life insurance trust (ILIT), which, unlike a taxable IRA or Roth IRA, would render the proceeds estate tax-exempt. If access to the policy's cash surrender value is deemed necessary (which would be unlikely, in today's high federal estate tax exemption environment), the ILIT can be structured as a spousal access trust or as a WRAP Trust, described more fully in Chapter 7.[54]

One potential disadvantage of Alternative 3 is that, during the owner's lifetime, he'll have less available funds to spend. For example, when the owner reaches age 80, the cash value of the life insurance product assumed in this article is projected to be only approximately $200,000. This amount, when added to the remaining after-tax value of the IRA (assuming the maximum 45 percent combined tax rate) and the after capital gain tax value of the non-qualified portfolio, would equal approximately $1.1 million, whereas under Alternative 1, the owner would have approximately $1.45 million available to spend at age 80, after taxes.

If this lifetime use issue is a significant concern to the owner, he may elect to structure the life insurance policy so that it will produce a larger cash value, but a lower projected death benefit, thus allowing the owner to access significant income tax free withdrawals and loans on the policy for his or her retirement. This type of "lifetime use" planning will produce even greater income tax free retirement benefits to the

---

54. *See* James Blase, "The WRAP Trust" Journal of the American Society of CLU & ChFC, Vol. LI, No. 5, at p. 92 (September 1997).

owner the earlier he or she begins the life insurance plan.[55] A life insurance policy with hybrid long-term care features can also be considered, for even greater income tax leveraging.

Another potential disadvantage to Alternative 3 is that the owner may live substantially beyond age 80, in which case an unchanging face amount life insurance policy may not keep pace with the value of otherwise available investments. To address this concern, the universal policy can be structured to provide an increasing death benefit, rather than a stagnant $1.1 million face amount.

Whether the tax advisor looks to the Roth IRA solution, the life insurance solution or some other solution or combination of solutions, the disparity in the post-death income tax treatment of non-qualified portfolios of investments versus qualified portfolios must be addressed. While it's fair and proper to eventually tax the owner's pre-tax contributions to a qualified plan or IRA at ordinary income tax rates, taxing all growth in the same at the ordinary income tax rates can't be justified, especially when juxtaposed against the much more favorable income tax treatment of non-qualified portfolios. The planner's goal should be to use all resources at her disposal to achieve post-death tax results that mirror as closely as possible the capital gain tax rates and income tax basis step-up available generally for non-qualified portfolios.

---

55. *Ibid.*

Chapter 6

Optimum Planning for Business Owners and Professionals

One of the most important goals in business owner estate planning, whether the business be a production business or a service business or profession (even a law practice!), is for the business owner to reap the benefits of his or her hard and expert efforts over the years, both for the business owner and for the business owner's family. Too often this aspect of business owner estate planning is overlooked in favor of other also important issues such as succession planning and retirement planning. There will be no need for a succession plan, and there will be no need for a retirement plan, nor will there even be much of a need for an estate plan at all, if there is not first an overall "exit" plan.

In large situations this may involve a complicated plan such as an ESOP, but in most cases this is simply a matter of first identifying the proper and best "successors," and then building a simple but successful exit plan. If children are involved in the business and want to continue to be involved, the exit plan is obviously simpler. If children are not involved but there are natural successors within the business (including but not limited to one or more co-owners), the situation gets a little harder. And if children are not involved in the business and there are no natural successors within the business, the owner must look outside the business for his or her "equity." One thing is for sure, it make no sense for the business owner not to enjoy the same fruits of his or her labor as an employee or executive of a public company enjoys, e.g., through the receipt of stock in the public enterprise.

Assuming there are no children interested in the business and the business has not already been sold to one or more employees or co-owners during the client's lifetime, look to structure a buy-sell agreement with one or more of the involved individuals, or even with a competitor. Keep it simple at first, without all of the typical buy-sell agreement bells and whistles involving disability, retirement, divorce, etc., which so often complicate buy-sell agreements to the point that nothing ever gets signed. If possible, fund the plan with life insurance, and structure the plan as a cross-purchase plan rather than a corporate redemption plan, in order to avoid unnecessary adverse income tax consequences to the surviving corporation and owners.

If family members are involved in the business, the owner first needs to decide whether to transfer all or part of the business to the involved children now, or in the near future. If the owner has accumulated sufficient retirement savings, the interest can be gifted; it not, the interest will either need to be sold or gifted in conjunction with some form of consulting or deferred compensation arrangement.

Regardless of whether the business is sold or gifted to the involved children, optimum estate planning will structure the arrangement so that the original owner can retain an element of control. This will not only make it more likely that the original owner will be willing to embark upon a lifetime succession plan, but it will allow the original owner to make "corrections" or "modifications" along the way, where necessary.

If the business interest is sold to the active family members, the proceeds from the same, including amount owed under installment promissory notes, can be used to provide liquidity for the non-active members, including the surviving spouse who was not involved in the business. In other situations life insurance will become an important tool to provide for the spouse and/or provide other non-active family members with a fair share of the owner's estate.

Flexible Tax Planning Needed

The most popular tax strategy in succession planning over the past 35 years has been to create minority interest discounts in an effort to lower the value of the client's business for federal estate and gift tax purposes. With federal estate tax rates as high as 70 percent during this period, and with a federal estate tax exemption as low as $175,000, this strategy no doubt made common sense.

This raises the obvious question: With a federal estate tax exemption currently over 30 times its 1981 level, and with the potential for the complete repeal of the federal estate tax on the horizon, does it still make sense to focus exclusively on creating minority interest discounts as the best succession planning tax strategy?

Far less than half of all family businesses survive to the third generation, which means that a significant percentage of closely-held businesses are sold at some point during the second generation's lifetime. Given all of the above, for most closely-held businesses does it still make sense to adopt a strategy of creating minority interest discounts, or is a more flexible tax strategy for succession planning now in order?

One Basic Optimum Planning Idea

Assume, for example, that in 2005 a family created a basic discounting technique by having the husband and wife each gift 0.5% of their respective 50% interests in the company to their children. The business is currently worth $6 million on a majority basis, but less than $4 million on a minority basis. The balance of the parents' estate is worth approximately $2 million. Is this succession plan still a good one? If not, what can be done about it now, to make it better?

The problem is that although the plan should help avoid estate taxes for the parents, assuming the parents utilize a traditional two-trust approach for a husband and wife, it may also cause a loss of full income tax basis step-up for the company shares (i.e., from their control premium value) at the parents' death. This loss of full income tax basis step-up may be unnecessary because the parents' combined taxable estate, had they retained all of the stock, would have been approximately $3 million less than their combined federal estate tax exemptions.

A simple yet flexible strategy to avoid this result would be for the children to gift the 1% stock back to the parents, leaving them each with 50% control of the company. There would be some taxable gift by the children to the parents (potentially covered by the annual gift tax exclusion), when the former transferred their interests in the company back to the parents.

The total value of the parents' estate would then be over the current federal estate tax exemption amount. Unless they were willing to gamble that the spousal portability election would protect the survivor from estate tax, they would still need to fund two separate revocable trusts. Each would fund their separate trusts with half of the stock in the company and with $1 million in assets other than the stock. For most small business owners this simple step of returning the parents to their original ownership positions in the company will be enough to avoid estate taxes while simultaneously avoiding minority interest discounts in the inherited income tax basis of the shares. The revised tax strategy for the parents' succession planning would end here.

But there is a potential problem for many closely-held business owners: the surviving spouse could still end up with a taxable estate, depending on the value of the company (and other separate assets) and the size of the federal and estate tax exemptions at the survivor's death. Also, the plan may not maximize the income tax basis of the shares at the surviving spouse's death, because half of the shares would be in the bypass or credit shelter trust. What can be done to improve this situation?

Here is just one thought: Husband and wife each gift shares in the company to one or more irrevocable trusts for their children sufficient to cause each of the spouses to become a minority owner in the company (e.g., 0.5% each). The couple's estate plans then each establish a bypass or credit shelter trust for the other, funded with each of their remaining interests in the company and other assets.

The irrevocable trusts for the children are for the latter's sole and exclusive benefit, and the trustees are given the sole and absolute power to make distributions of income and principal to the children. However, each grantor retains a conditional testamentary general power of appointment over the balance of the trust assets at death, to their respective estates.[56] Under IRS Chief Counsel Memorandum

---

56. A general power of appointment to the transferor's spouse's estate is required because a limited power of appointment will most likely not

2012080262,[57] each spouse makes a taxable gift of the full value of the stock transferred to the irrevocable trust or trusts, despite the conditional testamentary general power of appointment.

Although husband and wife should not serve as trustees of the irrevocable trust or trusts, they may retain the ability to remove and replace the trustee with another independent trustee. In taxable estate situations, the original owner will be comforted by Revenue Ruling 95-58,[58] where the IRS ruled that an owner may transfer assets in trust and retain the ability to change the trustee of the trust to an independent trustee (within the meaning of Section 672(c) of the Code, without risk of the transferred interest being included in the owner's gross estate under either Section 2036 or 2038 of the Code. In drafting any such retained right to change the trustee, however, care should be taken not to refer to the provisions of Section 672(c) which are in effect at the time of the removal and replacement, but rather the provisions of said section which existed in 1995 (or at the time of the establishment of the trust, if the Code section has not changed since then).

The general powers of appointment are conditional in that they are only exercisable to the extent they will not raise the value of the transferor spouse's taxable estate plus adjusted

---

result in the aggregation of the stock for estate tax valuation purposes. *See* Estate of Bonner v. United States, 84 F.3d 196 (5th Cir. 1996).

57. Dated September 28, 2011, and first released on February 24, 2012.

58. 1995-2 C.B. 191.

taxable gifts over the federal (or state, if lower) estate tax exemption level at the time of his or her death. This in turn should cause this portion of the trust, and only this portion, to be included in the transferor's spouse's gross estate, under IRC Section 2038. Another important condition would be that the powers would only be exercisable to the extent they would not cause the imposition of any type of "built-in gains" tax at the transferor's spouse's death.

It is vital that the retained conditional testamentary general power of appointment in the grantor spouse be a full general power of appointment, i.e., not one limited to the creditors of the grantor spouse's estate. Based on the Fifth Circuit's decision in Estate of Bonner v. United States,[59] if at the time of the decedent's death his or her estate lacked control over the disposition of the trust assets such that it could act as a hypothetical seller negotiating with willing buyers free of the limitations associated with fractional undivided interests, the trust assets will not be aggregated with the decedent's own assets for valuation purposes. Limiting the grantor spouse's retained testamentary general power of appointment over the children's trusts to the creditors of the grantor spouse's estate only presents the potential for the IRS to argue that the shares of the two trusts, while aggregated for estate tax inclusion purposes, should not be aggregated for estate tax valuation purposes.

After factoring in the potential Section 2038 inclusion in the surviving spouse's gross estate for the value of the children's irrevocable trusts, the surviving spouse is then also

---

59. 84 F.3d 196 (5th Cir. 1996).

granted a conditional testamentary general power of appointment (to his or her estate) over the remaining trust assets in the bypass or credit shelter trust, again limited so that the total amount included (after first factoring in the value included for the children's trust or trusts) will not cause the surviving spouse's taxable estate plus adjusted taxable gifts to exceed the federal estate tax exemption (or state estate tax exemption, if lower) level at the time of his or her death. This second step in effect creates a control premium for all the shares which are includible in the surviving spouse's gross estate at death, thus increasing their income tax basis step-up potential beyond a mere 50% ownership value.

Assume, for example, that the husband dies with the 49.5% interest in the company, and that this interest passes to the bypass or credit shelter trust for the wife. Wife later dies with her independent 49.5% interest. Assume also that, when the wife dies, the company is worth $5 million on a control basis and $3 million on a minority basis. Finally assume that the size of the estate tax exemption is $7 million at the time of the wife's subsequent death, and that she owns $2 million in other assets at that time.

Because the wife's conditional testamentary general powers of appointment are drafted to intentionally avoid the result in Estate of Bonner v. United States, i.e., so that the wife has a full power to appoint the 49.5% interest in the bypass trust and a full power to appoint the .5% interest in the children's irrevocable trust or trusts to her estate, all interests are aggregated into one 99.5% control interest for valuation purposes. The inherited stock receives a $4.975 million income tax basis in the hands of the children. Had the stock been valued as three separate minority interests, the inherited income tax basis would have been only $2.985 million.

One potential negative of allowing the surviving spouse a full power of disposition over all or a portion of the bypass trust at death is that the surviving spouse may then presumably appoint these trust assets to a new spouse, etc. This risk thus needs to be explained to the clients up front. It may also be advisable to authorize an independent trustee or trust protector to pull back on the surviving spouse's general power of appointment over the irrevocable trust or trusts for children, as well as over the bypass or credit shelter trust, in the event the surviving spouse has remarried. This is because maximum utilization of the spousal portability election in the new spouse's estate may then become preferable to income tax basis step-up to the surviving spouse's estate, depending on all the facts and circumstances.

Other conditions may need to be attached to the surviving spouse's contingent testamentary general power of appointment over the bypass or credit shelter trust. For example, the surviving spouse's general power of appointment should normally be over the most appreciated assets of the trust first (which will not necessarily include the shares of stock in the company), and should not be over any trust assets which have depreciated in value. Also, and as already alluded to above, a clause should be included to address proposals to tax built-in gains at death, such that the general power of appointment would not attach to any assets where the proposed tax would be incurred or to any assets which would, as a result of such legislation, carry with them a carryover income tax basis, even if includible in the surviving spouse's gross estate.

Note that the decedent's Section 2038 conditional general power of appointment over the shares of stock he or she transferred to the children's trusts will eliminate the adjusted taxable gift characteristic of the same, under IRC Section 2001(b)(2), at least to the extent the conditional power does become effective and the shares are actually included under Section 2038.[60]

A Possible Further Refinement

The plan outlined above eliminates the minority interest estate tax discount to the transferor spouse where the discount ends up not being necessary, but it does not create a control premium which could further enhance the income tax basis of the shares. This may be relevant where surviving spouse intends to sell the business after the first spouse's death.

A possible solution to this problem would be to grant the first spouse to die an additional conditional testamentary general power of appointment to his or her estate over the stock which was transferred to the children's by his or her spouse, only to the extent that the power will not cause the value of the

---

60. Although it is clear the reciprocal trust doctrine professed by the Supreme Court in Estate of Grace, 395 U.S. 316 (1969), should not apply on these facts, to cause the automatic inclusion of the trust or trusts established by the decedent's spouse in the decedent's gross estate, advisors who are concerned about this issue can include a clause in each trust agreement which voids the spouse's general power to the extent it would cause automatic inclusion in the spouse's gross estate.

spouse's gross estate plus adjusted taxable gifts to exceed the federal (or state) estate tax exemption at the date of death. The first spouse to die would now potentially own a 50.5% control interest in the company for estate tax valuation purposes, potentially significantly increasing the income tax basis of the 50.5% interest in the hands of the surviving beneficiaries.

The conditional general powers of appointment must be applied in two steps, primarily because the estate tax valuation methodologies at each step are different. The first step is the general power of appointment over the stock that was transferred by the decedent. This puts the decedent's estate in a 50% veto position, and thus is valued differently from a minority position. The second step is the general power of appointment over the stock that was transferred by the decedent's spouse. This now places the decedent's estate in a 50.5% control position, which is valued differently from a veto position.

Under this refined plan, the surviving spouse would also possess a conditional testamentary general power of appointment to his or her estate over the shares of stock that he or she transferred to the children's trusts, as well as over the shares that were transferred to the trust or trusts by the predeceased spouse. This would cause the surviving spouse to potentially also own a 50.5% controlling interest in the company.

The shares in the bypass trust established by the predeceased spouse would be subject to a third conditional testamentary general power of appointment to his or her estate in the hands of the surviving spouse, but again only to the extent the power does not cause the survivor's taxable estate to exceed the federal or state estate tax exemption at date of death.

This third conditional testamentary general power of appointment would apply only after application of the first two conditional testamentary general powers of appointment applicable to the children's trusts. The three separate powers may each be valued differently for federal estate tax purposes, e.g., if the step three general powers give the decedent even greater control over the company than a mere majority interest would provide.

If the surviving spouse remarries, an independent trustee or trust protector may be empowered to further restrict the surviving spouse's powers of appointment to provide additional assurances for the remainder beneficiaries or if it makes more sense to use part of the deceased spouse's unused exemption (DSUE) amount.

One More Possibility

In situations where the combined value of the couple's estates is less than the estate tax exemption, a full income tax basis step-up can be achieved at the death of the first spouse to die by allowing each spouse to transfer his or her interest to a joint revocable trust, and then grant each of them a full and unrestricted lifetime power of withdrawal over the entire interest. The entire interest would then continue to be subject to the surviving spouse's right of withdrawal, yet he or she would have received a full income tax basis step-up at the first spouse's death, as a result of a combination of IRC Sections 2038 and 2041.[61]

One may argue that the interest that was transferred to the joint trust by the surviving spouse should not receive a step-up in income tax basis, under the theory that it was gifted to the decedent spouse at the moment of death by the surviving spouse, and then reacquired by the surviving spouse within one year, under IRC Section 1014(e). The problem with this argument is that the surviving spouse never made the Section 1014(e) required "gift" to the decedent spouse, under the IRS regulations.[62]

A similar joint revocable trust basis step-up strategy should also be available to large estates. After first utilizing the valuation discounting technique of transferring a portion of the business to children's trusts, the couple then funds their separate revocable trusts with assets equal in value to at least the federal estate tax exemption amount, and then transfer the balance of their assets (including, to the extent possible, their respective interests in their company) to the type of joint revocable trust described immediately above.[63]

---

61. See, in this regard, J. Blase, "The Minimum Income Tax Trust," Trusts & Estates (May 2014), at pp. 36-39.

62. Id. at 37.

63. Id. at 37-38.

Estates that are larger than one full estate tax exemption, but less than two, may utilize a combination of these strategies, e.g., by only transferring to the joint revocable trust enough of the business interest that will not cause the surviving spouse estate to potentially be subject to estate tax.[64]

Continued Role of Life Insurance

The above-outlined plan involving the establishment and funding of irrevocable trusts for children, while flexible, will not necessarily eliminate all estate taxes at the older generation's death. An additional tax-sensitive strategy of utilizing income and estate tax-exempt life insurance planning, in order to pay any estate taxes that may still be due upon the death of the older generation, should be considered in these situations. Clients should also consider making larger lifetime transfers to children or to a spousal access trust in order to remove future appreciation from the older generation's estate.

Any life insurance planning program should continue to be coupled with income tax basis step-up planning involving the bypass, credit shelter or irrevocable life insurance trust, in order to achieve maximum income tax basis step-up at the surviving spouse's death, as well as with the possible utilization of the joint revocable trust technique described above for achieving maximum income tax basis step-up at the first spouse's death.

---

64. Ibid.

Finally, for some clients utilizing life insurance exclusively may be the best succession planning solution, at least in the short-term. It is no doubt simpler than engaging in lifetime gift planning, and will allow the client maximum control over the business during her or her lifetime.

Special S Trust Form Language

Similar to the manner in which a trust which is a beneficiary of qualified plan or IRA benefits can be divided into two separate shares, in order to gain optimum income tax deferral results, so too a trust which owns stock in an S corporation can be divided into two portions - a portion which will own S stock and a portion which will not.

Set forth below is some sample form language for a traditional bypass or credit shelter trust, a QTIP Trust, and a trust for children.

Family Trust Form

The assets to be held in the trust estate with the income and principal administered and distributed pursuant to the provisions of this ARTICLE shall be held by the trustee as a separate trust estate, and the assets in said trust estate shall at all times during the term of the trust be divided into two separate trusts. Trust "A" shall consist solely of an interest in any entity which is taxed as an "S corporation," as such term is defined in Section 1361(a)(1) of the Internal Revenue

Code, or any successor section thereto (hereafter "S corporation"), and the proceeds and reinvested proceeds from any subsequent sale of such interest in any "S corporation" by the trustee of Trust "A," and Trust "B" shall consist of all other assets. It is the intent of the grantors that Trust A shall qualify as a "Qualified Subchapter S Trust" under Section 1361(d) of the Internal Revenue Code, or any successor section thereto, for federal income tax purposes and it is contemplated that the primary current beneficiary will make the necessary election under the federal Internal Revenue Code to qualify Trust A as a permissible shareholder of an S corporation. The assets of both Trust A and Trust B shall be held in trust with the income and principal administered and distributed as follows:

Section 1. Distribution of Income of Trust A During Surviving Spouse's Lifetime

1.1   During any period in which the trust owns an interest in any "S corporation" as defined in Section 1361(a)(1) of the Internal Revenue Code, or any successor section thereto, all of the net income derived from the assets of Trust A shall be distributed to the surviving spouse, in regular installments not less frequently than quarter-annually. At the point, if any, at which the trust shall no longer own any interest in an "S corporation," all accrued and undistributed income up to said point shall be distributed to the surviving spouse.

1.2 During any period in which the trust owns no interest in an "S corporation" as defined in Section 1361(a)(1) of the Internal Revenue Code, or any successor section thereto, the income of Trust A shall be administered and distributed as follows:

a. During the surviving spouse's lifetime the surviving spouse (including any legal representative acting on behalf of the surviving spouse) shall have the annual noncumulative power to withdraw all or any portion of the trust accounting income derived from the assets of Trust A on or before December 31 of the calendar year; PROVIDED, HOWEVER, that (i) the foregoing power of withdrawal shall not extend to the portion of the trust accounting income which, for the calendar year, would be either exempt from federal income tax or subject to federal income tax to the trust, after all deductions and exemptions (but determined as though the trustee made no other income or principal distributions or encroachments during the year other than for trust expenses and taxes), at less than the general maximum federal income tax rate applicable to trusts (and for this purpose said excluded portion (I) shall begin with any dividends, capital gains or other items of trust accounting income which are subject to a maximum federal income tax rate which is lower than the general maximum federal income tax rate applicable to trusts, (II) shall next include any items of trust accounting income filling out the lower income tax brackets of the trust which do not constitute "net investment income" as defined in Section 1411(c) of the Internal Revenue Code, or any successor section thereto,

(III) shall next include any additional items of trust accounting income filling out the lower income tax brackets of the trust which constitute "net investment income" as defined in Section 1411(c) of the Internal Revenue Code, or any successor section thereto, and (IV) shall assume that all items of federal gross income of the trust which do not constitute trust accounting income and which are not subject to a maximum federal income tax rate which is lower than the general maximum federal income tax rate applicable to trusts, are using up the lower income tax brackets of the trust first, before the aforesaid items of trust accounting income) and (ii) if Section 2514(e) of the Internal Revenue Code, or any successor section thereto, is in effect during the calendar year, the amount of trust accounting income subject to the foregoing power of withdrawal during the calendar year shall not exceed five percent (5%) (or such other percentage as shall be provided for in Section 2514(e)(2) of the Internal Revenue Code, or any successor section thereto) of the combined value of the principal and income of Trust A on December 31 of the calendar year (or on the date of the surviving spouse's death, if earlier). If more than one item of trust accounting income is withdrawable by the surviving spouse pursuant to the foregoing provisions of this subsection 1.2.a (for example, taxable interest from corporate bonds and distributions from retirement assets (as defined in ARTICLE __, below)), but the above-described limitation of Section 2514(e) of the Internal Revenue Code, or any successor section thereto, shall apply, the surviving spouse's power of withdrawal shall extend to a pro rata portion of each of such items based upon the ratio in which the total amount of each of such items bears to the total amount of all of such items (assuming the above-described limitation of Section 2514(e) of the Internal Revenue Code, or any successor section thereto, does not apply). Any such withdrawable trust accounting income which is not withdrawn by the surviving spouse or by the surviving spouse's legal representative by the end of any calendar year (or by the time of the surviving spouse's death, if earlier) shall be added to the principal of Trust A, and the surviving spouse's power of withdrawal for such calendar year shall lapse. For purposes of this subsection 1.2.a, the term "trust accounting income" shall include all retirement assets (as defined in ARTICLE __, below, but ignoring the last proviso of the definition) paid to the trust during the year regardless of whether all of said retirement assets paid to the trust during the year are otherwise considered to be trust accounting income, and the principal of Trust A shall include the underlying value of all retirement assets (as defined in ARTICLE __, below, but ignoring the last proviso of the definition) and other assets which are payable to the trust over time and not yet paid to the trust. The trustee other than a trustee having any beneficial interest in the trust (other than solely as a contingent taker under ARTICLE __, below) may, in the sole and absolute discretion of said trustee, suspend the surviving spouse's withdrawal power under this subsection 1.2.a, in whole or part, by instrument in writing executed by said trustee before January 1 of the calendar year in which such withdrawal power would otherwise exist. Reasons for such suspension may include, but shall not be limited to, overall tax savings for the trust and its beneficiaries (including remainder beneficiaries) and creditor protection for the surviving spouse.

b.   During the surviving spouse's lifetime the surviving spouse (including any legal representative acting on behalf of the surviving spouse) shall also have the annual noncumulative power to withdraw all or any portion of the "net investment income" of Trust A (as defined in Section 1411(c) of the Internal Revenue Code, or any successor section thereto) which is not already withdrawable pursuant to the provisions of subsection 1.2.a, above, and which is not described in clause (III) of subsection 1.2.a, above (hereinafter "the excess net investment income"), on or before December 31 of the calendar year; PROVIDED, HOWEVER, that (i) the foregoing power of withdrawal shall not extend to the portion of the excess net investment income of Trust A which, for the calendar year, is less than the dollar amount at which the highest tax bracket in section 1(e) of the Internal Revenue Code, or any successor section thereto, begins for such calendar year (but with said dollar amount being reduced, but not below zero, by (A) any net investment income, as defined in Section 1411(c) of the Internal Revenue Code, or any successor section thereto, which is not withdrawable by the surviving spouse pursuant to the provisions of clause (III) of paragraph 1.2.a, above, and (B) an amount equal to the total of any costs which are deductible for purposes of determining the taxable income of the trust but not for purposes of determining the adjusted gross income of the trust, after the application of Section 67(e) of the Internal Revenue Code, or any successor section thereto), and (ii) if Section 2514(e) of the Internal Revenue Code, or any successor section thereto, is in effect during the calendar year, the amount of the excess net investment income subject to the foregoing power of withdrawal during the calendar year shall not exceed (A) five percent (5%) (or such other percentage as shall be provided for in Section 2514(e)(2) of the Internal Revenue Code, or any successor section thereto) of the combined value of the principal and income of Trust A on December 31 of the calendar year (or on the date of the surviving spouse's death, if earlier), less (B) any amount which is withdrawable by the surviving spouse during the calendar year pursuant to the provisions of subsection 1.2.a, above. If more than one item of excess net investment income is withdrawable by the surviving spouse pursuant to the foregoing provisions of this subsection 1.2.b (for example, capital gains from the sale of various corporate stocks and dividend distributions on various corporate stocks), but the above-described limitation of Section 2514(e) of the Internal Revenue Code, or any successor section thereto, shall apply, the surviving spouse's power of withdrawal shall extend to a pro rata portion of each of such items based upon the ratio in which the total amount of each of such items bears to the total amount of all of such items (assuming the above-described limitation of Section 2514(e) of the Internal Revenue Code, or any successor section thereto, does not apply). Any such withdrawable excess net investment income which is not withdrawn by the surviving spouse or by the surviving spouse's legal representative by the end of any calendar year (or by the time of the surviving spouse's death, if earlier) shall not be withdrawable by the surviving spouse in any subsequent calendar year. For purposes of this subsection 1.2.b, the principal of Trust A shall include the underlying value of all retirement assets (as defined in ARTICLE __, below, but ignoring the last proviso of the definition) and other assets which are payable to the trust over time and not yet paid to the trust. The trustee other than a trustee having any beneficial interest in the trust (other than solely as a contingent taker under ARTICLE __, below) may, in the sole and absolute discretion of said trustee, suspend the surviving spouse's withdrawal power under this subsection 1.2.b, in whole or part, by instrument in writing executed by said trustee before January 1 of the calendar year in which such withdrawal power would otherwise exist. Reasons for such suspension may include, but shall not be limited to, overall tax savings for the trust and its beneficiaries (including remainder beneficiaries) and creditor protection for the surviving spouse.

     c.   The trustee may, in the trustee's sole discretion, distribute, use or apply so much of the income of Trust A (which is not withdrawable by the surviving spouse or by the surviving spouse's legal representative pursuant to the provisions of subsections 1.2.a and 1.2.b, above) as the trustee may deem necessary to provide for the maintenance, support and health care of the surviving spouse, in the surviving spouse's accustomed manner of living.

Section 2.   Distribution of Income of Trust B During Surviving Spouse's Lifetime

2.1   During the surviving spouse's lifetime the surviving spouse (including any legal representative acting on behalf of the surviving spouse) shall have the annual noncumulative power to withdraw all or any portion of the trust accounting income derived from the assets of Trust B on or before December 31 of the calendar year; PROVIDED, HOWEVER, that (i) the foregoing power of withdrawal shall not extend to the portion of the trust accounting income which, for the calendar year, would be either exempt from federal income tax or subject to federal income tax to the trust, after all deductions and exemptions (but determined as though the trustee made no other income or principal distributions or encroachments during the year other than for trust expenses and taxes), at less than the general maximum federal income tax rate applicable to trusts (and for this purpose said excluded portion (I) shall begin with any dividends, capital gains or other items of trust accounting income which are subject to a maximum federal income tax rate which is lower than the general maximum federal income tax rate applicable to trusts, (II) shall next include any items of trust accounting income filling out the lower income tax brackets of the trust which do not constitute "net investment income" as defined in Section 1411(c) of the Internal Revenue Code, or any successor section thereto, (III) shall next include any additional items of trust accounting income filling out the lower income tax brackets of the trust which constitute "net investment income" as defined in Section 1411(c) of the Internal Revenue Code, or any successor section thereto, and (IV) shall assume that all items of federal gross income of the trust which do not constitute trust accounting income and which are not subject to a maximum federal income tax rate which is lower than the general maximum federal income tax rate applicable to trusts, are using up the lower income tax brackets of the trust first, before the aforesaid items of trust accounting income) and (ii) if Section 2514(e) of the Internal Revenue Code, or any successor section thereto, is in effect during the calendar year, the amount of trust accounting income subject to the foregoing power of withdrawal during the calendar year shall not exceed five percent (5%) (or such other percentage as shall be provided for in Section 2514(e)(2) of the Internal Revenue Code, or any successor section thereto) of the combined value of the principal and income of Trust B on December 31 of the calendar year (or on the date of the surviving spouse's death, if earlier). If more than one item of trust accounting income is withdrawable by the surviving spouse pursuant to the foregoing provisions of this subsection 2.1 (for example, taxable interest from corporate bonds and distributions from retirement assets (as defined in ARTICLE __, below)), but the above-described limitation of Section 2514(e) of the Internal Revenue Code, or any successor section thereto, shall apply, the surviving spouse's power of withdrawal shall extend to a pro rata portion of each of such items based upon the ratio in which the total amount of each of such items bears to the total amount of all of such items (assuming the above-described limitation of Section 2514(e) of the Internal Revenue Code, or any successor section thereto, does not apply). Any such withdrawable trust accounting income which is not withdrawn by the surviving spouse or by the surviving spouse's legal representative by the end of any calendar year (or by the time of the surviving spouse's death, if earlier) shall be added to the principal of Trust B, and the surviving spouse's power of withdrawal for such calendar year shall lapse. For purposes of this subsection 2.1, the term "trust accounting income" shall include all retirement assets (as defined in ARTICLE__, below, but ignoring the last proviso of the definition) paid to the trust during the year regardless of whether all of said retirement assets paid to the trust during the year are otherwise considered to be trust accounting income, and the principal of Trust B shall include the underlying value of all retirement assets (as defined in ARTICLE __, below, but ignoring the last proviso of the definition) and other assets which are payable to the trust over time and not yet paid to the trust. The trustee or trustees other than a trustee having any beneficial interest in the trust (other than solely as a contingent taker under ARTICLE __, below) may, in the sole and absolute discretion of said trustee(s), suspend the surviving spouse's withdrawal power under this subsection 2.1, in whole or part, by instrument in writing executed by said trustee(s) before January 1 of the calendar year in which such withdrawal power would otherwise exist. Reasons for such suspension may include, but shall not be limited to, overall tax savings for the trust and its beneficiaries (including remainder beneficiaries) and creditor protection for the surviving spouse.

2.2   During the surviving spouse's lifetime the surviving spouse (including any legal representative acting on behalf of the surviving spouse) shall also have the annual noncumulative power to withdraw all or any portion of the "net investment income" of Trust B (as defined in Section 1411(c) of the Internal Revenue Code, or any successor section thereto) which is not already withdrawable pursuant to the provisions of subsection 2.1, above, and which is not described in clause (III) of subsection 2.1, above (hereinafter "the excess net investment income"), on or before December 31 of the calendar year; PROVIDED, HOWEVER, that (i) the foregoing power of withdrawal shall not extend to the portion of the excess net investment income of Trust B which, for the calendar year, is less than the dollar amount at which the highest tax bracket in section 1(e) of the Internal Revenue Code, or any successor section thereto, begins for such calendar year (but with said dollar amount being reduced, but not below zero, by (A) any net investment income, as defined in Section 1411(c) of the Internal Revenue Code, or any successor section thereto, which is not withdrawable by the surviving spouse pursuant to the provisions of clause (III) of paragraph 2.1, above, and (B) an amount equal to the total of any costs which are deductible for purposes of determining the taxable income of the trust but not for purposes of determining the adjusted gross income of the trust, after the application of Section 67(e) of the Internal Revenue Code, or any successor section thereto), and (ii) if Section 2514(e) of the Internal Revenue Code, or any successor section thereto, is in effect during the calendar year, the amount of the excess net investment income subject to the foregoing power of withdrawal during the calendar year shall not exceed (A) five percent (5%) (or such other percentage as shall be provided for in Section 2514(e)(2) of the Internal Revenue Code, or any successor section thereto) of the combined value of the principal and income of Trust B on December 31 of the calendar year (or on the date of the surviving spouse's death, if earlier), less (B) any amount which is withdrawable by the surviving spouse during the calendar year pursuant to the provisions of subsection 2.1, above. If more than one item of excess net investment income is withdrawable by the surviving spouse pursuant to the foregoing provisions of this subsection 2.2 (for example, capital gains from the sale of various corporate stocks and dividend distributions on various corporate stocks), but the above-described limitation of Section 2514(e) of the Internal Revenue Code, or any successor section thereto, shall apply, the surviving spouse's power of withdrawal shall extend to a pro rata portion of each of such items based upon the ratio in which the total amount of each of such items bears to the total amount of all of such items (assuming the above-described limitation of Section 2514(e) of the Internal Revenue Code, or any successor section thereto, does not apply). Any such withdrawable excess net investment income which is not withdrawn by the surviving spouse or by the surviving spouse's legal representative by the end of any calendar year (or by the time of the surviving spouse's death, if earlier) shall not be withdrawable by the surviving spouse in any subsequent calendar year. For purposes of this subsection 2.2, the principal of Trust B shall include the underlying value of all retirement assets (as defined in ARTICLE __, below, but ignoring the last proviso of the definition) and other assets which are payable to the trust over time and not yet paid to the trust. The trustee or trustees other than a trustee having any beneficial interest in the trust (other than solely as a contingent taker under ARTICLE __, below) may, in the sole and absolute discretion of said trustee(s), suspend the surviving spouse's withdrawal power under this subsection 2.2, in whole or part, by instrument in writing executed by said trustee(s) before January 1 of the calendar year in which such withdrawal power would otherwise exist. Reasons for such suspension may include, but shall not be limited to, overall tax savings for the trust and its beneficiaries (including remainder beneficiaries) and creditor protection for the surviving spouse.

2.3   The trustee may, in the trustee's sole discretion, distribute, use or apply so much of the income of Trust B (which is not withdrawable by the surviving spouse or by the surviving spouse's representative pursuant to the provisions of subsections 2.1 and 2.2, above) as the trustee may deem necessary to provide for the maintenance, support and health care of the surviving spouse, in the surviving spouse's accustomed manner of living. In addition, the trustee may, in the trustee's sole discretion, distribute, use or apply the income of Trust B (which is not withdrawable by the surviving spouse or by the surviving spouse's legal representative pursuant to the provisions of subsections 2.1 and 2.2, above) as the trustee may deem necessary for the maintenance, support, health care and education of any descendant of the grantors;

PROVIDED, HOWEVER, that (i) the needs of the surviving spouse as specified above shall be the primary concern of the trustee, and (ii) the income of Trust B may not be used to limit, relieve or otherwise discharge, in whole or in part, the legal obligation of any individual to support and maintain any other individual. In determining the amounts to be distributed, used or applied for the grantors' descendants, the trustee shall not be required to treat each of such persons equally but shall be governed more by the particular needs and interests of each of them.

Section 3. Encroachment on Principal During Surviving Spouse's Lifetime

3.1 The trustee may, in the trustee's sole discretion, encroach upon the principal of Trust A and Trust B (which is not withdrawable by the surviving spouse or by the surviving spouse's legal representative pursuant to the provisions of subsections 1.2.a, 1.2.b, 2.1 and 2.2, above) for the maintenance, support, education and health care of the surviving spouse in the surviving spouse's accustomed manner of living; PROVIDED, HOWEVER, that the principal of Trust A and Trust B may not be used to limit, relieve or otherwise discharge, in whole or in part, the legal obligation of any individual to support and maintain the surviving spouse. Further, the trustee other than the surviving spouse and other than a trustee designated by the surviving spouse who is "related or subordinate" to the surviving spouse within the meaning of current Section 672(c) of the Internal

Revenue Code (substituting "the surviving spouse" for "the grantor" in said Section), may, in such trustee's sole discretion, utilize the principal of Trust A and Trust B (which is not withdrawable by the surviving spouse or by the surviving spouse's legal representative pursuant to the provisions of subsections 1.2.a, 1.2.b, 2.1 and 2.2, above) for the purpose of reimbursing the surviving spouse for any income tax liability accruing to the surviving spouse as a result of the surviving spouse's power of withdrawal under subsections 1.2.a, 1.2.b, 2.1 and 2.2, above; PROVIDED, HOWEVER, that the trustee shall not possess the discretionary power described in this sentence if, as a consequence of possessing said power, the surviving spouse is deemed to possess the same power for federal or state estate tax, gift tax, generation-skipping transfer tax, inheritance tax or other transfer tax purposes.

3.2   In addition, the trustee may, in the trustee's sole discretion, encroach upon the principal of Trust B (which is not withdrawable by the surviving spouse or by the surviving spouse's legal representative pursuant to the provisions of subsections 2.1 and 2.2, above) for the maintenance, support, education and health care of any descendant of the grantors; PROVIDED, HOWEVER, that (i) the needs of the surviving spouse as specified in subsection 3.1, above, shall be the primary concern of the trustee, and (ii) the principal of Trust B may not be used to discharge, relieve or limit, wholly or partially, the legal obligation of any individual to support and maintain any other individual.

3.3   In addition, if the trustee shall at any time during the term of Trust A and Trust B desire to purchase any additional interest in an "S corporation," the trustee of Trust B shall encroach upon the principal of Trust B (which is not withdrawable by the surviving spouse or by the surviving spouse's legal representative pursuant to the provisions of subsections 2.1 and 2.2, above) and distribute to the trustee of Trust A any funds which the trustee of Trust A shall deem necessary for such purpose.

Section 4.   Distribution of Principal at Death of Surviving Spouse

4.1   Upon the death of the surviving spouse, all of the accrued and undistributed income of Trust A shall be distributed to the then acting trustee or trustees under any revocable trust established by the surviving spouse during his or her lifetime (e.g. the Survivor's Trust under this Trust Agreement), to be held and distributed by said trustee or trustees pursuant to the provisions of the instrument establishing said revocable trust; PROVIDED, HOWEVER, that if no such revocable trust shall be in existence at the time of the surviving spouse's death, or if the foregoing provisions of this subsection 4.1 shall disqualify Trust A or prevent Trust A from qualifying as a "Qualified Subchapter S Trust" under Section 1361(d) of the Internal Revenue Code, or any successor section thereto, all of the accrued and undistributed income of Trust A shall be distributed to the surviving spouse's domiciliary probate estate.

4.2   Upon the death of the surviving spouse, all of the remaining assets of the trust which are not disposed of pursuant to the provisions of subsection 4.1, above, including the principal of Trust A and both the principal and accumulated and undistributed income of Trust B, shall be distributed to or among any of the grantors' descendants, in trust or otherwise, and in such proportions, as shall be designated by the surviving spouse in the surviving spouse's Last Will and Testament (having the most recent date of execution by the surviving spouse) and which is filed with the probate court of the relevant jurisdiction within six (6) months following the surviving spouse's death, but if such Last Will and Testament shall be contested within the aforementioned six (6) month period, then as shall be designated in the surviving spouse's Last Will and Testament which is finally admitted to probate after the period for contesting the surviving spouse's Last Will and Testament has expired, and referring specifically to this provision, excluding, however, the surviving spouse, the surviving spouse's estate, the surviving spouse's creditors and the creditors of the surviving spouse's estate.   In addition, if the surviving spouse is not survived by a surviving spouse (as that term is defined for purposes of Section 2056 of the Internal Revenue Code, or any successor section thereto), then to the extent it will not result in the surviving spouse's estate being liable for any federal or state estate or inheritance taxes, and except as otherwise provided in Section __ of ARTICLE __ hereof, the surviving spouse shall also have the power to appoint those remaining assets of Trust A and Trust B, beginning with the asset or assets having the greatest amount of built-in appreciation (calculated by subtracting the trust's income tax basis from the fair market value on the date of death of the surviving spouse), as a percentage of the fair market value of such asset or assets on the date of death of the surviving spouse, to the creditors of the surviving spouse's estate (or to the surviving spouse's estate if the power to distribute such assets to the creditors of the surviving spouse's estate is not sufficient to include such assets in the surviving spouse's estate for federal estate tax purposes), utilizing the same appointment procedure described immediately above; PROVIDED, HOWEVER, that if this trust has been or will be divided into two separate trusts for federal generation-skipping transfer tax purposes, the surviving spouse's aforesaid general power of appointment shall apply (i) first to the trust having an inclusion ratio, as defined in Section 2642(a) of the Internal Revenue Code, or any successor section thereto, of other than zero, but only to the extent such trust is not otherwise already includible in the surviving spouse's estate for federal or state estate or inheritance tax purposes, pursuant to the other provisions of this instrument, and (ii) next to the trust having an inclusion ratio, as defined in Section 2642(a) of the Internal Revenue Code, or any successor section thereto, of zero; PROVIDED FURTHER, HOWEVER, that if the surviving spouse is the beneficiary of more than one trust which includes a provision similar to this sentence (including but not limited to Trust A and Trust B under this ARTICLE), the extent of the foregoing power of appointment shall be reduced by multiplying the value of the assets otherwise subject to the foregoing power of appointment by a fraction the numerator of which shall equal the value of the assets otherwise subject to the foregoing power of appointment and the denominator of which shall equal the value of all assets subject to the foregoing and to the similar power(s) of appointment, the intent being that under no circumstance shall the surviving spouse's estate be liable for any federal or state estate or inheritance tax as a consequence of the foregoing power of appointment. If the surviving spouse is survived by a surviving spouse (as that term is defined for purposes of Section 2056 of the Internal Revenue Code, or any successor section thereto), the surviving spouse shall only possess the power of appointment described in the immediately preceding sentence to the same or lesser extent that the trustee (other than the surviving spouse and other than a trustee who is "related or subordinate" to the surviving spouse within the meaning of current Section 672(c) of the Internal Revenue Code (substituting "the surviving spouse" for "the grantor" in said Section)) shall direct by instrument in writing filed with the trust during the surviving spouse's lifetime and not revoked by said trustee prior to the surviving spouse's death; PROVIDED, HOWEVER, that the trustee shall not possess the aforedescribed power to direct if the surviving spouse appointed the trustee who or which possesses the aforedescribed power to direct, and if as a consequence the surviving spouse is deemed to possess the aforedescribed power to direct for federal or state estate tax, gift tax, generation-skipping transfer tax, inheritance tax or other transfer tax purposes. In exercising said trustee's broad discretionary power in determining whether and to what extent the surviving spouse shall possess the aforesaid power of appointment if the surviving spouse is survived by a surviving spouse, said trustee shall be primarily concerned with minimizing overall income and transfer taxes to the surviving spouse's estate and to recipients of the trust assets after the surviving spouse's death.

4.3   Upon the death of the surviving spouse, all of the remaining assets of the trust estate which are not disposed of pursuant to the provisions of subsection 4.1, above, or effectively appointed by the surviving spouse pursuant to the provisions of subsection 4.2, above, shall be distributed as follows:_____.

QTIP Trust Form

The assets to be held in the trust estate with the income and principal administered and distributed pursuant to the provisions of this ARTICLE shall be held by the trustee as a separate trust estate, and the assets in said trust estate shall at all times during the term of the trust be divided into two separate trusts. Trust "A" shall consist solely of an interest in any entity which is taxed as an "S corporation," as such term is defined in Section 1361(a)(1) of the Internal Revenue Code, or any successor section thereto (hereafter "S corporation"), and the proceeds and reinvested proceeds from any subsequent sale of such interest in any "S corporation" by the trustee of Trust "A," and Trust "B" shall consist of all other assets. It is the intent of the grantors that Trust A shall qualify as a "Qualified Subchapter S Trust" under Section 1361(d) of the Internal Revenue Code, or any successor section thereto, for federal income tax purposes and it is contemplated that the primary current beneficiary will make the necessary election under the federal Internal Revenue Code to qualify Trust A as a permissible shareholder of an S corporation. The assets of both Trust A and Trust B shall be held in trust with the income and principal administered and distributed as follows:

Section 1. Distribution and Use of Income During Surviving Spouse's Lifetime

1.1   The trustee shall distribute all of the net income derived from the assets of Trust A and Trust B from and after the death of the deceased spouse to the surviving spouse in regular periodic installments, not less frequently than quarter-annually, for and during the remainder of the surviving spouse's life; PROVIDED, HOWEVER, if the trustee, at any time or times, shall consider the surviving spouse to be unable to properly use such income in the surviving spouse's own best interest because of the surviving spouse's physical or mental infirmity, or for any other reason, the trustee may use and apply part or all of such net income for the benefit of the surviving spouse. Any income not so used and applied shall be distributed directly to the surviving spouse at least as frequently as annually. At the point, if any, at which the trust shall no longer own any interest in an "S corporation," all accrued and undistributed income up to said point shall be distributed to the surviving spouse.

1.2 During the surviving spouse's lifetime the surviving spouse (including any legal representative acting on behalf of the surviving spouse) shall have the annual noncumulative power to withdraw all or any portion of the trust accounting income derived from the assets of Trust B which is not required to be distributed to the surviving spouse pursuant to the provisions of subsection 1.1, above (as deemed apportioned pursuant to the provisions of Section 652(b) or 662(b), as applicable, of the Internal Revenue Code, or any successor sections thereto), on or before December 31 of the calendar year; PROVIDED, HOWEVER, that (i) the foregoing power of withdrawal shall not extend to the portion of the trust accounting income which, for the calendar year, would be either exempt from federal income tax or subject to federal income tax to the trust, after all deductions and exemptions (but determined as though the trustee made no other income or principal distributions or encroachments during the year other than for trust expenses and taxes), at less than the general maximum federal income tax rate applicable to trusts (and for this purpose said excluded portion (I) shall begin with any dividends, capital gains or other items of trust accounting income which are subject to a maximum federal income tax rate which is lower than the general maximum federal income tax rate applicable to trusts, (II) shall next include any items of trust accounting income filling out the lower income tax brackets of the trust which do not constitute "net investment income" as defined in Section 1411(c) of the Internal Revenue Code, or any successor section thereto, (III) shall next include any additional items of trust accounting income filling out the lower income tax brackets of the trust which constitute "net investment income" as defined in Section 1411(c) of the Internal Revenue Code, or any successor section thereto, and (IV) shall assume that all items of federal gross income of Trust B which do not constitute trust accounting income and which are not subject to a maximum federal income tax rate which is lower than the general maximum federal income tax rate applicable to trusts, are using up the lower income tax brackets of the trust first, before the aforesaid items of trust accounting income) and (ii) if Section 2514(e) of the Internal Revenue Code, or any successor section thereto, is in effect during the calendar year, the amount of trust accounting income subject to the foregoing power of withdrawal during the calendar year shall not exceed five percent (5%) (or such other percentage as shall be provided for in Section 2514(e)(2) of the Internal Revenue Code, or any successor section thereto) of the combined value of the principal and income of Trust B on December 31 of the calendar year (or on the date of the surviving spouse's death, if earlier). If more than one item of trust accounting income is withdrawable by the surviving spouse pursuant to the foregoing provisions of this subsection 1.2 (for example, taxable interest from corporate bonds and distributions from retirement assets (as defined in ARTICLE __, below)), but the above-described limitation of Section 2514(e) of the Internal Revenue Code, or any successor section thereto, shall apply, the surviving spouse's power of withdrawal shall extend to a pro rata portion of each of such items based upon the ratio in which the total amount of each of such items bears to the total amount of all of such items (assuming the above-described limitation of Section 2514(e) of the Internal Revenue Code, or any successor section thereto, does not apply). Any such withdrawable trust accounting income which is not withdrawn by the surviving spouse or by the surviving spouse's legal representative by the end of any calendar year (or by the time of the surviving spouse's death, if earlier) shall be added to the principal of Trust B, and the surviving spouse's power of withdrawal for such calendar year shall lapse. For purposes of this subsection 1.2, the term "trust accounting income" shall include all retirement assets (as defined in ARTICLE __, below, but ignoring the last proviso of the definition) paid to the trust during the year regardless of whether all of said retirement assets paid to the trust during the year are otherwise considered to be trust accounting income, and the principal of Trust B shall include the underlying value of all retirement assets (as defined in ARTICLE __, but ignoring the last proviso of the definition) and other assets which are payable to the trust over time and not yet paid to the trust. The trustee other than a trustee having any beneficial interest in the trust (other than solely as a contingent taker under ARTICLE __, below) may, in the sole and absolute discretion of said trustee, suspend the surviving spouse's withdrawal power under this subsection 1.2, in whole or part, by instrument in writing executed by said trustee before January 1 of the calendar year in which such withdrawal power would otherwise exist. Reasons for such suspension may include, but shall not be limited to, overall tax savings for the trust and its beneficiaries (including remainder beneficiaries) and creditor protection for the surviving spouse.

1.3 During the surviving spouse's lifetime the surviving spouse (including any legal representative acting on behalf of the surviving spouse) shall also have the annual noncumulative power to withdraw all or any portion of the "net investment income" of Trust B (as defined in Section 1411(c) of the Internal Revenue Code, or any successor section thereto) which is not required to be distributed to the surviving spouse pursuant to the provisions of subsection 1.1, above (as deemed apportioned pursuant to the provisions of Section 652(b) or 662(b), as applicable, of the Internal Revenue Code, or any successor sections thereto) which is not already withdrawable pursuant to the provisions of subsection 1.2, above, and which is not described in clause (III) of subsection 1.2, above (hereinafter "the excess net investment income"), on or before December 31 of the calendar year; PROVIDED, HOWEVER, that (i) the foregoing power of withdrawal shall not extend to the portion of the excess net investment income of the trust which, for the calendar year, is less than the dollar amount at which the highest tax bracket in section 1(e) of the Internal Revenue Code, or any successor section thereto, begins for such calendar year (but with said dollar amount being reduced, but not below zero, by (A) any net investment income, as defined in Section 1411(c) of the Internal Revenue Code, or any successor section thereto, which is not withdrawable by the surviving spouse pursuant to the provisions of clause (III) of subsection 1.2, above, and (B) an amount equal to the total of any costs which are deductible for purposes of determining the taxable income of the trust but not for purposes of determining the adjusted gross income of the trust, after the application of Section 67(e) of the Internal Revenue Code, or any successor section thereto), and (ii) if Section 2514(e) of the Internal Revenue Code, or any successor section thereto, is in effect during the calendar year, the amount of the excess net investment income subject to the foregoing power of withdrawal during the calendar year shall not exceed (A) five percent (5%) (or such other percentage as shall be provided for in Section 2514(e)(2) of the Internal Revenue Code, or any successor section thereto) of the combined value of the principal and income of Trust B on December 31 of the calendar year (or on the date of the surviving spouse's death, if earlier), less (B) any amount which is withdrawable by the surviving spouse during the calendar year pursuant to the provisions of subsection 1.2, above. If more than one item of excess net investment income is withdrawable by the surviving spouse pursuant to the foregoing provisions of this subsection 1.3 (for example, capital gains from the sale of various corporate stocks and dividend distributions on various corporate stocks), but the above-described limitation of Section 2514(e) of the Internal Revenue Code, or any successor section thereto, shall apply, the surviving spouse's power of withdrawal shall extend to a pro rata portion of each of such items based upon the ratio in which the total amount of each of such items bears to the total amount of all of such items (assuming the above-described limitation of Section 2514(e) of the Internal Revenue Code, or any successor section thereto, does not apply). Any such withdrawable excess net investment income which is not withdrawn by the surviving spouse or by the surviving spouse's legal representative by the end of any calendar year (or by the time of the surviving spouse's death, if earlier) shall not be withdrawable by the surviving spouse in any subsequent calendar year. For purposes of this subsection 1.3, the principal of Trust B shall include the underlying value of all retirement assets (as defined in ARTICLE __, below, but ignoring the last proviso of the definition) and other assets which are payable to the trust over time and not yet paid to the trust. The trustee other than a trustee having any beneficial interest in the trust (other than solely as a contingent taker under ARTICLE __, below) may, in the sole and absolute discretion of said trustee, suspend the surviving spouse's withdrawal power under this subsection 1.3, in whole or part, by instrument in writing execued by said trustee before January 1 of the calendar year in which such withdrawal power would otherwise exist. Reasons for such suspension may include, but shall not be limited to, overall tax savings for the trust and its beneficiaries (including remainder beneficiaries) and creditor protection for the surviving spouse.

Section 2. Encroachment on Principal During Surviving Spouse's Lifetime

2.1 The trustee may, in the trustee's sole discretion, encroach upon the principal of Trust A and Trust B (which is not withdrawable by the surviving spouse or by the surviving spouse's legal representative pursuant to the provisions of subsections 1.2 and 1.3, above) for the maintenance, support, education and health care of the surviving spouse in the surviving spouse's accustomed manner of living; PROVIDED,

HOWEVER, that the principal of Trust A and Trust B may not be used to limit, relieve or otherwise discharge, in whole or in part, the legal obligation of any individual to support and maintain the surviving spouse. Further, the trustee other than the surviving spouse and other than a trustee designated by the surviving spouse who is "related or subordinate" to the surviving spouse within the meaning of current Section 672(c) of the Internal Revenue Code (substituting "the surviving spouse" for "the grantor" in said Section), may, in such trustee's sole discretion, utilize the principal of Trust A and Trust B (which is not withdrawable by the surviving spouse or by the surviving spouse's legal representative pursuant to the provisions of subsections 1.2 and 1.3, above) for the purpose of reimbursing the surviving spouse for any income tax liability accruing to the surviving spouse as a result of the surviving spouse's powers of withdrawal under subsections 1.2 and 1.3, above; PROVIDED, HOWEVER, that the trustee shall not possess the discretionary power described in this sentence if, as a consequence of possessing said power, the surviving spouse is deemed to possess the same power for federal or state estate tax or inheritance tax purposes.

2.2   In addition, if the trustee shall at any time during the term of Trust A and Trust B desire to purchase any additional interest in an "S corporation," the trustee of Trust B shall encroach upon the principal of Trust B (which is not withdrawable by the surviving spouse or by the surviving spouse's legal representative pursuant to the provisions of subsections 2.1 and 2.2, above) and distribute to the trustee of Trust A any funds which the trustee of Trust A shall deem necessary for such purpose.

Section 3. Distribution of Principal at Death of Surviving Spouse

Upon the death of the surviving spouse, all of the remaining assets of the trust estate, including both principal and accrued and undistributed income, shall be held or distributed as follows:

3.1 **Payment of Death Taxes.** Unless specific provision is made by the surviving spouse under the surviving spouse's Last Will and Testament directing the payment of the following taxes, then, to the extent such taxes are not in fact paid by the trustee under any trust created by the surviving spouse during the surviving spouse's lifetime, the trustee shall use the assets of Trust B (and, to the extent necessary, the principal of Trust A) for the payment of all estate, inheritance, succession, transfer or other death taxes of any kind, including any penalties or interest thereon, assessed against the surviving spouse's estate, or against any beneficiary of this trust, which are attributable to the remaining assets of this trust; PROVIDED, HOWEVER, such death taxes shall not be payable from or charged against retirement assets (as defined in ARTICLE __, below) unless all other assets passing under this ARTICLE at the death of the surviving spouse are insufficient to pay all of such death taxes. The amount of such taxes which shall be considered attributable to the remaining assets of this trust shall be the difference between the amount of such taxes as finally determined and the amount which would have been due if none of the remaining assets of this trust were included in the estate of the surviving spouse for the purpose of computing such taxes. The taxes which are to be paid by the trustee out of the remaining assets of Trust B (and, to the extent necessary, the principal of Trust A) may be paid either to the personal representative of the estate of the surviving spouse or may be paid directly to the appropriate governmental agencies charged with the collection of such taxes, and the trustee may rely on the certification of the personal representative of the estate of the surviving spouse as to the amount of such taxes payable. If this trust has been divided or will be divided into two separate trusts for federal generation-skipping transfer tax purposes, then all of such death taxes shall first be paid out of, apportioned to and charged against, without right of contribution or reimbursement, the trust having an inclusion ratio, as defined in Section 2642(a) of the Internal Revenue Code, or any successor section thereto, of other than zero.

3.2 **Disposition of Balance of Trust Assets.** All of the assets remaining in Trusts A and B of this trust estate which are not disposed of pursuant to the provisions of subsection 3.1, above, shall be held or distributed as follows:

a. The trustee shall distribute all of the accrued and undistributed income of Trust A to the then acting trustee or trustees under any revocable trust established by the surviving spouse during his or her lifetime, e.g. the Survivor's Trust under this Trust Agreement, to be held and distributed by said trustee or trustees pursuant to the provisions of the instrument establishing said revocable trust; PROVIDED, HOWEVER, that if no such revocable trust shall be in existence at the time of the surviving spouse's death, or if the foregoing provisions of this paragraph a shall disqualify Trust A or prevent Trust A from qualifying as a "Qualified Subchapter S Trust" under Section 1361(d) of the Internal Revenue Code, or any successor section thereto, all of the accrued and undistributed income of Trust A shall be distributed to the surviving spouse's domiciliary probate estate.

b.   The trustee shall distribute all of the remaining assets of Trust A and Trust B not disposed of pursuant to the provisions of paragraph a, above, including both principal and accumulated and undistributed income, if any, to or among any descendants of the grantors, in trust or otherwise, and in such proportions, as shall be designated by the surviving spouse in the surviving spouse's Last Will and Testament (having the most recent date of execution by the surviving spouse) and which is filed with the probate court of the relevant jurisdiction within six (6) months following the surviving spouse's death, but if such Last Will and Testament shall be contested within the aforementioned six (6) month period, then as shall be designated in the surviving spouse's Last Will and Testament which is finally admitted to probate after the period for contesting the surviving spouse's Last Will and Testament has expired, and referring specifically to this provision, excluding, however, the surviving spouse, the surviving spouse's estate, the surviving spouse's creditors and the creditors of the surviving spouse's estate.

     c.   All of the remaining assets of the trust estate which are not disposed of pursuant to the provisions of paragraph a, above, or effectively appointed by the surviving spouse pursuant to the provisions of paragraph b, above, including both principal and accumulated and undistributed income, if any, shall be distributed to the grantors' descendants who survive the surviving spouse, per stirpes; PROVIDED, HOWEVER, that (i) the share of either child of the grantors shall be held in trust for the benefit of such child with income and principal administered and distributed pursuant to the provisions of ARTICLE __ hereof to the extent the share is derived from a trust under this ARTICLE having an inclusion ratio, as defined in Section 2642(a) of the Internal Revenue Code, or any successor section thereto, of zero, and/or if there is neither a federal estate tax nor a federal generation-skipping transfer tax in effect which applies to the grantor's wife's estate at the time of the grantor's wife's death, otherwise pursuant to the provisions of ARTICLE __ hereof, and (ii) the share of any grandchild or more remote descendant of the grantors who is then less than thirty-five (35) years of age shall be held in trust for the benefit of such grandchild or more remote descendant with income and principal administered and distributed pursuant to the provisions of ARTICLE __ hereof.

Lifetime Trust for Child

The assets to be held in a trust estate for the benefit of either child of the grantors pursuant to the provisions of this ARTICLE shall be held by the trustee as a separate trust estate for the primary benefit of such child (hereinafter in this ARTICLE referred to as "the beneficiary"), and shall at all times during the term of the trust be divided into two separate trusts. Trust "A" shall consist solely of an interest in any entity which is taxed as an "S corporation," as such term is defined in Section 1361(a)(1) of the Internal Revenue Code, or any successor section thereto (hereafter "S corporation"), and the proceeds and reinvested proceeds from any subsequent sale of such interest in any "S corporation" by the trustee of Trust "A," and Trust "B" shall consist of all other assets. It is the intent of the grantors that Trust A shall qualify as a "Qualified Subchapter S Trust" under Section 1361(d) of the Internal Revenue Code, or any successor section thereto, for federal income tax purposes and it is contemplated that the primary current beneficiary will make the necessary election under the federal Internal Revenue Code to qualify Trust A as a permissible shareholder of an S corporation. The assets of both Trust A and Trust B shall be held in trust with the income and principal administered and distributed as follows:

Section 1. Distribution of Income of Trust A During Lifetime of Beneficiary

1.1   During any period in which the trust owns an interest in any "S corporation" as defined in Section 1361 of the Internal Revenue Code, or any successor section thereto, all of the net income derived from the assets of Trust A shall be distributed to the beneficiary, in regular installments not less frequently than quarter-annually, for and during the term of the Trust. At the point, if any, at which the trust shall no longer own an interest in an "S corporation," all accrued and undistributed income up to said point shall be distributed to the beneficiary.

1.2   During any period in which the trust owns no interest in an "S corporation" as defined in Section 1361(a)(1) of the Internal Revenue Code, or any successor section thereto, the income of Trust A shall be administered and distributed as follows:

a.   During the beneficiary's lifetime the beneficiary (including any legal representative acting on behalf of any beneficiary under a legal incapacity) shall have the annual noncumulative power to withdraw all or any portion of the trust accounting income of Trust A on or before December 31 of the calendar year; PROVIDED, HOWEVER, that (i) the foregoing power of withdrawal shall not extend to the portion of the trust accounting income which, for the calendar year, would be either exempt from federal income tax or subject to federal income tax to the trust, after all deductions and exemptions (but determined as though the trustee made no other income or principal distributions or encroachments during the year other than for trust expenses and taxes), at less than the general maximum federal income tax rate applicable to trusts (and for this purpose said excluded portion (I) shall begin with any dividends, capital gains or other items of trust accounting income which are subject to a maximum federal income tax rate which is lower than the general maximum federal income tax rate applicable to trusts, (II) shall next include any items of trust accounting income filling out the lower income tax brackets of the trust which do not constitute "net investment income" as defined in Section 1411(c) of the Internal Revenue Code, or any successor section thereto, (III) shall next include any additional items of trust accounting income filling out the lower income tax brackets of the trust which constitute "net investment income" as defined in Section 1411(c) of the Internal Revenue Code, or any successor section thereto, and (IV) shall assume that all items of federal gross income of the trust which do not constitute trust accounting income and which are not subject to a maximum federal income tax rate which is lower than the general maximum federal income tax rate applicable to trusts, are using up the lower income tax brackets of the trust first, before the aforesaid items of trust accounting income) and (ii) if Section 2514(e) of the Internal Revenue Code, or any successor section thereto, is in effect during the calendar year, the amount of trust accounting income subject to the foregoing power of withdrawal during the calendar year shall not exceed five percent (5%) (or such other percentage as shall be provided for in Section 2514(e)(2) of the Internal Revenue Code, or any successor section thereto) of the combined value of the principal and income of Trust A on December 31 of the calendar year (or on the date of the beneficiary's death, if earlier). If more than one item of trust accounting income is withdrawable by the beneficiary pursuant to the foregoing provisions of this subsection 1.2.a (for example, taxable interest from corporate bonds and distributions from retirement assets (as defined in ARTICLE __, below)), but the above-described limitation of Section 2514(e) of the Internal Revenue Code, or any successor section thereto, shall apply, the beneficiary's power of withdrawal shall extend to a pro rata portion of each of such items based upon the ratio in which the total amount of each of such items bears to the total amount of all of such items (assuming the above-described limitation of Section 2514(e) of the Internal Revenue Code, or any successor section thereto, does not apply). Any such withdrawable trust accounting income which is not withdrawn by the beneficiary or by the beneficiary's legal representative by the end of any calendar year (or by the time of the beneficiary's death, if earlier) shall be added to the principal of Trust A, and the beneficiary's power of withdrawal for such calendar year shall lapse. For purposes of this subsection 1.2.a, the term "trust accounting income" shall include all retirement assets (as defined in ARTICLE __, below, but ignoring the last proviso of the definition) paid to the trust during the year regardless of whether all of said retirement assets paid to the trust during the year are otherwise considered to be trust accounting income, and the principal of Trust A shall include the underlying value of all retirement assets (as defined in ARTICLE __, below, but ignoring the last proviso of the definition) and other assets which are payable to the trust over time and not yet paid to the trust. The trustee or trustees other than a trustee having any beneficial interest in the trust (other than solely as a contingent taker under ARTICLE __, below) may, in the sole and absolute discretion of said trustee(s), suspend the beneficiary's withdrawal power under this subsection 1.2.a, in whole or part, by instrument in writing executed by said trustee(s) before January 1 of the calendar year in which such withdrawal power would otherwise exist. Reasons for such suspension may include, but shall not be limited to, overall tax savings for the trust and its beneficiaries (including remainder beneficiaries), creditor protection for the beneficiary, and unwise or immature use of withdrawn funds by the beneficiary.

b.   During the beneficiary's lifetime the beneficiary (including any legal representative acting on behalf of any beneficiary under a legal incapacity) shall also have the annual noncumulative power to withdraw all or any portion of the "net investment income" of Trust A (as defined in Section 1411(c) of the Internal Revenue Code, or any successor section thereto) which is not already withdrawable pursuant to the provisions of subsection 1.2.a, above, and which is not described in clause (III) of subsection 1.2.a, above (hereinafter "the excess net investment income"), on or before December 31 of the calendar year; PROVIDED, HOWEVER, that (i) the foregoing power of withdrawal shall not extend to the portion of the excess net investment income of the trust which, for the calendar year, is less than the dollar amount at which the highest tax bracket in section 1(e) of the Internal Revenue Code, or any successor section thereto, begins for such calendar year (but with said dollar amount being reduced, but not below zero, by (A) any net investment income, as defined in Section 1411(c) of the Internal Revenue Code, or any successor section thereto, which is not withdrawable by the beneficiary pursuant to the provisions of clause (III) of subsection 1.2.a, above, and (B) an amount equal to the total of any costs which are deductible for purposes of determining the taxable income of the trust but not for purposes of determining the adjusted gross income of the trust, after the application of Section 67(e) of the Internal Revenue Code, or any successor section thereto), and (ii) if Section 2514(e) of the Internal Revenue Code, or any successor section thereto, is in effect during the calendar year, the amount of the excess net investment income subject to the foregoing power of withdrawal during the calendar year shall not exceed (A) five percent (5%) (or such other percentage as shall be provided for in Section 2514(e)(2) of the Internal Revenue Code, or any successor section thereto) of the combined value of the principal and income of Trust A on December 31 of the calendar year (or on the date of the beneficiary's death, if earlier), less (B) any amount which is withdrawable by the beneficiary during the calendar year pursuant to the provisions of subsection 1.2.a, above. If more than one item of excess net investment income is withdrawable by the beneficiary pursuant to the foregoing provisions of this subsection 1.2.b (for example, capital gains from the sale of various corporate stocks and dividend distributions on various corporate stocks), but the above-described limitation of Section 2514(e) of the Internal Revenue Code, or any successor section thereto, shall apply, the beneficiary's power of withdrawal shall extend to a pro rata portion of each of such items based upon the ratio in which the total amount of each of such items bears to the total amount of all of such items (assuming the above-described limitation of Section 2514(e) of the Internal Revenue Code, or any successor section thereto, does not apply). Any such withdrawable excess net investment income which is not withdrawn by the beneficiary or by the beneficiary's legal representative by the end of any calendar year (or by the time of the beneficiary's death, if earlier) shall not be withdrawable by the beneficiary in any subsequent calendar year. For purposes of this subsection 1.2.b, the principal of Trust A shall include the underlying value of all retirement assets (as defined in ARTICLE __, below, but ignoring the last proviso of the definition) and other assets which are payable to the trust over time and not yet paid to the trust. The trustee or trustees other than a trustee having any beneficial interest in the trust estate (other than solely as a contingent taker under ARTICLE__, below) may, in the sole and absolute discretion of said trustee(s), suspend the beneficiary's withdrawal power under this subsection 1.2.b, in whole or part, by instrument in writing executed by said trustee(s) before January 1 of the calendar year in which such withdrawal power would otherwise exist. Reasons for such suspension may include, but shall not be limited to, overall tax savings for the trust and its beneficiaries (including remainder beneficiaries), creditor protection for the beneficiary, and unwise or immature use of

272

withdrawn funds by the beneficiary.

c.   The trustee may, in the trustee's sole discretion, distribute, use or apply so much of the income of Trust A (which is not withdrawable by the beneficiary or by the beneficiary's legal representative pursuant to the provisions of subsections 1.2.a and 1.2.b, above) as the trustee may deem necessary to provide for the maintenance, support, health care and education of the beneficiary, in the beneficiary's accustomed manner of living.

Section 2.   Distribution of Income of Trust B During Lifetime of Beneficiary

2.1   During the beneficiary's lifetime the beneficiary (including any legal representative acting on behalf of any beneficiary under a legal incapacity) shall have the annual noncumulative power to withdraw all or any portion of the trust accounting income of Trust B on or before December 31 of the calendar year; PROVIDED, HOWEVER, that (i) the foregoing power of withdrawal shall not extend to the portion of the trust accounting income which, for the calendar year, would be either exempt from federal income tax or subject to federal income tax to the trust, after all deductions and exemptions (but determined as though the trustee made no other income or principal distributions or encroachments during the year other than for trust expenses and taxes), at less than the general maximum federal income tax rate applicable to trusts (and for this purpose said excluded portion (I) shall begin with any dividends, capital gains or other items of trust accounting income which are subject to a maximum federal income tax rate which is lower than the general maximum federal income tax rate applicable to trusts, (II) shall next include any items of trust accounting income filling out the lower income tax brackets of the trust which do not constitute "net investment income" as defined in Section 1411(c) of the Internal Revenue Code, or any successor section thereto, (III) shall next include any additional items of trust accounting income filling out the lower income tax brackets of the trust which constitute "net investment income" as defined in Section 1411(c) of the Internal Revenue Code, or any successor section thereto, and (IV) shall assume that all items of federal gross income of the trust which do not constitute trust accounting income and which are not subject to a maximum federal income tax rate which is lower than the general maximum federal income tax rate applicable to trusts, are using up the lower income tax brackets of the trust first, before the aforesaid items of trust accounting income) and (ii) if Section 2514(e) of the Internal Revenue Code, or any successor section thereto, is in effect during the calendar year, the amount of trust accounting income subject to the foregoing power of withdrawal during the calendar year shall not exceed five percent (5%) (or such other percentage as shall be provided for in Section 2514(e)(2) of the Internal Revenue Code, or any successor section thereto) of the combined value of the principal and income of Trust B on December 31 of the calendar year (or on the date of the beneficiary's death, if earlier). If more than one item of trust accounting income is withdrawable by the beneficiary pursuant to the foregoing provisions of this subsection 2.1 (for example, taxable interest from corporate bonds and distributions from retirement assets (as defined in ARTICLE __, below)), but the above-described limitation of Section 2514(e) of the Internal Revenue Code, or any successor section thereto, shall apply, the beneficiary's power of withdrawal shall extend to a pro rata portion of each of such items based upon the ratio in which the total amount of each of such items bears to the total amount of all of such items (assuming the above-described limitation of Section 2514(e) of the Internal Revenue Code, or any successor section thereto, does not apply). Any such withdrawable trust accounting income which is not withdrawn by the beneficiary or by the beneficiary's legal representative by the end of any calendar year (or by the time of the beneficiary's death, if earlier) shall be added to the principal of Trust B, and the beneficiary's power of withdrawal for such calendar year shall lapse. For purposes of this subsection 2.1, the term "trust accounting income" shall include all retirement assets (as defined in ARTICLE __, below, but ignoring the last proviso of the definition) paid to the trust during the year regardless of whether all of said retirement assets paid to the trust during the year are otherwise considered to be trust accounting income, and the principal of Trust B shall include the underlying value of all retirement assets (as defined in ARTICLE __, below, but ignoring the last proviso of the definition) and other assets which are payable to the trust over time and not yet paid to the trust. The trustee or trustees other than a trustee having any beneficial interest in the trust (other than solely as a contingent taker under ARTICLE __, below) may, in the sole and absolute discretion of said trustee(s), suspend the beneficiary's withdrawal power under this subsection 2.1, in whole or part, by instrument in writing executed by said trustee(s) before January 1 of the calendar year in which such withdrawal power would otherwise exist. Reasons for such suspension may include, but shall not be limited to, overall tax savings for the trust and its beneficiaries (including remainder beneficiaries), creditor protection for the beneficiary, and unwise or immature use of withdrawn funds by the beneficiary.

2.2 During the beneficiary's lifetime the beneficiary (including any legal representative acting on behalf of any beneficiary under a legal incapacity) shall also have the annual noncumulative power to withdraw all or any portion of the "net investment income" of Trust B (as defined in Section 1411(c) of the Internal Revenue Code, or any successor section thereto) which is not already withdrawable pursuant to the provisions of subsection 2.1, above, and which is not described in clause (III) of subsection 2.1, above (hereinafter "the excess net investment income"), on or before December 31 of the calendar year; PROVIDED, HOWEVER, that (i) the foregoing power of withdrawal shall not extend to the portion of the excess net investment income of the trust which, for the calendar year, is less than the dollar amount at which the highest tax bracket in section 1(e) of the Internal Revenue Code, or any successor section thereto, begins for such calendar year (but with said dollar amount being reduced, but not below zero, by (A) any net investment income, as defined in Section

1411(c) of the Internal Revenue Code, or any successor section thereto, which is not withdrawable by the beneficiary pursuant to the provisions of clause (III) of subsection 2.1, above, and (B) an amount equal to the total of any costs which are deductible for purposes of determining the taxable income of the trust but not for purposes of determining the adjusted gross income of the trust, after the application of Section 67(e) of the Internal Revenue Code, or any successor section thereto), and (ii) if Section 2514(e) of the Internal Revenue Code, or any successor section thereto, is in effect during the calendar year, the amount of the excess net investment income subject to the foregoing power of withdrawal during the calendar year shall not exceed (A) five percent (5%) (or such other percentage as shall be provided for in Section 2514(e)(2) of the Internal Revenue Code, or any successor section thereto) of the combined value of the principal and income of Trust B on December 31 of the calendar year (or on the date of the beneficiary's death, if earlier), less (B) any amount which is withdrawable by the beneficiary during the calendar year pursuant to the provisions of subsection 2.1, above. If more than one item of excess net investment income is withdrawable by the beneficiary pursuant to the foregoing provisions of this subsection 2.2 (for example, capital gains from the sale of various corporate stocks and dividend distributions on various corporate stocks), but the above-described limitation of Section 2514(e) of the Internal Revenue Code, or any successor section thereto, shall apply, the beneficiary's power of withdrawal shall extend to a pro rata portion of each of such items based upon the ratio in which the total amount of each of such items bears to the total amount of all of such items (assuming the above-described limitation of Section 2514(e) of the Internal Revenue Code, or any successor section thereto, does not apply). Any such withdrawable excess net investment income which is not withdrawn by the beneficiary or by the beneficiary's legal representative by the end of any calendar year (or by the time of the beneficiary's death, if earlier) shall not be withdrawable by the beneficiary in any subsequent calendar year. For purposes of this subsection 2.2, the principal of Trust B shall include the underlying value of all retirement assets (as defined in ARTICLE __, below, but ignoring the last proviso of the definition) and other assets which are payable to the trust over time and not yet paid to the trust. The trustee or trustees other than a trustee having any beneficial interest in the trust estate (other than solely as a contingent taker under ARTICLE __, below) may, in the sole and absolute discretion of said trustee(s), suspend the beneficiary's withdrawal power under this subsection 2.2, in whole or part, by instrument in writing executed by said trustee(s) before January 1 of the calendar year in which such withdrawal power would otherwise exist. Reasons for such suspension may include, but shall not be limited to, overall tax savings for the trust and its beneficiaries (including remainder beneficiaries), creditor protection for the beneficiary, and unwise or immature use of withdrawn funds by the beneficiary.

2.3 The trustee may, in the trustee's sole discretion, distribute, use or apply so much of the income of Trust B (which is not withdrawable by the beneficiary or by the beneficiary's legal representative pursuant to the provisions of subsections 2.1 and 2.2, above) as the trustee may deem necessary to provide for the maintenance, support, health care and education of the beneficiary, in the beneficiary's accustomed manner of living. In addition, the trustee may, in the trustee's sole discretion, distribute, use or apply the income of Trust B (which is not withdrawable by the beneficiary or by the beneficiary's legal representative pursuant to the provisions of subsections 2.1 and 2.2, above) as the trustee may deem necessary for the maintenance, support, health care and education of any descendant of the beneficiary; PROVIDED, HOWEVER, that (i) the needs of the beneficiary as specified above shall be the primary concern of the trustee, and (ii) the income of Trust B may not be used to limit, relieve or otherwise discharge, in whole or in part, the legal obligation of any individual to support and maintain any other individual. In determining the amounts to be distributed, used or applied for the beneficiary's descendants, the trustee shall not be required to treat each of such persons equally but shall be governed more by the particular needs and interests of each of them.

Section 3. Encroachment on Principal During Lifetime of Beneficiary

3.1   The trustee may, in the trustee's sole discretion, encroach upon the principal of Trust A and Trust B (which is not withdrawable by the beneficiary or by the beneficiary's legal representative pursuant to the provisions of subsections 1.2.a, 1.2.b, 2.1 and 2.2, above) for the maintenance, support, education and health care of the beneficiary in the beneficiary's accustomed manner of living; PROVIDED, HOWEVER, that the principal of Trust A and Trust B may not be used to limit, relieve or otherwise discharge, in whole or in part, the legal obligation of any individual to support and maintain the beneficiary.

3.2   In addition, the trustee may, in the trustee's sole discretion, encroach upon the principal of Trust B (which is not withdrawable by the beneficiary or by the beneficiary's legal representative pursuant to the provisions of subsections 2.1 and 2.2, above) for the maintenance, support, education and health care of any descendant of the beneficiary; PROVIDED, HOWEVER, that (i) the needs of the beneficiary as specified in subsection 3.1, above, shall be the primary concern of the trustee, and (ii) the principal of Trust B may not be used to discharge, relieve or limit, wholly or partially, the legal obligation of any individual to support and maintain any other individual.   In determining the amounts to be distributed, used or applied for the beneficiary's descendants, the trustee shall not be required to treat each of such persons equally but shall be governed more by the particular needs and interests of each of them.

3.3   In addition, if the trustee shall at any time during the term of Trust A and Trust B desire to purchase any additional interest in an "S corporation," the trustee of Trust B shall encroach upon the principal of Trust B (which is not withdrawable by the beneficiary or by the beneficiary's legal representative pursuant to the provisions of subsections 2.1 and 2.2, above) and distribute to the trustee of Trust A any funds which the trustee of Trust A shall deem necessary for such purpose.

Section 4.   Investment in Business of Beneficiary

The trustee may, in the trustee's sole discretion, apply the principal of the trust (which is not withdrawable by the beneficiary or by the beneficiary's legal representative pursuant to the provisions of Sections 1 and 2, above) for the purpose of investing in a business or profession operated by, or to be operated by, the beneficiary or the beneficiary's spouse and owned or to be owned by the trust and/or may make secured or unsecured loans of principal (which is not withdrawable by the beneficiary or by the beneficiary's legal representative pursuant to the provisions of Sections 1 and 2, above) to the beneficiary for the purpose of enabling the beneficiary to purchase, start up or invest in a business or profession operated by, or to be operated by, the beneficiary or the beneficiary's spouse and owned or to be owned by the beneficiary.

Section 5.   Acquisition of Residence for Beneficiary

The trustee may, in the trustee's sole discretion,

apply the principal of the trust (which is not withdrawable by the beneficiary or by the beneficiary's legal representative pursuant to the provisions of Sections 1 and 2, above) for the purpose of purchasing a home to be owned by the trust and used and occupied by the beneficiary and/or may make secured or unsecured loans of principal (which is not withdrawable by the beneficiary or by the beneficiary's legal representative pursuant to the provisions of Sections 1 and 2, above) to the beneficiary for the purpose of enabling the beneficiary to purchase a home to be used and occupied by the beneficiary. In the case of a home owned by the trust, the trustee may pay and charge to the income or principal account, or partly to each, in the trustee's sole discretion, the taxes, insurance payments, maintenance costs and other expenses required in order to keep such residence in proper repair and free of liens.

Section 6. Distribution of Principal at Death of Beneficiary

6.1   Upon the death of the beneficiary, all of the accrued and undistributed income of Trust A shall be distributed to the then acting trustee or trustees under any revocable trust established by the beneficiary during the beneficiary's lifetime, to be held and distributed by said trustee or trustees pursuant to the provisions of the instrument establishing said revocable trust; PROVIDED, HOWEVER, that if no such revocable trust shall be in existence at the time of the beneficiary's death, or if the foregoing provisions of this subsection 6.1 shall disqualify the trust from qualifying as a

"Qualified Subchapter S Trust" under Section 1361(d) of the Internal Revenue Code, or any successor section thereto, all of the accrued and undistributed income of the trust shall be distributed to the beneficiary's domiciliary probate estate.

6.2 Upon the death of the beneficiary, and except as otherwise provided in Section __ of ARTICLE __ hereof, all of the remaining assets of the trust which are not disposed of pursuant to the provisions of subsection 6.1, above, including the principal of Trust A and both the principal and accumulated and undistributed income of Trust B, shall be distributed to or among the beneficiary's surviving spouse and the grantors' descendants (other than the beneficiary), in trust or otherwise, and in such proportions, as shall be designated by the beneficiary by and in the beneficiary's Last Will and Testament (having the most recent date of execution by the beneficiary) and which is filed with the probate court of the relevant jurisdiction within six (6) months following the beneficiary's death, but if such Last Will and Testament shall be contested within the aforementioned six (6) month period, then as shall be designated in the beneficiary's Last Will and Testament which is finally admitted to probate after the period for contesting the beneficiary's Last Will and Testament has expired, and referring specifically to this provision, excluding, however, the beneficiary, the beneficiary's estate, the beneficiary's creditors and the creditors of the beneficiary's estate; PROVIDED, HOWEVER, if the beneficiary is survived by one or more descendants, no more than fifty percent (50%) of such remaining trust assets may be appointed to or in trust for the benefit of the beneficiary's surviving spouse. In addition, if the beneficiary is not survived by a surviving spouse (as that term is defined for purposes of Section 2056 of the Internal Revenue Code, or any successor section thereto, or for purposes of the law of the state or other jurisdiction in which the beneficiary was domiciled at the time of his or her death, if said state or other jurisdiction has an estate or inheritance tax in effect at the time of the beneficiary's death), then to the extent it will not result in the beneficiary's estate being liable for any federal or state estate or inheritance taxes, and except as otherwise provided in Section __ of ARTICLE __ hereof, the beneficiary shall also have the power to appoint those remaining trust assets, if any, beginning with the asset or assets having the greatest amount of built-in appreciation (calculated by subtracting the trust's income tax basis from the fair market value on the date of death of the beneficiary), as a percentage of the fair market value of such asset or assets on the date of death of the beneficiary, to the creditors of the beneficiary's estate (or to the beneficiary's estate if the power to distribute such assets to the creditors of the beneficiary's estate is not sufficient to include su assets in the beneficiary's estate for federal estate tax purposes), utilizing the same appointment procedure described immediately above; PROVIDED, HOWEVER, that if this trust has been or will be divided into two separate trusts for federal generation-skipping transfer tax purposes, the beneficiary's aforesaid general power of appointment shall apply (i) first to the trust having an inclusion ratio, as defined in Section 2642(a) of the Internal Revenue Code, or any successor section thereto, of other than zero, but only to the extent such trust is not otherwise already includible in the beneficiary's estate for federal or state estate or inheritance tax purposes, pursuant to the other provisions of this trust instrument, and (ii) next to the trust having an inclusion ratio, as defined in Section 2642(a) of the Internal Revenue Code, or any successor section thereto, of zero; PROVIDED FURTHER, HOWEVER, that if the beneficiary is the beneficiary of more than one trust (including but not limited to Trust A and Trust B under this ARTICLE) which includes a provision similar to this sentence, the extent of the foregoing power of appointment shall be reduced by multiplying the value of the assets otherwise subject to the foregoing power of appointment by a fraction the numerator of which shall equal the value of the assets otherwise subject to the foregoing power of appointment and the denominator of which shall equal the value of all assets subject to the foregoing and to the similar power(s) of appointment, the intent being that under no circumstance shall the beneficiary's estate be liable for any federal or state estate or inheritance tax as a consequence of the foregoing power of appointment. If the beneficiary is survived by a surviving spouse (as that term is defined for purposes of Section 2056 of the Internal Revenue Code, or any successor section thereto, or for purposes of the law of the state or other jurisdiction in which the beneficiary was domiciled at the time of his or her death, if said state or other jurisdiction has an estate or inheritance tax in effect at the time of the beneficiary's death), the beneficiary shall only possess the power of appointment described in the immediately preceding sentence to the same or lesser extent that the trustee (other than the beneficiary and other than a trustee who is "related or subordinate" to the beneficiary within the meaning of current Section 672(c) of the Internal Revenue Code (substituting "the beneficiary" for "the grantor" in said Section)) shall direct by instrument in writing filed with the trust during the beneficiary's lifetime and not revoked by said trustee prior to the beneficiary's death; PROVIDED, HOWEVER, that the trustee shall not possess the aforedescribed power to direct if the beneficiary appointed the trustee who or which possesses the aforedescribed power to direct, and if as a consequence the beneficiary is deemed to possess the aforedescribed power to direct for federal or state estate tax, gift tax, generation-skipping transfer tax, inheritance tax or other transfer tax purposes. In exercising said trustee's broad discretionary power in determining whether and to what extent the beneficiary shall possess the aforesaid power of appointment if the beneficiary is survived by a surviving spouse, said trustee shall be primarily concerned with minimizing overall income and transfer taxes to the beneficiary's estate, to the beneficiary's surviving spouse's estate, and to recipients of the trust assets after the beneficiary's death.

     6.3   Upon the death of the beneficiary, all of the remaining assets of the trust estate which are not disposed of pursuant to the provisions of subsection 6.1, above, or effectively appointed by the beneficiary pursuant to the provisions of subsection 6.2, above, shall be distributed.

Chapter 7

Optimum Gift and Valuation Discount Planning

When large gifting is involved, the typical goals of optimum gift planning are to cause a significant reduction in the size of the client's taxable estate at death, but while also minimizing income taxes, protecting the gifted assets from lawsuits, and maintaining maximum control over and even an economic interest in the gifted assets. The following are some examples of how these optimum estate planning goals can be achieved in a large gift environment. As a result of the 2016 Presidential, Senate and House elections, it is possible that the federal estate tax could be repealed in 2017. If this should happen, and there is not a federal gift tax penalty involved, for large estates the focus will be on gifting to irrevocable trusts in order to, in effect, "grandfather" the transferred assets from federal estate tax as long as the applicable rule against perpetuities period will allow.

WRAP Trust

The WRAP Trust has been around for approximately 20 years.[65] It is an irrevocable trust established for the benefit of the client's spouse and/or other heirs, but with economic benefits indirectly retained by the client. The letters W.R.A.P. stand for Wealth, Retirement and Asset Protection.

The trust is drafted so that the client is treated as the complete owner of the income and principal of the trust for federal income tax purposes, under the principles discussed in Chapter 2, but the trust corpus is still excluded from the client's gross estate for estate tax purposes. Normally this is accomplished utilizing a power to substitute principal under Section 675(4) of the Code.[66]

The trust can be funded with a life insurance policy on the client's life or with any other combination of assets. If the trust is funded with a survivorship or second-to-die policy, neither spouse should be a trustee or beneficiary of the trust. The trust also includes typical *Crummey* withdrawal powers in order to maximize the amount which may be gifted to the trust on a transfer tax-free basis.

---

65. *See, e.g.,* James G. Blase, The WRAP Trust™, Journal of the American Society of CLU & ChFC, Vol. LI, No. 5 (September 1997), at page 92.

66. *See* Rev. Rul. 2008-22, 2008-1 C.B. 796; Rev. Rul. 2011-28, 2011-2 C.B. 830.

Indirect control of the trust corpus is achieved if the client's spouse is the trustee. For further control, the grantor also retains the right to remove and replace the trustee with an independent trustee.[67] Trust assets are removed from the client's gross estate, and the client may even decide to pay the income taxes on the trust income (including capital gains), for further estate tax leveraging. As an irrevocable trust without any direct economic interest in the grantor, the trust corpus is also protected from the grantor's creditors.

Although the grantor's spouse can be a beneficiary of the trust (the so-called "spousal access" feature, discussed below), a better alternative may be for the grantor to borrow from the trust, because bona fide loans potentially even further reduce the size of the grantor's gross estate at death, i.e., by the total amount of the estate tax deductible debt owed back to the trust, which is essentially the grantor's family. Given the IRS' position that the grantor may retain the right to remove and replace the trustee with an independent trustee, the need to possess an actual right to borrow from the trust is negated. Annual interest payments on the loans are really no more than disguised gifts, since they are ignored for both income and gift tax purposes.

If the trust is funded with one or more life insurance policies on the life of the grantor, loans to the grantor can be made by the trustee taking withdrawals or loans from the policy, and "re-lending" these funds to the grantor. The WRAP Trust thus becomes an outstanding vehicle for allowing

---

67. Rev. Rul 95-58, 1995-2 C.B. 191.

a grantor-insured to remove the death benefit of a policy on his or her life from his or her gross estate, while still retaining access to the policy's cash value. What is more, the access is on an estate tax leveraged basis, because the benefit is received in the form of estate tax deducible loans from the trust.

The assets of the trust, including any life insurance policy, are protected from creditors because the grantor retains no direct economic interest in the trust. However, if the grantor does borrow from the trust, he or she will typically be required to secure these loans with other assets, e.g., with a mortgage on the grantor's residence, thereby creating a level of asset protection for the grantor's assets owned outside of the trust, also.

Double Spousal Access Trusts ("DSATs")

Many married couple clients utilize all or a portion of their lifetime $5.5 gift tax exemptions by transferring assets to a so-called "spousal access trust" (or "SAT," for short), with the goal of moving all growth in the trust assets outside of their taxable estates, while indirectly maintaining an economic interest in the trust assets, i.e., through the non-transferor spouse. For some, the goal is to double the amount of the current gift and corresponding indirect economic benefit, to up to $11 million. The problem comes in attempting to accomplish this lofty goal without violating the Supreme Court's reciprocal trust doctrine.

Reciprocal Trusts

It is of course a simple matter for one spouse to establish a $5.5 million irrevocable SAT for his or her spouse, and for the other spouse to establish a $5.5 million trust or trusts for the benefit of the children. But for many married couple clients, however, this plan is not satisfactory, because it does not allow spousal access to the income or principal from the second trust. These couples then ask the logical next question: "Why can't we each just establish a reciprocal SAT for the other spouse, with up to $5.5 million in trust assets each?"

The problem is that the U.S. Supreme Court ruled against these type of "reciprocal trust arrangements" in 1969, in its Estate of Grace decision,[68] holding that the trusts were includible in the spouses' gross estates under Section 2036 of the Internal Revenue Code. Although many creative estate planning attorneys have devised a variety of techniques for married couples to establish reciprocal trust arrangements without running afoul of the Supreme Court's 1969 decision, many other estate planning attorneys view any type of lifetime reciprocal trust arrangement for their married couple clients as risky from a federal estate tax perspective. As the attorney authors of one recent reciprocal trust doctrine article summarized the situation: "There's no clearly defined line or

---

68. United States v. Estate of Joseph P. Grace, 395 U.S. 316 (1969).

291

safe harbor as to what constitutes a sufficient difference between two trusts to avoid the reciprocal trust doctrine."[69]

Gift-Splitting

If the clients are not enamored with the possibility that their reciprocal gifting plan may fail in the end, the next logical question which presents itself is whether the husband or wife may transfer up to $11 million in assets to a trust for the benefit of his or her spouse and descendants, and then have his or her spouse consent to gift-splitting on the couples' federal gift tax returns for the calendar year, thus allowing the transfer to be treated as though each of the spouses made a gift of up to $5.5 million. If this plan were to work, as long as the "transferee spouse" is living the couple will have access to the trust assets.

Unfortunately, the short answer to this question is that the Internal Revenue Code only allows spouses to "gift-split" on gifts made to persons other than the transferor's spouse,[70] and in general a gift by the transferor spouse to a trust which benefits both the other spouse and third parties, is not a gift to "other than the transferor's spouse."[71]

---

69. Steiner and Shenkman, "Beware of the Reciprocal Trust Doctrine," April, 2012 issue of Trusts & Estates 14 at 17.

70. I.R.C. § 2513(a)(1).

71. This point was raised by the attorney authors of the article cited in footnote 70, *supra*, and their proposed solution was to attempt to draft reciprocal trusts which did not run afoul of the Supreme Court's decision in *Grace*. Steiner and Shenkman, *supra* at 14.

DSAT Design

Enter the double spousal access trust, or DSAT. Here is an example of how the DSAT would operate, assuming the husband is the transferor spouse:

- Husband ("H") transfers up to $11 million worth of assets to an irrevocable trust for the benefit of his wife and children (and grandchildren, if any).

- The couples' children (and grandchildren, if any), but not the wife, are each granted an immediate "Crummey" withdrawal power over an equal percentage of the entire $11 million transfer.

- 30 days after the transfer, each of the Crummey withdrawal rights lapse as to five percent of the then current value of the trust.[72]

---

72. Per Section 25.2514-3(c)(4) of the federal gift tax regulations: "Section 2514(e) provides that a lapse during any calendar year is considered as a release so as to be subject to the gift tax only to the extent that the property which could have been appointed by exercise of the lapsed power of appointment exceeds the greater of (i) $5,000, or (ii) 5 percent of the aggregate value, at the time of the lapse, of the assets out of which, or the proceeds of which, the exercise of the lapsed power could be satisfied. For example, if an individual has a noncumulative right to withdraw $10,000 a year from the principal of a trust fund, the failure to exercise this right of withdrawal in a particular year will not constitute a gift if the fund at the end of the year equals or exceeds $200,000. If, however, at the end of the particular year the fund should be worth only $100,000, the failure to exercise the power will be considered a gift to the

- Assuming the first lapse occurred in 2017, on January 31, 2018, the Crummey withdrawal powers each lapse as to another five percent.

- This same lapsing pattern continues on January 31 of each succeeding year, until Crummey powers in the up to $11 million worth of assets transferred to the DSAT no longer exist.

- During the entire period of the DSAT, income and principal will be available to both the wife and to the children (and grandchildren, if any), to the extent not subject to the unlapsed portion of the Crummey withdrawal powers. Thus, if we assume the couple has 10 children and grandchildren, after the first partial lapse of the Crummey withdrawal powers in 30 days, $5.5 million of the $11 million will be fully available for use by the wife, as trustee, and January 31, 2018, the second $5.5 million will be fully available to her. Of course, prior to the full lapse of all of the Crummey withdrawal powers, the remaining trust funds would also be available, though to the children (and grandchildren, if any), i.e., via exercise of the unlapsed portions of their withdrawal powers.

---

extent of $5,000, the excess of $10,000 over 5 percent of a fund of $100,000. Where the failure to exercise a power, such as a right of withdrawal, occurs in more than a single year, the value of the taxable transfer will be determined separately for each year."

294

- If this plan is implemented, the children (and adult grandchildren, if any) may wish to consider carrying additional umbrella liability insurance, at least during their Crummey withdrawal right period, because their Crummey withdrawal rights may be subject to the claims of potential future creditors.[73]

- Depending upon applicable state law, the Crummey withdrawal rights will most likely be considered separate property for marital or community property division purposes in the event any of the children or grandchildren should ever divorce,[74] but notwithstanding this fact if possible the children and grandchildren should cover this issue fully with a premarital agreement, if any of them should become engaged, or with a post-marital agreement, if any of them is already married.

- If the above plan is implemented, the husband and wife would each be able to apply the balance of his or her $5.5 million lifetime gift and GST

73. Note that for beneficiaries who are residents of a "domestic asset protection trust" state, it may be possible to structure the Crummey withdrawal rights so that the lapsed portions will thereafter be protected from the withdrawal power holder's creditors, at least outside of federal bankruptcy and its potential 10-year waiting period for transfers to a self-settled trust.

74. Although in many states the income off of separate property is considered marital or community property.

exemption to the DSAT, thus rendering the trust completely exempt from both estate and GST tax forever, or at least for the entire applicable rule against perpetuities period. Because the Crummey withdrawal powers in the hands of the children (and grandchildren, if any) would absorb the entire gift tax value of the $11 million transfer to the trust, the above-referenced limitations on gift-splitting which would normally govern when the transferor's spouse is a beneficiary of the trust, should not apply to transfers to a DSAT.[75]

- An obvious significant potential drawback to the DSAT approach is that, during the unlapsed

---

75. Per Section 25.2513-1(b)4) of the federal gift tax regulations: "If one spouse transferred property in part to his spouse and in part to third parties, the consent is effective with respect to the interest transferred to third parties only insofar as such interest is ascertainable at the time of the gift and hence severable from the interest transferred to his spouse. See § 25.2512-5 for the principles to be applied in the valuation of annuities, life estates, terms for years, remainders and reversions." *See also* Section 2632-1(b)(2)(i) of the federal generation-skipping transfer tax regulations: "An indirect skip is a transfer of property to a GST trust as defined in section 2632(c)(3)(B) provided that the transfer is subject to gift tax and does not qualify as a direct skip. In the case of an indirect skip made after December 31, 2000, to which section 2642(f) (relating to transfers subject to an estate tax inclusion period (ETIP)) does not apply, the transferor's unused GST exemption is automatically allocated to the property transferred (but not in excess of the fair market value of the property on the date of the transfer). The automatic allocation pursuant to this paragraph is effective whether or not a Form 709 is filed reporting the transfer, and is effective as of the date of the transfer to which it relates. An automatic allocation is irrevocable after the due date of the Form 709 for the calendar year in which the transfer is made."

portion of the Crummey withdrawal rights period, the children (and grandchildren, if any, including parents acting on behalf of minor grandchildren) will have the right to withdraw substantial assets from the trust. If this is a significant concern to the couple, the DSAT approach either should not be employed or, if it is utilized, should be modified so that Crummey withdrawal rights are eliminated or limited in the case of any particular child or grandchild where a significant concern exists or later arises. Note also that, as illustrated above, in many instances the Crummey withdrawal right period under a DSAT may actually only extend for a few years, which may reduce somewhat the couple's concern that one or more of the Crummey withdrawal right holders will exercise his or her withdrawal power.

• Another potential disadvantage to the DSAT approach is that, if any of the children or grandchildren should die during the Crummey withdrawal right period, the unlapsed portion of his or her Crummey withdrawal right will be subject to estate tax in his or her estate. Due to the $5.5 million federal estate tax exemption, however, combined with the significant annual lapsing of the Crummey withdrawal powers in the hands of the children and grandchildren, for practical purposes estate tax issues for the children and grandchildren may not be a significant concern in most instances, at least after a few years of the trust's existence. Nevertheless, cheap term (or reducing term) life insurance on the lives of the children and grandchildren can normally be easily purchased to insure over any short-term risk.

- A final obvious potential disadvantage of putting "all one's eggs in a single DSAT basket" occurs if the "transferee spouse" dies first, thus leaving the transferor spouse with none of the DSAT assets in which to live on. This concern can be alleviated by allowing the transferor spouse to borrow from the DSAT (for full value, of course) and/or by purchasing life insurance on the life of the transferee spouse.

- Of course, and as is always the case when one spouse gifts assets to an irrevocable trust which benefits the other spouse, in whole or in part, it is important that any assets being transferred by the transferor spouse be his or her independent assets, and not community property or jointly-owned assets. Also, in order to avoid the potential application of the step transaction doctrine, the gifted assets should not have been only very recently transferred into the independent name and ownership of the transferor spouse. A 90-day "waiting period" would appear to be normal recommended minimum time frame that the transferred assets should be in the independent name and ownership of the transferor spouse.

Additional Estate Tax Benefit of the DSAT

In addition to the significant non-tax benefit of maintaining "spousal access" to up to $11 million worth of assets in the DSAT, as opposed to only half of this amount, utilizing the DSAT eliminates any potential IRS estate tax inclusion argument based on the concept of "reciprocal trustees," which argument is especially worrisome when the same or similar property is transferred by the husband and wife to each of two separate trusts.[76] There is only one trust involved with a DSAT, and therefore only one set of trustees. In contrast, obviously two sets of trustees would be required if there is a second trust for the benefit of descendants only, or if there is an attempt at a "qualified" reciprocal trust arrangement. If either or both of the latter forms of trust arrangements are utilized, cautious clients would need to consider utilizing outside trustees for the second trust, in order to ward off any potential IRS "reciprocal trustee" attack.

Additional Wealth Shifting

Other estate planning techniques can be nicely combined with either the SAT or the DSAT to further enhance its estate tax benefits.

---

76. Estate of Bischoff v. Commissioner, 69 T.C. 9 32 (1977); Exchange Bank & Trust v. U.S., 694 F.2d 1261 (Fed. Cir. 1982); contra: Estate of Green, 68 F.3d 151 (6th Cir. 1995).

Addition of Low-Interest Rate Loan Element

Not to be overlooked when funding an SAT or DSAT is the ability to also take advantage of today's historically low IRS required minimum interest rates on intra-family loans. The IRS long term rate is currently in the low 2s, so locking into a long-term loan arrangement today could allow the SAT or DSAT to accumulate even more assets estate tax free. For example, if in August, 2012 the transferor spouse loans the trust $1,000,000 for 10 years at an interest rate of 2-1/4 percent, and the overall growth rate of the trust during this same 10-year period turned out to be 7 percent, the estate tax-exempt SAT or DSAT will have grown by another $600,000, for an additional federal estate tax savings of approximately $240,000 (at a 40 percent estate tax rate), assuming both spouses die at the expiration of the 10-year period.

Further, because an SAT (and especially a DSAT) allows for a larger initial funding of the trust, more funds can be loaned to the trust, at a low interest rate, without the fear that the IRS could successfully attack the loans as illusory. Thus, assuming the same 2-1/4 percent interest rate and 7 percent growth rate, a 10-year loan for $5 million could reduce federal estate taxes by an additional $1.35 million and a $10 million loan could reduce federal estate taxes by an additional $2.7 million, if both spouses were to die 10 years after the date of the loan.

Structuring SAT or DSAT as a Grantor Trust

In order to minimize both income and estate taxes, the SAT or DSAT should be structured as a complete grantor trust as to the transferor spouse, during the transferor spouse's lifetime. This step will not only avoid income taxes to the transferor spouse on any loan which he or she makes to the trust, but it will also allow the SAT or DSAT to grow estate tax free, unreduced by income taxes, while the transferor spouse's gross estate is reduced each year by the income taxes attributable to the income of the trust.

The SAT or DSAT should also be structured so that the surviving spouse, if any, is taxed on all or part of the income of the trust under the third-party grantor trust rules, and specifically under Section 678 of the Internal Revenue Code, which provides that a beneficiary of a trust is taxed on any trust income he or she has the sole right to withdraw. This additional trust drafting technique will preserve all or most of the estate tax free growth inside of the SAT or DSAT after the transferor spouse's death, while reducing the size of the surviving spouse's taxable estate by the income taxes he or she pays each year on the trust income which he or she chooses not withdraw.

Note that the use of the Section 678 third-party grantor trust technique requires a careful coordination with Section 2514 of the Internal Revenue Code, in order to ensure that the surviving spouse does not make a taxable gift when all or a portion of his or her income withdrawal rights lapse at the end of each year.

Note also that, in some situations, it may actually be advisable not to structure the trust as a grantor trust, in order to shift income to lower income tax bracket children and grandchildren. If the latter is the case, the trust needs to be carefully structured so as to not run afoul of the grantor trust rules (at least as to the ordinary income portion of the trust), e.g., by restricting the ability of the trustee to apply all or a portion of the trust income to or for the benefit of the transferee spouse.

Use of the DSAT technique should be considered by any married couple who is contemplating making a gift of more than $5.4 million (or at least more than either spouse's remaining lifetime gift tax exemption), but who is hesitant to do so without maintaining access to all or most of the gifted assets. As described above, the only significant potential disadvantage of the DSAT which cannot be easily solved (in addition to the fact that the couple may divorce or the transferee spouse may die prematurely) concerns the ability of the Crummey withdrawal power holders to withdraw significant trust funds, at least for a limited period of time. If the couple views this as a significant concern in their particular family, they should either not employ the DSAT device or, if the couple nevertheless still desires to utilize the DSAT, they should eliminate or limit Crummey withdrawal rights in the case of any particular child or grandchild where there is a significant concern.

Compare: Beneficiary Defective Inheritor's Trust

The beneficiary defective inheritor's trust ("BDIT") arguably offers the client even greater control, because, except in situations where the trust owns an insurance policy on his or her life, the client can serve as the trustee of trust and as direct beneficiary. It therefore provides the client with direct control and a direct economic benefit in the trust, rather than just indirect control and an indirect economic benefit, e.g., the spouse as trustee or at least an ability to change the trustee, and the spouse as beneficiary or the ability to receive loans from the trust.

The BDIT operates by having another individual (typically a parent) do the initial funding of the trust, granting the client a complete withdrawal power over the same. The trust therefore becomes a complete grantor trust to the client under Section 678 of the Code, and the grantor is therefore taxed on all of the income of the trust, including capital gains. The client's withdrawal power over the trust corpus apparently lapses annually, under a "5 and 5" lapsing provision; therefore only the portion of the withdrawal power which has not lapsed prior to the client's death is includible in his or her gross estate.

From there, the client sells assets to the income tax defective trust, for an installment note. Since obviously the promissory note and all accrued interest on the same is includible in the client's gross estate at death, the estate tax play is the hope for growth in the trust corpus which exceeds this amount, as well as the client's payment of the income tax on the trust's income, including capital gains.

There are several major admitted issues associated with the BDIT, however, among which are the following:

- The third party contribution to the BDIT will need to be considerable, in order to justify the sales by the client to the trust as not being disguised gifts with a retained interest. In today's uncertain stock market, assuming a 10 percent "liquid seed" is always going to pass muster with the IRS is risky, at best. There is some suggestion that it may be possible to have a third party or parties guarantee any installment notes of the trust, and then have the trustee obtain an appraisal for the gift tax value of those guarantees (which, in an uncertain stock market, could be considerable), and pay this fee to the guarantor. The point is there are a lot of issues here, and as a consequence there is absolutely no certainty that the arrangement will work. The estate tax stakes are considerable.

- The plan assumes that the annual lapses of the power of withdrawal will be treated as partial releases for purposes of Code Section 678(a)(2), and that therefore the client will continue to be taxed on all of the income of the trust. There is considerable risk here, too, especially since the related federal gift tax section of the Code, Section 2514(e), expressly provides that a lapse can be treated as a release, for gift tax purposes. If Congress felt the need to expressly treat certain lapses as a release for federal gift tax purposes, why did they not do the same for federal income tax purposes? Relying solely on a private letter ruling or rulings for authority in this area would appear troublesome, at best.

Therefore, when compared to either the WRAP Trust or the DSAT approaches for making larger gifts, the BDIT does not exclude as much from the client's taxable estate, i.e., because the accrued interest on the installment promissory notes must be included and any outstanding withdrawal powers will be included, and carries with its considerable more complexity, tax risks, and need for cooperation by others. Assuming direct control and economic benefit (i.e., as trustee and as direct beneficiary) vs indirect control (i.e., with the spouse as trustee and/or the ability to remove and replace the trustee) and economic benefit (i.e., through the spouse as beneficiary and/or the ability to take estate tax deductible loans from the trust) is vital enough to the client, he or she may be willing to incur the risks associated with the BDIT.

Impact of Proposed Valuation Regulations on Lifetime and Testamentary Gifting

The new proposed Internal Revenue Code Section 2704 proposed regulations[77] contain three sets of new rules aimed at family-controlled entities and gifting. As a result of the 2016 Presidential, Senate and House election results, it would appear likely that the final regulations will, at best, substantially deviate from the regulations in their currently proposed form.

---

77. 26 CFR Part 25 [REG-163113-02].

Nevertheless, here is a brief summary of each of these new sets of proposed rules.

Transfers Within Three Years Rule

The first set of new rules begins with an extension of the Tax Court's decision in *Estate of Murphy v. Commissioner.*[78] Rather than a subjective test relating to deathbed transfers of voting stock to achieve minority interest status, however, the Internal Revenue Service has chosen to impose a bright line "transfers within three years of death rule," similar to the rule for gifts of life insurance policies within three years of death of the lapse or release of a Section 2036-type retained interest within three years of death.[79] The only difference is that there doesn't appear to be an exception to the three-year rule for transfers for adequate and full consideration in money or money's worth.[80] If transfers within three years of death result in a lapse of a liquidation right in the transferor, the transferred shares will effectively be included in the transferor's gross estate for federal estate tax purposes.

Although one could argue it's questionable whether Congress granted the IRS authority to unilaterally add this new three-year rule, the IRS could just as easily argue that the new three-year rule represents nothing more than an easing of the already-imposed IRC rules, rather than an expansion of the

---

78. 60 T.C.M. 645 (1990).

79. Proposed Regulation Section 25.2704-1(c)(1).

80. Internal Revenue Code Section 2035(d).

same. IRC Section 2704(a)(2) provides:

(2) Amount of transfer

For purposes of paragraph (1), the amount determined under this paragraph is the excess (if any) of—

(A) the value of all interests in the entity held by the individual described in paragraph (1) immediately before the lapse (determined as if the voting and liquidation rights were nonlapsing), over

(B) the value of such interests immediately after the lapse.

Thus, because the transferor would have possessed the valuable right to liquidate the entity before the transfer of the interest, but as a result of the transfer, the transferees no longer retain the same right, the value of the lapsed right may be considered an additional transfer under the IRC. See, however, the discussion below, which challenges the IRS' ability to have the lapse treated as occurring at the transferor's date of death versus at the date of the actual lapse.

The proposed regulations also clarify that a transfer that results in the restriction or elimination of the transferee's ability to exercise the voting or liquidation rights that were associated with the interest while held by the transferor is a lapse of those rights. For example, the transfer of a partnership interest to an assignee that neither has nor may exercise the voting of liquidation rights of a partner is a lapse of the voting and liquidation rights associated with the transferred interest.[81]

Applicable Restrictions

Under the second set of new rules, state-imposed "applicable restrictions" on the ability to liquidate an entity that can be changed by family members are no longer excepted from the term. Thus, if state law provides that a limited partner doesn't have a right to have the partnership purchase his/her limited interest for fair value, but this aspect of the state law can be overridden by agreement among the family members, then the state law restriction is ignored for valuation purposes, and it's assumed that each family member possesses this liquidation right.

Further, even if the restriction is mandated by state law and couldn't be removed, it still won't be given effect for valuation purposes if either: (1) the state law restriction is limited to family-controlled entities, or (2) the state law provides an optional provision or an alternative statute for the creation and governance of the same type of entity that doesn't mandate the restriction.

---

81. Prop. Reg. Section 25.2704-1(a)(5).

Disregarded Restrictions

The basic concept of the third set of new rules is to go beyond the ability to liquidate itself and look at the value of what the interest holder would receive if they did liquidate their interest. Thus, these "disregarded restrictions" cover any restriction that: (1) limits the ability of the holder of the interest to liquidate the interest (this is, the potential overlap section); (2) limits the liquidation proceeds to an amount that's less than a "minimum value"; (3) defers payment of the liquidation proceeds for more than six months; or (4) allows for payment of the liquidation proceeds in any form other than cash or other property, other than certain secured notes. The "minimum value" of an interest is the net value of the entity multiplied by the interest's share of the entity.

Significantly, the preamble to the proposed regulations provides that: "if a restriction is disregarded under proposed §25.2704-3, the fair market value of the interest in the entity is determined assuming . . . any appropriate discounts or premiums," but also assuming the disregarded restrictions didn't exist, either in the governing documents or applicable law. Thus, it would appear that the proposed regulations haven't done away with lack of marketability and minority interest discounts in their entirety.

An "applicable restriction" is defined to mean "a limitation on the ability to liquidate the entity, in whole or in part (as opposed to a particular holder's interest in the entity), if, after the transfer, that limitation either lapses or may be removed by the transferor, the transferor's estate, and/or any member of the transferor's family, either alone or collectively."[82] A "disregarded restriction," on the other hand, is defined generally to include a restriction that's "a limitation on the ability to redeem or liquidate an interest in an entity . . . if the restriction, in whole or in part, either lapses after the transfer or can be removed by the transferor or any member of the transferor's family . . ., either alone or collectively."[83] A disregarded restriction is therefore one that places restrictions on the particular holder of the interest in the entity, rather than on the holders of the entity generally.

For purpose of determining whether the restriction can be removed by the transferor or any member of the transferor's family . . ., either alone or collectively," the proposed regulations disregard an interest held by a non-family member that: (1) has been held less than three years before the date of the transfer, (2) constitutes less than 10 percent of the value of all of the equity interests, (3) when combined with the interests of other non-family members constitutes less than 20 percent of the value of all the equity interests, or (4) lacks a right to put the interest to the entity and receive a minimum value.[84]

Similar to the applicable restriction rule, restrictions imposed under federal or state law won't constitute a "disregarded restriction" provided the law is one that may not be superseded with regard to a particular entity (whether by the

---

82. Prop. Reg. Section 25.2704-2(b)(1).

83. Prop. Reg. Section 25.2704-3(b)(1).

84. Prop. Reg. Section 25.2704-3(b)(4).

shareholders, partners, members and/or managers of the entity or otherwise) and isn't limited in its application to certain narrow classes of entities, particularly those types of entities (such as family-controlled entities) most likely to be subject to what is described in Section 2704.

Strategies to Prepare for Implementation of Proposed 2704 Regulations

The proposed regulations to Internal Revenue Code Section 2704, while generally retroactive to restrictions created after Oct. 8, 1990, apply only to lapses and transfers occurring on or after the date the proposed regulations are published as final regulations. The only exception is that the new rule on disregarded restrictions only applies to transfers occurring 30 or more days after the date the proposed regulations are published as final regulations. Thus, one obvious planning technique would be to transfer, either by gift or by sale (including sales to a trust that's "defective" for income tax purposes), affected interests before the date the proposed regulations become final. This would appear to include even interests that are newly created after the date of the proposed regulations.

As a consequence of the recent Presidential, Senate and House election results, it would appear likely that the final regulations will deviate substantially from their currently proposed form, and could actually be removed in their entirety. This factor is obviously relevant in advising clients on which actions to take, if any, in light of the (now lesser) possibility that the proposed regulations *could* become final soon, in roughly their current form.

Sales to a defective trust should be effective under the grandfathering sections of the proposed regulations despite the fact that grantor/seller will continue to be a holder of the entity interest for purposes of determining whether the grantor/seller and members of their family were or are in control of the entity.[85] That's because the relevant lapse or transfer of the interest to or for the benefit of a member of the transferor's family will have occurred prior to the date the regulations become final, which is all that's required under the proposed regulations' grandfathering rules. No lapse of rights in the interest or transfer of the interest occurs on or after the date the regulations become final.

Use of an Incomplete Gift Trust

Assuming the proposed regulations will eventually be finalized and upheld in substantially their current form, all future lapsing rights and restrictions on liquidation will need to somehow fall within their cracks. Here's a planning idea that shouldn't only avoid the proposed regulations, but also IRC Section 2704 completely.

The client first establishes and funds an irrevocable trust in which he retains no interest other than the exclusive lifetime and testamentary power to determine all distributions of

---

85. Internal Revenue Code Section 2704(c)(3); Treasury Regulations Section 25.2701-6(a)(4)(ii)(C).

principal or income to other persons, including the client's descendants. Because there's no completed gift on the establishment of the trust,[86] the rules of IRC Section 2702 don't apply.[87] To avoid having the client considered the owner of any trust assets for Section 2704 purposes, the trust document is drafted to eliminate any ability to distribute trust income or principal to or for the benefit of the client. The trust serves the additional important business purpose of insulating the trust assets from creditor attack in most states.

According to the proposed regulations, "[a]n individual, the individual's estate, and members of the individual's family are treated as also holding any interest held indirectly by such person through a corporation, partnership, trust, or other entity under the rules contained in §25.2701-6."[88] As applied to estates and trusts, Treasury Regulations Section 25.2701-6(a)(4)(i) includes the following attribution rules (emphasis supplied):

> A person is considered to hold an equity interest held by or for an estate or trust to the extent the person's beneficial interest therein may be satisfied by the equity interest held by the estate or trust, or the income or proceeds thereof, assuming the maximum exercise of discretion in favor of the person. A beneficiary of an estate or trust who cannot receive any distribution with

---

86. Treas. Regs. Section 25.2511-2(f).

87. IRC Section 2702(a)(3)(A)(i).

88. Proposed Regulations Section 25.2704-2(d).

respect to an equity interest held by the estate or trust, including the income therefrom or the proceeds from the disposition thereof, is not considered the holder of the equity interest. Thus, if stock held by a decedent's estate has been specifically bequeathed to one beneficiary and the residue of the estate has been bequeathed to other beneficiaries, the stock is considered held only by the beneficiary to whom it was specifically bequeathed. However, any person who may receive distributions from a trust is considered to hold an equity interest held by the trust if the distributions may be made from current or accumulated income from or the proceeds from the disposition of the equity interest, even though under the terms of the trust the interest can never be distributed to that person. This paragraph applies to any entity that is not classified as a corporation, an association taxable as a corporation, or a partnership for federal income tax purposes.

Also according to the regulations, "[a] person holds a beneficial interest in a trust or an estate so long as the person may receive distributions from the trust or estate other than payments for full and adequate consideration."[89] The grantor may not receive distributions from the type of "incomplete gift" trust described above.

The regulations add that "[a]n individual holds as equity interest held by or for a trust if the individual is considered an owner of the trust (a "grantor trust") under subpart E, part 1,

---

89. Treas. Regs. Section 25.2701-6(a)(4)(ii)(B).

subchapter J of the Internal Revenue Code (relating to grantors and others treated as substantial owners)."[90] It's therefore also necessary to structure transfers to the irrevocable trust, and the trust instrument itself, so that it doesn't run afoul of IRC Section 674, relating to powers to control beneficial enjoyment.

The easiest Section 674 exception to use will typically be the one found in Section 674(b)(5)(A), a power to distribute corpus "to or for a beneficiary or beneficiaries or to or for a class of beneficiaries (whether or not income beneficiaries) provided that the power is limited by a reasonably definite standard which is set forth in the trust instrument." Remembering that "a reasonably definite standard" isn't the same as an "ascertainable standard" applicable in the federal estate and gift tax context, if the trust document requires that all trust accounting income is to be added to corpus, and that corpus can only be distributed as the grantor (in a non-fiduciary capacity) directs for the education, support, maintenance or health of a beneficiary, for a beneficiary's reasonable support and comfort or to enable a beneficiary to maintain their accustomed standard of living[91], the grantor shouldn't be treated as an owner of any portion of the trust under subchapter J.

The gift should also be incomplete for federal gift tax purposes, in accordance with Treas. Regs. Section 25.2511-2(c): "A gift is also incomplete if and to the extent

---

90. Treas. Regs. Section 25.2701-6(a)(4)(ii)(C).

91. Treas. Regs. Section 1.674(b)-1(b)(5)(i).

that a reserved power gives the donor the power to name new beneficiaries or to change the interests of beneficiaries as between themselves, unless the power is a fiduciary power limited by a fixed or ascertainable standard" (emphasis supplied). One issue to bear in mind is that if the grantor only has one child and no other descendants, it will be necessary to broaden the class of permissible beneficiaries and/or remaindermen of the trust (other than the grantor or the grantor's spouse, or their respective estates, creditors or creditors of their estates), to satisfy the requirements of this section of the regulations.

A principal requirement of Section 2704(a) is that: "the individual holding such right immediately before the lapse and members of such individual's family hold, both before and after the lapse, control of the entity." Similarly, a primary requirement of Section 2704(b) is that "the transferor and members of the transferor's family hold, immediately before the transfer, control of the entity." As a consequence of the IRS' above-outlined trust attribution rules, if a corporate or partnership interest is owned inside the type of incomplete gift trust described above, for Section 2704 purposes, no portion of the interest is owned by the grantor of the trust. The Section 2704(a) lapsing rules and the Section 2704(b) applicable and disregarded restriction rules therefore can't apply when a transfer of the interests is deemed made by the grantor, either for gift tax purposes as a result of the lapse, exercise or release of the grantor's retained powers or for estate tax purposes as a result of a completed transfer of an interest included in the grantor's gross under IRC Section 2038.

The individual's spouse shouldn't be a beneficiary of the trust under this formulation, because the application of IRC Section 677 could then render the grantor an owner of the trust under subchapter J. However, either the individual or the individual's spouse should be able to receive bona fide loans from the trust, since fair market value loans wouldn't constitute a beneficial interest in the trust. The drafter would only need to be careful not to violate any of the defective loan provisions of IRC Section 675.

It may be postulated: If a partial exercise or release (and therefore a completed gift) occurs during the grantor's lifetime, Section 2702 applies. However, Section 2702(d) provides: "In the case of a transfer of an income or remainder interest with respect to a specified portion of the property in a trust, only such portion shall be taken into account in applying this section to such transfer." (Emphasis supplied) Under the above-described incomplete gift trust arrangement, neither the grantor nor any applicable family member will have retained any interest in the transferred portion, and therefore Section 2702 doesn't apply to the deemed transfer or to the remaining portion of the trust in which the grantor hasn't made a completed gift.

Treas. Regs. Section 25.2511-2(f) also makes clear that "[t]he relinquishment or termination of a power to change the beneficiaries of transferred property, occurring otherwise than by the death of the donor (the statute being confined to transfers by living donors) is regarded as the event which completes the gift and causes the tax to apply." Section 2702 therefore can't apply at the death of the grantor, since the section only applies to lifetime gifts.

What does this all mean for Section 2704 purposes and the proposed regulations? It means simply that if the corporation or partnership arrangement contemplated by Section 2704 and the proposed and final Section 2704 regulations is established by a trust in which the grantor owns no ability to receive distributions of either income or principal, Sections 2704(a) and (b) can't apply to gifts or estate tax inclusion with respect to the grantor's interest in the trust. Thus, although there will still be a taxable gift by the grantor when he exercises or releases his retained rights, or estate tax inclusion when his retained rights lapse at death, the valuation of the gifts of the included interest shouldn't be limited by the rules under Section 2704, because the interests aren't considered owned by the grantor for purposes of determining the requisite Section 2704 concurrent control in the grantor and their family.

Of course, efforts should be made to avoid any potential step-transaction argument stemming from situations in which, for example, the client transfers his entity interest to the incomplete gift trust, and then follows the transfer up shortly thereafter by exercising his retained power to direct that trust assets be distributed for the trust beneficiaries' reasonable support and comfort, or the client transfers his interest to the incomplete gift trust in contemplation of death.[92] Subject to the step-transaction doctrine, the mere exercise or release of the client's retained powers within three years of his death

---

92. Note the distinction between the latter situation and Internal Revenue Service's proposed rule for transfers within three years of the transferor's death that result in the lapse of a voting or liquidation right. In the latter situation, no transfer occurs during the decedent's lifetime.

shouldn't run afoul of the IRS' proposed rule treating a lapse of a voting or liquidation rights that results from a transfer that occurs within three years of the decedent's death as a lapse which occurs on the date of the transferor's death. The reason for this conclusion is that, immediately before the exercise or release of the client's retained powers (that is, the transfer which potentially resulted in the loss of voting or liquidation rights), the client and his family didn't hold control of the entity.[93]

Significant Portions of the Proposed Regulations are Invalid

The "and/or" Addition

A potential issue with the type of incomplete gift trust discussed above arises because the IRS has attempted to add regulations that change the law so that no longer must the control of the entity immediately before the lapse or transfer be in the hands of the transferor and members of their family, as required by both Internal Revenue Code Section 2704(a) and 2704(b), but instead control immediately before the transfer need only be in "the transferor and/or members of the transferor's family."[94] The Conference Committee Report that accompanied the passage of IRC Section 2704 in 1990 was

---

93. Treas. Regs. Section 25.2704-1(a)(1). ("This section applies only if the entity is controlled by the holder and members of the holder's family immediately before and after the lapse.")

94. Proposed Regulations Section 25.2704-2(a). Prop. Reg. Section 25.2704-1(a)(1).

very specific in including the requirement that control of the corporation or partnership immediately before the lapse or transfer be in "the transferor and family members,"[95] and included this concurrent arrangement in all three of its examples illustrating the application of IRC Section 2704(a) and 2704(b):

> Example 6—Parent and Child control a corporation. Parent's stock has a voting right that lapses on Parent's death. Under the conference agreement, Parent's stock is valued for Federal estate tax purposes as if the voting right of the parent's stock were nonlapsing.

> Example 7—Father and Child each own general and limited interests in a partnership. The general partnership interest carries with it the right to liquidate the partnership; the limited partnership interest has no such right. The liquidation right associated with the general partnership interest lapses after 10 years. Under the conference agreement, there is a gift at the time of the lapse equal to the excess of (1) the value of Father's partnership interests determined as if he held the right to liquidate over (2) the value of such interests determined as if he did not hold such right.

> Example 8—Mother and Son are partners in a two-person partnership. The partnership agreement provides that the partnership cannot be terminated. Mother dies and leaves her partnership interest to

---

95. Conference Committee Report at p. 158. (emphasis supplied).

Daughter. As the sole partners, Daughter and Son acting together could remove the restriction on partnership termination. Under the conference agreement, the value of Mother's partnership interest in her estate is determined without regard to the restriction. Such value would be adjusted to reflect any appropriate fragmentation discount.[96]

The Internal Revenue Service has clearly exceeded its regulatory authority by changing the Congressionally-imposed "and" to an IRS-imposed "and/or." Congress granted the IRS certain regulatory authority in Section 2704(b)(4):

The Secretary may by regulations provide that other restrictions shall be disregarded in determining the value of the transfer of any interest in a corporation or partnership to a member of the transferor's family if such restriction has the effect of reducing the value of the transferred interest for purposes of this subtitle but does not ultimately reduce the value of such interest to the transferee.

Congress thus gave the IRS authority to disregard other restrictions, which the IRS clearly has done by proposing new Treasury Regulations Section 25.2704-3, but Congress didn't grant the IRS authority to make other unilateral changes to the IRC, which it clearly has also done by changing the key concurrent word "and" to the concurrent or disjunctive phrase "and/or."

Ibid., at pp. 157-158. (emphasis supplied).

Evidence that Congress knew how to employ the concurrent and disjunctive "and/or" concept can be found in the separate IRC Section 2704(b)(2)(B)(ii), which deals with the situation after the transfer: "The transferor or any member of the transferor's family, either alone or collectively, has the right after such transfer to remove, in whole or in part, the restriction." (emphasis supplied) The IRS itself has also demonstrated that it understands the difference between the "immediately before" and "after" sections and the use of the word "and" versus the phrase "and/or," by choosing to employ the following language in proposed regulation Section 25.2704-2(b)(1): ". . . if, after the transfer, that limitation either lapses or may be removed by the transferor, the transferor's estate, and/or any member of the transferor's family, either alone or collectively." (emphasis supplied)

The preamble to the proposed regulations likewise illustrates that the IRS recognizes that Congress intended the word "and" to mean concurrent ownership only (emphasis supplied):

The legislative history of section 2704 states that the provision is intended, in part, to prevent results similar to that in Estate of Harrison v. Commissioner, T.C. Memo. 1987-8 . . . In Harrison, the decedent and two of his children each held a general partner interest in a partnership immediately before the decedent's death. . . .

Thus, attempts to argue the *Chevron*[97] line of cases where the IRS is given broad authority in drafting regulations fall short in the instant case. While Section 2704 of the Internal Revenue Code grants the IRS limited "legislative" authority, the IRS has clearly exceeded its authority by issuing proposed regulations which not only exceed the scope of the IRS' legislative authority, but which also exceeds its general authority under the *Chevron* line of decisions to interpret ambiguous language in the Code.

Finally, note that the IRS' current "immediately before" regulations do not employ the proposed "and/or" wording, but rather track the Code's "and" wording.[98] Thus, for whatever the reasons, the decision was apparently made to change the concurrent word "and" to the concurrent and disjunctive phrase "and/or."

Lapse Within Three Years of Death Rule

Assume A owns 100 percent of a corporation and gifts 25 percent each to his three children, taking a minority interest discount for each of the three separate gifts (the transfer resulting in the lapse of voting and liquidation rights). A dies two years later owning the remaining 25 percent interest in the corporation, with no evidence that the transfer two years earlier

---

97. Chevron U.S.A. Inc. v. Natural Resources Defense Council Inc., 467 U.S. 837 (1984).

98. Treasury Regulations Section 25.2704-1(a)(1). Treas. Reg. Section 25.2704-2(a).

was in contemplation of A's death. In this situation, when only A controlled the corporation immediately before the lapse of the voting and liquidation rights (that is, the date A transferred the 25 percent interest each to A's three children), when there's no evidence that the transfer two years earlier was in contemplation of A's death, does the IRS have authority to unilaterally impose a new three-year rule treating the resulting lapse of the voting and liquidation rights as occurring at A's death, for purposes of IRC Section 2704(a)?

This question is relevant because immediately before the actual lapse date, only A was in control of the corporation, while at the time of A's death (that is, the "deemed" lapse date, under the proposed regulations), both A and A's children controlled the corporation. The IRS' only regulatory authority under Section 2704(a)(3) is to "apply this subsection to rights similar to voting and liquidation rights." (emphasis supplied) But the rights at issue here aren't rights "similar to" voting and liquidation rights; they are voting and liquidation rights. Considering a resulting lapse of voting and liquidation rights as a transfer under Section 2704(a) under the IRS' general grant of authority to render reasonable interpretations of the IRC isn't the issue, because such a construction of the IRC is at least arguable; deeming the lapse to have occurred at death, however, is a problem, because this construction constitutes an impermissible change in the IRC.

Therefore, if the IRS' proposed "three-year rule" is ultimately determined to constitute an invalid exercise of the IRS' regulatory power, lifetime gifts of minority interests by a transferor who is the sole owner of the entity, even if made within three years of the transferor's death, would not be subject to IRC Section 2704(a), because of the balance of the proposed regulations which do not tax other "resulting" lapses. A question remains whether IRC Section 2704(b) would apply, however, because although there is no applicable restriction on the transferor's ability to liquidate the entity or the transferor's interest therein at the time of the gifts, there are applicable restrictions in the hands of the transferees. An obvious relevant factor will be whether the above-discussed "and/or" change is valid.

Disregarded Restrictions Generally

The entire proposed regulation (PR) Section 25.2704-3 on disregarded restrictions misses a vital requirement of the enabling Internal Revenue Code Section 2704(b)(4). That section includes the prerequisite that the disregarded restriction "not ultimately reduce the value of such interest to the transferee." In each of the four situations described in PR subparagraphs (i) through (iv) of Section 25.2704-3(b)(1) involving various limitations on the ability to redeem or liquidate an interest in any entity, however, the value of the interest in the transferee is ultimately reduced. Therefore, all of the "disregarded restrictions" listed in PR Section 25.2704-3 are invalid.

Removal of Applicable and Disregarded Restrictions

The PRs incorrectly extend the attribution rules (including the trust attribution rules) referenced at Section

2704(c)(3) to the requirement that the restrictions must be removable after the transfer by the transferor and/or members of the transferor's family.

Section 2704(c)(3) provides that "[t]he [attribution] rule of section 2701(e)(3) shall apply for purposes of determining the interests held by any individual." (Emphasis supplied.) The "interests held by any individual" language is referenced in the IRC Sections 2704(a)(1)(B) and (b)(1)(B) prerequisites that the transferor and members of the transferor's family "hold" control of the entity, and in the Section 2704(a)(2) determination of the value of the lapsed voting or liquidation right. This same "held" language isn't employed as part of the Section 2704(b)(2)(B)(ii) requirement that "[t]he transferor or any member of the transferor's family, either alone or collectively, has the right after such transfer to remove, in whole or in part, the restriction."

Thus, for example, if the limited entity interest is transferred, either during lifetime or at death, to an irrevocable trust that includes an independent trustee or co-trustee, how can it be said that: "[t]he transferor or any member of the transferor's family, either alone or collectively, has the right after such transfer to remove, in whole or in part, the restriction." To remove the restriction, the family members would need the consent of the independent trustee or co-trustee. There's nothing in the IRC that authorizes a "deemed" or "attributed" consent concept in the right to remove the restriction context.

Disregarding Nominal Interests Held by Nonfamily Members

Although the IRS arguably has the authority to disregard de minimis or nominal ownership interests generally, the question is whether the proposed regulations have exceeded this authority. The three-year, 10 percent, 20 percent and put right requirements add up to a very significant interest indeed, far exceeding what's generally thought to be a de minimis or nominal interest.

The Future of Discount Planning

Assuming the proposed Internal Revenue Code Section 2704 regulations are eventually finalized and upheld in substantially their current form, at first blush it would appear that future estate and gift tax discount planning should return to its original form of creating marketability and minority interest discounts for transferred and retained interests. That's because the preamble to the proposed regulations implies that the Internal Revenue Service will continue to honor the minority and lack of marketability discounts. The Conference Committee Report that accompanied the passage of Section 2704 in 1990 also makes it abundantly clear that "[t]hese rules do not affect minority discounts or other discounts available under present law."[99]

99. Conference Committee Report at p. 157.

The open question, however, will be determining the level of these discounts in the future. Because family members could always agree, even as shareholders in a corporation, to liquidate the entity, would the general state law majority, supermajority or unanimous shareholder voting requirements for liquidation now constitute "applicable restrictions" or "disregarded restrictions?" The proposed regulations for both applicable restrictions and disregarded restrictions imply that this is the case: "The manner in which the restriction may be removed is irrelevant for [the purpose of determining whether the ability to remove the restriction is held by any one or more family members], whether by voting, taking other action authorized by the governing documents or applicable local law, . . . terminating the entity, or otherwise."[100]

It would thus appear that the only type of entity that will benefit significantly from a lack of marketability or minority interest discount in the future will be one that is engaged in an active operation, that is, where the going concern value of the interest is significantly greater than its liquidation value. The entity's "liquidation value per unit" may be its future floor estate and gift tax value, or its "minimum value," employing the IRS' new term.

Per the proposed regulations, "[i]f a restriction is disregarded under this section, the fair market value of the transferred interest is determined under generally applicable valuation principles as if the disregarded restriction does not exist in the governing documents, local law, or otherwise."

---

100. Proposed Regulations Sections 25.2704-2(b)(3), 25.2704-3(b)(3) (emphasis supplied).

Thus, for example, as a 20% shareholder I may be deemed to have received a 20% interest in a photocopy machine. But as a minority owner of the machine, what can I really do with it?

Finally, and perhaps most importantly, it would now appear likely that, as a direct consequence of the recent Presidential, Senate and House elections, valuation discount planning will be restored to its current status, and the federal estate tax may actually be repealed.

Epilogue

"The Trump Effect"

OK, now scratch everything I just wrote, as President Trump plans to fire the federal estate, gift and generation-skipping transfer taxes. Just kidding - mostly at least.

As alluded to at various places throughout this text, President Trump and the Republican Party are proposing tax reduction in both the estate tax and income tax areas. The purpose of this chapter is to illustrate how these proposals, if passed, could ultimately affect the detailed discussion in the previous chapters of the book, and to provide some direction regarding how advisors should plan, today, while we await the eventual Congressional action.

As a preliminary matter, it would appear axiomatic that any estate plan prepared in the wake of tax reform anticipate not only the tax proposals which are currently on the table, but also other potential changes occurring during future administrations - even the possibility that the estate tax could return to the $3.5 million exemption and 50% or higher tax rate levels! And while President Trump has proposed the outright repeal of the federal estate tax, what about the potential for the return of carryover income tax basis at certain estate levels or, even worse, the potential for income tax on built-in gains at the client's death - which bring backs into play life insurance as a tax-efficient vehicle for paying these taxes? Finally, of course state estate and inheritances tax issues cannot be ignored, even if the federal estate tax were to be repealed.

Why are we even considering all of these various factors, when nothing has even been passed yet? As already alluded to above, there are several reasons. First, what happens if one of our clients were to become incapacitated now, but live until a point when the new laws have taken effect? And what if one spouse in a married couple dies before the laws are changed, but the surviving spouse is alive after the laws are changed, and as a consequence ends up being faced with provisions in a bypass or marital trust which may no longer make tax sense?

Is it even fair to "double bill" clients and have them pay for one plan today, with no conditional provision being made for potential tax laws which have already been proposed, only to make them pay again in 2018, after the changes take effect? Finally, is it arguably malpractice to wait until the already outlined changes take effect, say on December 31, 2017, and then argue that it is impossible for me to now immediately change hundreds of clients' estate plans, when at least we could be building these provisions in for clients who are doing their estate planning today?

Planning for Married Couples and The Trump Effect

Beginning at page 25 of this text, we outline drafting language which can be utilized in anticipation of the potential repeal of the federal estate tax before the first spouse's death. The keys in this situation are to "lock in" estate tax repeal in the event the federal estate tax is repealed prior to the first's spouse death, but to do so in a flexible manner so that maximum income tax basis step-up can be preserved - not only at the first spouse to die's death, but also at the surviving spouse's death - without causing a potential unnecessary income tax on built-in gains at either spouse's death, and without causing estate taxes in the event the federal estate tax in reinstated prior to the first spouse's to die death and/or the surviving spouse's death.

Note that the included forms make reference to sections of the Code which existed only during the federal estate tax repeal year of 2010, not because we think these exact same Code sections will be reinstated during 2017, but rather because it is the best we can do, at this time. (Thus the included language: "or similar section.") If nothing similar to these sections gets passed again, and the federal estate tax is repealed, then everything just passes to the bypass trust, unless the trust document is further amended.

Again, why not just wait until the new law is actually passed to include this "conditional" form of drafting? The main reasons are that one of our clients may become incapacitated in the meantime, or the spouse may die and an irrevocable bypass trust may be established the terms of which may not make tax sense if the surviving spouse is alive after the rules are changed. More practically speaking, it will be impossible to amend hundreds of estate plans immediately, if an estate tax repeal law is passed, likely at the stroke of midnight on December 31.

Planning for Children and Other Non-Spouse Beneficiaries - The Trump Effect

It is doubtful that any legislation introduced by President Trump or by the Republican party will directly address the gross disparity in the current income tax treatment of trusts versus individuals. However, President Trump is at least calling for the lowering of the maximum individual income tax rate (and presumably, therefore the maximum trust rate) from 39.6% to 35%, eliminating the 5% penalty tax on dividends and capital gains, and eliminating of the 3.8% tax on net investment income.

It may therefore be best to clarify in the trust document that the special net investment income and dividend/capital gains minimization provisions are applicable *only* in the event the applicable sections of the Code are then in existence. However, remember that it is conceivable President Trump (or some future administration) could be successful in eliminating the tax on net investment income, but not the 5% penalty tax on dividends and/or capital gains, or in eliminating the 5% penalty tax on either or both dividends and/or capital gains, but not the tax on net investment income. How should these possibilities be addressed in our drafting?

One approach would be to add a sentence at the end of the trust subsection which addresses these taxes to the effect that, if the tax on net investment income is repealed, but not both of the penalty taxes, the income withdrawal provisions of the document shall continue to apply for purposes of determining the beneficiary's withdrawal rights over dividends and/or capital gains subject to the penalty tax, and for this purpose the tax on net investment income sections of the Code shall be deemed to continue to exist. If, on the other hand, the tax on net investment income is retained, but either or both of the penalty taxes on capital gains and/or dividends are/is repealed, there would normally be no need to limit the application of the subsection, except potentially in rare instances where the client is certain the trust income beneficiary or beneficiaries will have income(s) in excess of the $200,000 and $250,000 thresholds.

Of course, since it is impossible to anticipate all of the potential future scenarios involved, it is still necessary that we include the independent trustee "amendment" form language already set forth at pages 51 - 55 of this text. This is the purpose of the independent trustee "amendment" form language.

Trust forms for children and other individual beneficiaries must also continue to address the basis step-up issues at death with the conditional testamentary general powers already described. Recall that these conditional general powers provide specific protections for potential cases where there may be a deemed sale of properties having built-in gain involved, or a potential "step down" in income tax basis.

When it comes to charitable beneficiaries, the only real difference in the foregoing analysis is that now potentially *all* situations (i.e., not just those with nontaxable estates) will require an analysis of whether it is makes tax sense to leave amounts directly to charity under a will or revocable trust. Depending on how the new law plays out, there may be an advantage to leaving appreciated assets directly to charity at death, i.e., if this were to result in the avoidance of a tax on built-in gains at death. With so much uncertainty on this point right now, however, the preference would be to wait on these high net worth charitable situations, until the final law is passed.

Planning for Retirement Benefits - The Trump Effect

The most relevant point here is that, for high net worth clients at least, the fact that retirement benefits do not receive an income tax basis step-up at death will have less significance than it does currently and, in fact, these the former forms of benefits may actually turn out to be *more* beneficial than other forms of "non-IRD" retirement savings. The reason for this is that income tax deferral is available for retirement assets, whereas "non-IRD" forms of investment savings may be subject to the tax on built-in gains upon the client's passing. Of course, this potential renewed benefit will be negated if Congress also passes a law which eliminates or significantly restricts so-called "stretch" treatment for IRAs, qualified plan benefits, and/or non-qualified annuities - and there appears to be a Congressional groundswell of support to do exactly this.

For the more typical net worth client, obviously the lowering of income tax brackets proposed by President Trump could have a significant positive impact on the recipients of retirement benefits, whether those benefits be qualified or non-qualified. It will also make it easier for the participant/owner to do a Roth conversion and/or take distributions for other estate planning purposes.

Planning for Business Owners and Professionals - The Trump Effect

The proposed large lowering of the income tax rate for small businesses and corporations will of course be of significant benefit to our business owner clients as well as to their families after their passing. The impact on our professional clients has yet to be revealed, but hopefully there will be some relief there also, at least for the portion of the professional's earnings which are not directly attributable to his or her own efforts. It is also currently unclear what impact the proposals will have on the portion of the business owner's income attributable to rents, interest and dividends, but it appears fairly evident it will make no difference whether the business is operated as a sole proprietorship, partnership, limited liability company, C corporation or S corporation.

President Trump's immediate action to curtail all IRS regulatory projects obviously gave business and real estate owner estate and gift tax discount planning at least a temporary reprieve. But questions remain as to what actions, if any, should be taken in light of this temporary, and potentially permanent, slap on the hands of the IRS.

For example, should we be advising our high net worth business or real estate owner clients (i.e., those with otherwise taxable estates) to establish a family limited partnership with their children as the general partners? And, if so, should we also advise the clients to then gift all or a portion of the discounted interests to their children?

Assuming any attempt at repealing the federal estate tax will be completed by the end of 2017, it would generally appear to accomplish little to make significant lifetime gifts of appreciated assets at this time (i.e., because of carryover basis), unless there is a very large amount of built-in gains tax (i.e., at death) we would also potentially be avoiding in the process. It would also appear likely that business interests will not be subject to immediate built-in gains tax at the owner's death.

For the high net worth client, creating discounts now, i.e., while the Treasury's discount regulations are still in limbo, can make sense, because this step alone can potentially save estate taxes. Be sure to prepare the discount plan in a fashion which can be unwound without tax impact, however, because if the estate tax *is* repealed, *and* only carryover income tax basis is substituted in its place, merely establishing a lower income tax basis for the client's heirs at death would obviously not be prudent.

Gift and Valuation Discount Planning - The Trump Effect

As already alluded to in the immediately preceding section dealing with business and real estate owners, the obvious issue here is whether, in the short term at least, it makes sense to advise clients to enter into significant gift programs with their associated carryover income tax basis issues and their obviously irrevocable nature. Any significant gift plan should include the techniques previously outlined in this text which would include conditional powers of appointment to intentionally cause estate inclusion in the event this does not create an estate tax problem *and* does not trigger any tax on built-in gains. Gifting now can make sense if one of the goals is to avoid a potential built-in gains tax at death, although any built-in gains tax proposal would likely include a significant "exemption" amount, anyway, probably roughly equivalent to the current lifetime gift tax exemption.

All techniques which establish estate tax discounts at death should now be carefully structured to enable the income tax-free unwinding of the arrangement in the event it results only in the loss of income tax basis step-up at death, i.e., it does not result in any other tax benefit.

Of course, if the situation develops such that it becomes likely the Treasury Department's proposed anti-discount regulations could actually be finalized in roughly their current proposed form, all of the above-described techniques designed to "grandfather" any currently available estate and gift tax valuation discounts, would also be back on the table.

Made in the USA
Coppell, TX
17 August 2020

33689914R00187